PREMODERN JAPAN

PREMODERN JAPAN

A Historical Survey

Mikiso Hane
KNOX COLLEGE

Westview Press
BOULDER • SAN FRANCISCO • OXFORD

Cover art: Terra-cotta Haniwa figure, third–sixth centuries (*courtesy Cleveland Museum of Art, The Norweb Collection*)

Copyright © 1991 by Westview Press, Inc.

Published in 1991 in the United States of America by Westview Press, Inc., 5500 Central Avenue, Boulder, Colorado 80301, and in the United Kingdom by Westview Press, 36 Lonsdale Road, Summertown, Oxford OX2 7EW

An earlier version of this book, *Japan: A Historical Survey*, was published in 1972 by Charles Scribner's Sons.

Library of Congress Cataloging-in-Publication Data
Hane, Mikiso.
  Premodern Japan : a historical survey / Mikiso Hane.
    p. cm.
  Rev. ed. of: Japan, a historical survey. 1972.
  Includes bibliographical references and index.
  ISBN 0-8133-8066-9 (hardcover).—ISBN 0-8133-8065-0 (pbk.)
  1. Japan—History—To 1868. I. Hane, Mikiso. Japan, a
historical survey. II. Title.
DS850.H36 1991
952—dc20   90-41699
                                                                    CIP

Printed and bound in the United States of America

The paper used in this publication meets the requirements
of the American National Standard for Permanence of Paper
for Printed Library Materials Z39.48-1984.

10   9

To Rose, Laurie, and Jennifer

CONTENTS

MAPS

PREFACE

This account of the premodern period of Japan's history is, essentially, the first half of *Japan, A Historical Survey*, which was published in 1972, although revisions and modifications were made as described below. My objective in writing this history was to present a general picture of Japanese history for the benefit of nonspecialists—general readers as well as college students—in the hope of furthering their understanding of present-day Japan through the study of her past.

An ideal general history provides facts as well as analyses of significant events, conditions, and accomplishments. Some critics have commented that I included too many data in this history. But I am convinced that one cannot interpret or analyze history without a firm grasp of the essential facts. In rereading the 1972 edition carefully in preparing for this edition, I became even more persuaded that the data presented here are all necessary for a discerning perspective and appreciation of Japan's past and present.

I attempted to provide a balanced picture by incorporating all facets of history—political, social, economic, cultural, and intellectual. Naturally, the emphases vary from period to period, but throughout I tried to keep in mind the social conditions at the lower levels of the society. I also emphasized cultural and intellectual achievements because Japanese thinkers and artists have not been as devoid of creative achievements and ideas as is occasionally believed.

For this revised edition I have made a number of revisions and incorporated recent scholarly interpretations and findings. For example, more attention is given here to the influence of Korea on early Japan, especially on the origin and evolution of the imperial dynasty and on cultural developments. Recent interpretations of certain political and intellectual affairs have also been incorporated, and more recent translations of literary works, such as the *Tale of Genji*, have been utilized.

Japanese names have been given in the traditional style—that is, surname first and given name second. Historical personages in Japan have traditionally been identified by their given names, and I have followed this practice. For example, I refer to Tokugawa (surname) Ieyasu (given name) as Ieyasu.

For the transcriptions of Japanese names and terms, I have used the Hepburn system. Diacritical marks indicate long vowels; however, they are not used in geographical place names commonly known in the West. Singular and plural nouns are not distinguished in Japanese. Hence, samurai, diamyō, and shōgun, for example, could be either singular or plural.

In preparing the 1972 edition, I made extensive use of the works of other scholars and specialists, both Western and Japanese. In this revised edition also I am indebted directly and indirectly to the works of numerous scholars and to the scholars who read the revised manuscript and made invaluable suggestions. I am grateful to many friends and colleagues for their advice and assistance, especially my associates at Knox College. I thank my wife, Rose, and my daughters, Laurie and Jennifer, for their assistance and support.

I am also heavily indebted to the invaluable advice and assistance provided me by the staff at Westview Press—Susan McEachern, Peter Kracht, and especially Beverly LeSuer and Sarah Tomasek, who labored patiently over the manuscript to ferret out all the glitches and inconsistencies. And I owe the idea for writing the history of Japan to Frederick A. Praeger, who planted the idea in my head thirty years ago when I was browsing through books in the booths at the American Historical Association meeting in Chicago.

Mikiso Hane

INTRODUCTION

Today Japan is the seventh largest country in the world in terms of population. Over 123 million people are crowded into an area slightly smaller than the state of Montana. The islands that make up the nation are mountainous, and only slightly over 14 percent of the land is farmed. Although the country is poor in natural resources, it is the world's third most productive industrial nation.

Japan's position in the world was not as prominent in the past as it is today. It was not until the nineteenth and twentieth centuries that her presence in world affairs came to be felt. In the first half of the twentieth century Japan emerged as a major military power in East Asia, but following defeat in World War II, she renounced militarism and has been concentrating on economic development.

Prior to the middle of the nineteenth century, Japan was isolated from the external world, with contact restricted primarily to the Dutch and to Japan's neighbors, Korea and China, although relations with the other European countries did prevail briefly from the mid-sixteenth to the early seventeenth century. In a sense Japan was a cultural satellite of China, remaining under her influence for centuries following the introduction of Chinese culture in the fifth and sixth centuries. By adopting, adapting, and assimilating the fruits of Chinese civilization, Japan developed a culture and way of life and established institutions and values that were distinctly her own. In the nineteenth and twentieth centuries Japan was exposed to Western civilization, and another period of importation and assimilation ensued. Yet the traditional attitudes, ways, and institutions persisted; consequently, contemporary Japan cannot be adequately understood without an examination of her early history.

Before the massive influx of things Chinese that started in the fifth century, Japan had indigenous beliefs, institutions, and practices; some of these survived the "Sinification" process and persisted to the present. Among these was Shinto, an animistic folk religion that acknowledges the presence of sacred beings—gods and spirits—in nature. Myths about creator gods and the belief that the imperial dynasty was founded by the descendants of the Sun Goddess (Amaterasu-no-Ōmikami) were propagated by the clan that gained political hegemony. These beliefs formed the basis of "state" Shinto, which was used by the leaders of modern Japan to unify the people under the imperial family.

The emperor system came to be intimately associated with Shinto. The ancestors of the current imperial family established their political dominion around the late fifth or early sixth century; this family remains the central political entity today. This is not to say that it remained the actual source of power through the ages, but it did persist as an institution to which even the actual wielders of power, the shōgun, had to pay at least pro forma honor. Thus loyalty to the imperial court was stressed as a quintessential principle of Japanese behavior by proponents of imperial rule.

Another characteristic of the Japanese that persisted through the ages is a strong sense of group identity, whether it be with the clan, the family, or the community. Thus individualism in traditional Japan never developed into an acceptable mode of behavior. This suppression of individual interests for the good of the group was reinforced by the advent of Confucianism around the fifth century and built its moral code around the family system. The emphasis on group interests led to idealization of values such as submissiveness, obedience, self-sacrifice, responsibility, and duty. The emphasis on group interests also resulted in a parochial outlook with a strong demarcation between the "in-group" and the outsiders. This in-group versus others attitude applied not just to the family, clan, or village versus others but also ultimately to "we, the Japanese" versus foreigners. This insular mentality, a product of the island makeup of the country, fostered a pronounced ethnocentrism and a belief in the homogeneity and uniqueness of the Japanese people. This mode of thinking is manifested in the modern age as militant nationalism; traces of nationalism first began to surface from time to time after the seeds of cultural nationalism began to sprout in the Heian period (794–1185).

The Confucian emphasis on preserving the hierarchical order of "superior" and "inferior" persons and the maintenance of proper relationships to ensure social harmony (that is, the "inferior" person should behave in accordance with his or her station in the family and society) came to be strongly embedded in Japanese mores. This social imperative was reinforced by the emergence of the samurai as the dominant force in the late twelfth century. The proper order of things came to be reinforced by the edge of the sword, not simply by moral rectitude inculcated by learning, as the Confucian scholars taught.

The Confucian hierarchy based on sex and age came to define the place of women in Japan, for despite some evidence that early Japan may have been a matriarchal society, or at least a matrilineal society, the acceptance of the Confucian social philosophy and the ascendancy of the samurai class resulted in a steady decline in the social standing of women, although women still were accorded property rights even after samurai rule was established in the late twelfth century. It was not until the Tokugawa era (1600–1867) that gender discrimination came to be enforced stringently among the samurai class; as noted in Chapter 7, however, relationships between men and women among the townspeople remained less rigid.

The emergence of the samurai, and their ascendancy from the late twelfth to the mid-nineteenth century, was a significant factor in the formation of the Japanese way. The "militaristic" side of Japan emerged as the antipode to the "civilian" side that had been nurtured and fostered by the Heian court aristocrats who had adopted the Chinese code of propriety, decorum, moderation, composure, and so on. The samurai favored direct action and decisiveness. The code of the warriors (*Bushidō*) that came to be idealized in the years of shōgunal rule stressed such ideals as loyalty, self-sacrifice, courage, martial valor, honor, integrity, and other Spartan virtues. Such values functioned as counterpoints to the genteel ways of the court aristocrats as well as to the freer and more hedonistic ways of the townspeople in the Tokugawa era. Thus the Japanese value system, like those of other societies, evolved in a multifaceted manner. The disdain for materialism fostered by Confucian and samurai value systems were offset by the townspeople's unabashed pursuit of riches. Contemporary Japan's economic success is not surprising in light of this tradition.

Chinese ways affected more than Japan's social and political systems, institutions, and behavior: Chinese civilization had an immense impact in Japanese cultural, intellectual, and literary realms, also. The Chinese writing system, literary tradition, philosophical schools, arts, and crafts were incorporated into Japanese culture. (Most of these influences entered by way of Korea, after having gone through some modification there.) Nationalist scholars later asserted that before the advent of Chinese influence, with its emphasis on artificial rules of propriety, decorum, and rectitude, the cultural artifacts of Japan reflected the free and natural sentiments of the people. Here too we can see the two faces of traditional Japan: one that is more naturally Japanese and another that is heavily infused with Chinese culture. The influence of Chinese art and culture and the development of a distinctively Japanese style in art and literature—with aesthetic sensitivity toward nature that is reinforced, some would say, by Zen aesthetics—are discussed in Chapter 5.

Buddhism, which entered Japan about the same time that Chinese culture began to inundate the country, also shaped the Japanese outlook and culture in significant ways. Although it did not become a state religion (the Japanese, like the Chinese, believe that one can worship many gods and participate in many different religious practices at the same time), Buddhism did eventually permeate the entire land.

A significant economic factor that molded Japanese society and outlook is the near total reliance on agriculture as a means of subsistence in traditional Japan. Rice culture that entered Japan in the Yayoi period (circa 250 B.C.–A.D. 250) determined the style of farm work through the ages. Working the handkerchief-sized paddies and rugged hillside terraces to produce the necessary crops to feed the population taught the peasants patience, diligence, frugality, and discipline. These qualities were later reinforced by the samurai, who bound the peasants to the soil and insisted on a strict adherence to the virtues of frugality, hard work, and obedience to meet the economic needs of the feudal order. These characteristics persisted into the modern age and contributed to the creation of the modern economic "miracle."

But the peasants did not always remain docile and submissive: periodically they rose up in protest. Hence the revolutionary tradition is not totally absent from Japanese history. Widespread and large-scale peasant uprisings broke out in the Ashikaga (1336–1573) and Tokugawa years, even when such nonviolent acts as submitting petitions to the ruling class led to certain death.

Despite the resulting stress on Japan's harmony, propriety, and hierarchical order, the pattern of her political history is one of constant conflict and bloodshed, beginning with the struggle to establish a dynastic order from the third to fourth century A.D. This pattern continued through the power struggles in the Heian years, the emergence of the samurai in the outlying regions and the sanguinary power struggle among them, the establishment of military rule by the Minamoto clan, the conflict with the imperial forces, the struggles that continued into the Ashikaga years, and the Age of the Warring States of the latter part of the fifteenth century and throughout most of the sixteenth century. It was not until the Tokugawa family established its hegemony that peace and stability ensued for almost two and a half centuries. Thus one might say that the militaristic face of Japan remained a constant.

While the struggle for power was taking place in the political arena, the peasants continued to work the land, suffering privation, famines, epidemics, hunger, starvation, and repression. The townspeople were busy perfecting the arts and crafts.

During the years of turmoil and disaster, literature and the arts survived and enjoyed peaks of creative splendor. This is seen in the art and architecture that followed the introduction of Chinese culture and in the Japanization of this culture in the Heian period. The result was the golden age of literature produced by great Heian women writers like Lady Murasaki and the production of Japanese poems, diaries, essays, and military romances. The profound influence of Zen aesthetics is reflected in painting, architecture, landscape gardening, Nō theater, ceramics, tea ceremony, calligraphy, construction of multistoried picturesque castles, and the production of fine armor and swords in the Kamakura (1185–1333) and Ashikaga (1336–1573) years. In the Tokugawa era the culture of the townspeople flourished with woodblock prints, haiku, Kabuki theater, puppet theater, novels, and folk art.

Japanese history, like the history of all societies, is an unfolding of multifaceted developments, a montage of political, social, economic, cultural, and intellectual elements. But to give a coherent structure to this kaleidoscopic phenomena requires some sort of framework. The most convenient schema in a general historical survey is still a chronological sequence centered upon political developments. This historical survey of pre-Meiji Japan is organized in this conventional manner.

CHAPTER 1

THE EARLY YEARS

GEOGRAPHIC SETTING

The Japanese archipelago, consisting of the four main islands of Hokkaido, Honshu, Shikoku and Kyushu, and over one thousand smaller islands, juts into the Pacific Ocean in a convex arc. The total area of Japan is 145,834 square miles; it is about $\frac{1}{25}$ the size of the United States. To the north the Russian-administered Kuriles, a large number of small volcanic islands, extend to Kamchatka Peninsula, while to the south the Ryukyu Islands stretch out toward Taiwan.

The Japanese islands are mountainous, with considerable volcanic activity. Offshore on the eastern side there are great submarine trenches, 5 or 6 miles below sea level. Along the coast on the same side the mountain tops reach 2 miles above sea level. This great range of elevation from sea bottom to mountain peak causes enormous strains and stresses, resulting in constant shifts in the rock masses. Moreover, there are about five hundred volcanoes in the archipelago, and earthquakes, a related phenomenon, are commonplace occurrences, with an average of about fifteen hundred tremors annually. Since 1596 there have been twenty-one major earthquakes, each one resulting in the deaths of more than a thousand persons.

Seventy-two percent of the country is hilly or mountainous, with an average slope of more than 15 degrees. But nearly 65 percent of the land with a slope of 15 degrees or less is tilled. The total area under cultivation, however, amounts to less than 14.3 percent of the land mass. The highest elevations are located in the Gifu Node in central Honshu. A dozen or more mountains measuring 10,000 feet are located in these highlands known as the Japanese Alps. Mt. Fuji, 12,461 feet, is situated here.

There are no extensive lowlands in Japan. The typical plain is a small isolated area in a coastal indentation or in a mountain basin. The largest of the plains, the Kantō Plain, where Tokyo is located, has an area of only 5,000 square miles, or 3.2 million acres. Other major plains are the Nōbi Plain at the head of Ise Bay where Nagoya is situated (450,000 acres) and the Kinai Plain at the head of Osaka Bay where Kyoto, Osaka, and Kobe are located (310,000 acres). These are the most important plains, on which six of Japan's largest cities were built. Other fairly large plains are the Ishikari in southwestern Hokkaido, the Echigo in northwestern Honshu, the Sendai in northeastern Honshu, and the Tsukushi in northwestern Kyushu.

Rivers water most of these plains, but they are generally short, swift, and shallow and therefore not suitable for navigation. The two longest rivers are the Ishikari in Hokkaido (227 miles) and the Shinano in central Honshu (229 miles). The mountain rivers are important as sources of irrigation for the rice fields and hydroelectric power.

Japan proper has a remarkably long coastline, about 17,000 miles, or 1 linear mile of coast for each 8.5 square miles of area. The effect of this unusually long coastline is accentuated by the fact that most of the lowlands have sea frontage. This situation has fostered a strong maritime outlook in the Japanese. A large part of the coastline has indentations and irregularities that, together with the many tiny islands along the coastline, make the landscape strikingly beautiful and diverse.

Since the Japanese archipelago extends from 31 degrees to 45 degrees north latitude, there is a marked contrast in the climate between the northern and southern regions. Discrepancies in surface configurations, great differences in altitude, and diversity in the effects produced by the Pacific Ocean and the Japan Sea also account for notable differences in climate. A large part of Japan lies in subtropical latitudes. Consequently, in most areas climatic conditions are conducive to plant growth and are not too harsh for human comfort.

The monsoonal air masses affect the climate in a significant way. In the winter great waves of dry, cold polar air come from the Lake Baikal region of Siberia. In the summer moist tropical and subtropical maritime air masses, originating over the warmer parts of the Pacific Ocean, move into eastern Asia. Thus while the winter winds are prevailingly from the northwest, the summer winds come from the southeast. The winters are colder and the summers hotter and more humid than normal for regions with Japan's latitude.

The two ocean currents washing the shores of Japan also influence her climate. A cold current from the north, the Okhotsk Current, and a warm stream from the south, the Japan Current, converge off northern Honshu. A smaller stream from the Japan Current swings into the Japan Sea from the Tsushima Strait and flows northward as far as Hokkaido.

During late spring and early summer a period of abundant rain, high humidity, and cloudiness sets in. This is the so-called *bai-u*, or plum rains. In the late summer and early fall violent storms and typhoons strike the islands, causing much damage to the rice fields as well as to the dwellings and the general landscape.

Japan's climate is much like that of the United States Atlantic seaboard or the Mississippi Valley in similar latitudes. Temperatures in January range from about 10 degrees or 15 degrees in northern and central Hokkaido to 35 degrees or 40 degrees on the lowlands of central Honshu and 45 degrees

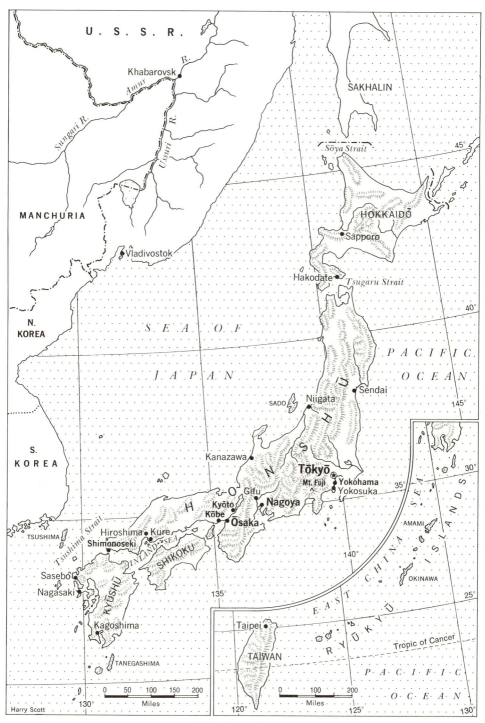

MODERN JAPAN.

in the extreme south of Kyushu. July temperatures in central and southern Japan range from 77 degrees to 80 degrees. August is slightly warmer than July in most areas. High temperatures combined with high humidity make the summers extremely sultry and oppressive.

Japan has a considerable amount of precipitation all year round; although it rains more in the warm months than in the winter, the difference in precipitation between summer and winter is not great. Even in the driest cool season there are 2 or 3 inches of precipitation each month and several times this amount in the warm months. Where precipitation is heaviest it may exceed 120 inches annually, while where it is lightest, in the Inland Sea region, it averages 40 inches per year.

Snow falls throughout the main islands, although it is light in the southern regions. It remains on the ground all winter in Hokkaido and in Honshu on the northern part of the Pacific side and all across the Japan Sea side. In the mountainous regions of western and northern Japan the snow reaches a depth of 6 or 7 feet in January.

The growing season varies from about 120 to 130 days in central and eastern Hokkaido to 250 days or more along the extreme southern and eastern littoral. The region around Tokyo has a growing season of 215 days.

Rice, grown in paddy fields, is the most important food crop produced. Today 55 percent of the cereal acreage consists of rice fields. Barley, wheat, oats, soybeans, potatoes, and a variety of vegetables are also grown. Tea and mulberry (for silkworms) constitute important supplementary income crops for farm families. Because only a little more than 15 million acres are arable, intensive cultivation is practiced, and terraced fields climb the hillsides of the Japanese landscape.

Since Japan is an island nation, the sea is an important source of food. Seafood is the chief source of protein in the Japanese diet. The warm Japan Current yields sardine, mackerel, tuna, bonito, skipjack, albacore, and seabream, while herring, salmon, cod, and crab are fished from the Okhotsk Current. Many edible seaweeds are also extracted from the sea.

Japan is one of the most completely forested countries in the world. About 55 percent of the island is forested and another 8 to 9 percent is potential forest land. The forests are a source not only of timber but of charcoal, wood fuel, wood pulp, and a variety of foods. Broadleaf forests occupy about 50 percent of the forest land, while coniferous and mixed forests occupy 29 and 21 percent, respectively.

Japan does not have an adequate supply of mineral resources. Because coal, the most important of her minerals, is of poor quality, a supply of better quality must be imported for heavy industrial use. Petroleum resources are extremely limited: in the mid-1980s 99.9 percent of the crude oil consumed came from abroad. Her iron mines supply only a small percentage of her industrial needs. The supply of copper, limestone, and sulfur is adequate, but lead, zinc, and phosphate and potassium materials for fertilizers must be imported.

THE MYTHOLOGICAL ORIGINS OF JAPAN

According to Japanese mythology—based upon the first historical accounts, the *Kojiki* (*Records of Ancient Matters;* completed in 712) and the *Nihongi* (*Chronicles of Japan;* completed in 720)—sky and heaven gradually separated from the primordial chaos in the universe, and five primal deities appeared. They were followed by a series of mated deities, ending with the creative pair, He-Who-Invites (Izanagi) and She-Who-Invites (Izanami). They stirred the sea with a spear and created an islet. Descending upon it, they created many other deities as well as the other islands of Japan.

Izanami died while giving birth to the Fire God and descended into the underworld of Yomi (darkness), where putrefaction and pollution prevailed. Longing to see his wife, Izanagi followed her into the land of darkness but was driven back by her because she was ashamed to be seen by him in her state of putrefaction. Returning from the land of darkness, Izanagi cleansed himself, and as he washed his left eye—left being the side of honor—the Sun Goddess, Amaterasu, was born, and from the right eye sprang the Moon God. As he washed his nose the Impetuous-Male-Deity (Susano-o), the Storm God, came into being.

The Sun Goddess and the Moon God ascended to the sky, the former to rule at Takamagahara (Plain of High Heaven) and the latter to serve as her consort. The Storm God was to rule over the earth. When Susano-o, who was an unruly character, visited his sister in the sky, he behaved obstreperously, damaging her rice fields and defiling her house with excrement. In anger Amaterasu shut herself up in a cave, darkening the world. To lure her out, the heavenly gods engaged in dancing and merrymaking. When Amaterasu opened the door of the cave to peek out to see what was taking place, the gods compelled her to leave the cavern, and the world was made radiant again. This story may be connected with ceremonies conducted during an eclipse of the sun or during the winter solstice to revive the waning power of the sun. It was also intended, some maintain, to signify the triumph of light over darkness, peace and order over savagery and destruction.

Susano-o was banished to the earth for his misconduct. He first traveled to Korea, then to Izumo in western Honshu. From Izumo, Susano-o's descendant, Ōkuninushi, ruled the earth. The Sun Goddess, wishing to extend her authority to the earth, sent several messengers to persuade the Great-Land-Master to abdicate in her favor. After resisting several of Amaterasu's attempts to persuade him, the ruler of the earth finally agreed to submit to her authority. The Sun Goddess then sent her grandson, Ninigi, to rule the earth.[1]

Ninigi descended to the earth at Tsukushi in northern Kyushu and brought with him three items that became symbols of the imperial rule: a bronze mirror (a symbol of the Sun Goddess and of purity); a sword (courage), which was used by Susano-o to slay a huge serpent; and a curved-bead necklace (benevolence), which warded off evil spirits.

Ninigi's great-grandson, Waka-mike-nu, left Kyushu to conquer the rest of Japan. Sailing through the Inland Sea, he entered the Kinki region (the area that encompasses Osaka, Kyoto, and Nara) and established his rule in Yamato in 660 B.C. He then became the first emperor of Japan, Jimmu.[2]

Among other mythological figures two deserve mention, since they came to be popularly regarded as actual historical personages of heroic stature. One is Yamato-takeru, who performed great military feats in conquering the rebellious people in the south (the Kumaso) and in the north (the Ezo). The other is the Empress Jingū, who is said to have led an expedition against Silla in Korea.

Mythological tales similar to those found in Japan are told in other parts of Asia, especially among the peoples of Korea and Southeast Asia and the nomads of northern Asia.[3] The models for the stories concerning the origin of the universe, the age of the gods, superhuman kings, and heroic men may have been taken from Chinese myths by the ancient Japanese, but in the opinion of Joseph Campbell, an authority on mythology, "the material that they dressed to this frame was of their own, comparatively childlike, folkloristic heritage, and the result was the most remarkable history of the world-as-fairytale" that the literature of mythology knows. This, according to Campbell, is particularly suitable to Japan, where "the extraordinary earnestness and profound gravity of the ideal of life is masked by the fashionable fiction that everything is only play."[4]

JAPANESE PREHISTORY

Archaeologists and historians fail to agree about the origins of the Japanese.[5] There is a consensus, however, that the early inhabitants came from different areas in several separate waves of immigration. Some of the early inhabitants are believed to have been a Tungusic people who came from the northeastern region of the continent by way of Hokkaido or Korea. It is also thought that people of Malayan origin came from the south—from South China or perhaps from Southeast Asia—by way of Formosa and the Ryukyus, while others of Mongoloid origin came by way of Korea.

The Japanese language seems to have links with both the Polynesian and Altaic languages. Some authorities theorize that in the Jōmon period a language of southern origin was spoken, while in the Yayoi period a new language, Altaic in character, entered from the continent.

Until very recently there was no concrete evidence to substantiate the existence of paleolithic man in Japan, but archaeological discoveries since 1947 indicate that this was the case. Tools made of roughly flaked stone dating from perhaps two hundred thousand years ago have been discovered. Archaeological remains of microlithic artifacts, that is, tools of sharp-edged stone flakes, indicate that mesolithic man was present in Japan around 5000 B.C.

Among the early inhabitants of neolithic Japan were, it is believed, ancestors of the Ainus, a people of Caucasian origin who inhabit Hokkaido today. (There are at present only about eighteen thousand Ainus in existence.)

The early stages of the neolithic age in Japan, known as the Jōmon period, extended from about 4500 B.C. to 250 B.C. On the basis of carbon 14 tests made on archaeological finds, some authorities now contend that the Jōmon period started around 7000 or 8000 B.C. The term Jōmon (cord-making) describes the type of decoration on pottery associated with this age. Most Jōmon earthenwares have designs of high relief made with cord impressions. This era is divided into several periods based upon the changing style of pottery.⁶ The patterns made by cord impressions became increasingly more complex in later stages.

Jōmon people, who may have numbered slightly over 100,000 five thousand years ago, lived near the sea coast and gathered shellfish for food. A large number of shell mounds, principally in the Tokyo Bay area, have been found at archaeological sites that had been inhabited by Jōmon men. Those living in mountainous areas hunted game and lived on fruits, nuts, berries, and edible roots. Fish hooks made of animal bones and ground and chipped stone tools were used by men of the Jōmon period. These early people lived in pit dwellings covered over with thatched roofs. Evidently the houses were circular, had several supporting pillars for the slanting roofs, and each had a fireplace of earthenware or stone. Clay figurines have been used to ensure fertility and guard against pernicious forces. It appears from the iconography of these idols that the sun and the spirits of stones were worshipped in this period.

The later years of the neolithic age are called the Yayoi period (ca. 250 B.C.–A.D. 250) because potteries belonging to this culture were first discovered at a place called Yayoi in Tokyo in 1884. The Yayoi pots, reddish in color, were wheel-made and are less elaborately decorated than Jōmon pieces. The designs are simple and neat, generally consisting of straight lines. Yayoi pottery, fired at a higher temperature, is technically superior to Jōmon pottery. A greater variety of earthenwares were produced in the Yayoi period. Basically there were three types: plain jars used for cooking, decorated urns for storing food, and more elaborately designed dishes on pedestals in which offerings to the gods were placed.

Yayoi culture is believed to have emerged around the third century B.C. in northern Kyushu. It would appear that it was influenced by two different cultural forces, one from the south and the other from the north. Rice cultivation, which was not yet practiced in northern China, came to Japan from the south. It may have been introduced from Southeast Asia or from South China by immigrants fleeing the Han conquerors, who were extending their control into South China. Perhaps it entered from South China by way of southern Korea. At any rate, the introduction of rice cultivation revolutionized the way of life of ancient Japan and established the basis for the economic life of the people until the industrial age.

While rice cultivation indicates a southern influence, the polished stone implements of Yayoi culture show links with Korea, Manchuria, and northern China. As we have already noted, it is possible that during this period Japan came under the influence of people who belonged to the Altaic world. The Yayoi decorative designs resemble ornaments found in areas where the Altaic languages were spoken. Around the second century B.C.

Terra-cotta Jōmon urn, ca. 200 B.C.—an example of prehistoric Japanese art. Courtesy of the Cleveland Museum of Art, John L. Severance Fund.

bronze and iron implements were introduced from China and Korea. Among the bronze artifacts were swords, halberds, and mirrors used for religious and ceremonial purposes.

The agricultural implements used in the Yayoi period were crude wooden and stone tools such as hoes, rakes, spades, semilunar knives, and adzes. In the later stages of the period, iron implements came to be used for household and agricultural purposes. For weapons, Yayoi men used bows and arrows and, after the introduction of iron, iron swords, spears, and halberds. Remnants of looms and fabrics indicate that weaving was also introduced from the continent in this period. Pits and caves were no longer utilized for dwellings. Huts were now constructed above the ground, and wooden posts and beams were used to hold up thatched roofs. The dead were buried in urns, dolmens, and stone cists; a variety of artifacts, many of Chinese origin, were buried with them.

In the Yayoi period, with the population numbering perhaps about 600,000, there were two population centers. One was near the present city of Nara in the Yamato Plain and the other was in northern Kyushu. Evidently they adhered to different religious cults. The people in Yamato used bronze bells for ceremonial purposes while those in Kyushu used gems and bronze spears, swords, halberds, and mirrors. While the swords and halberds are believed to have come from the continent, the bronze bells used in the Yamato region are not found on the continent. These bells were fairly large, some as long as four feet, and were decorated with engravings of farming and hunting scenes.

The ritualistic use of these artifacts was evidently linked with political control. An ancient account states that shields and spears sent to the governors and chiefs were interred in the sacred hills to ensure the protection of the frontiers; thus the bronze spear became a symbol of divine presence as well as of power. That the possession of ritual symbols endowed the possessor with special authority is seen in the fact that the imperial family traditionally used three symbols—the sacred sword, mirror, and gem—to assert its special authority and legitimacy.

The first written accounts of Japan are found in the historical chronicles of China, specifically in the *History of the Kingdom of Wei* (a kingdom in North China, A.D. 220–265), written in A.D. 297, and in the *History of the Later Han Dynasty*, compiled around A.D. 445. These histories mention the existence of more than one hundred communities in Japan and note that a number of envoys were sent from Japan to the Han court in what is the present-day city of Sian and to the Han governors in Korea. The first envoy is said to have arrived in the Han capital in A.D. 57. A golden seal presumably given to one of the rulers of northern Kyushu by an emperor of Later Han China in the first century was found in 1784. Its authenticity has been questioned, but many authorities now consider it to be genuine.

According to the Chinese records Japan underwent a period of civil strife in the second century A.D., but eventually the nation was unified under a queen referred to as Pimiku. Pimiku (or Himiko in Japanese, meaning daughter of the sun) was not a proper name but rather a term applied to female rulers in general. The Pimiku mentioned in the Chinese histories was a shaman, a priestess who served as an intermediary between supernatural forces and the people. The *History of Wei* states that Pimiku "occupied herself with magic and sorcery, bewitching the people. Though mature in age, she remained unmarried. She had a younger brother who assisted her in ruling the country. After she became the ruler, there were few who saw her. She had one thousand women as attendants, but only one man."[7]

Historians disagree about the location of the land ruled by Pimiku. The *History of Wei* states that Pimiku resided in Yamatai, located on an island southeast of Korea. This might indicate that Yamatai was in northern Kyushu, but if the distances given in the *History of Wei* were followed it would be located on the high seas. The similarity of the names might signify that Yamatai was actually Yamato in central Honshu, but Yamatai, which means gateway to the mountains, was not an uncommon place name.

All sorts of theories based upon mythological, linguistic, and archaeological evidence have been set forth to prove that Pimiku's kingdom was in either northern Kyushu or the Yamato Plain, but neither side has been able to substantiate its contention. It would appear that northern Kyushu had much greater contact with the continent, but the *History of Wei* states that when Pimiku died in the middle of the third century a great mound was constructed as her tomb. This, the proponents of the Yamato thesis argued, proves that Pimiku ruled in the Yamato Plain, because the practice of constructing large tombs did not prevail in northern Kyushu. In the late 1980s, however, archaeological excavations in northern Kyushu led to the discovery of a fortified town with a large burial mound. This finding has provided the Kyushu school with additional arguments to support its contention.

The hypothesis that Pimiku was the ancestor of the imperial family, or that she was a historical personage, is open to question. If she were, it might not be unreasonable to assume that she was located in Kyushu, because it appears that early clan chieftains contending for power moved from Kyushu to the Yamato region some time after Pimiku's reign. The fact that the symbols of imperial authority—swords, mirrors, and gems—have been found in abundance in the burial sites of northern Kyushu would tend to uphold the Kyushu theory. On the other hand, in 1986 a bronze mirror from the Wei dynasty was discovered in the Yamato region. It is argued that this may be one of the one hundred mirrors that the *History of Wei* states the Wei ruler presented to Pimiku.

It is possible that the Kyushu people had imported new weapons (such as long swords and iron armor) and had learned new techniques of warfare (such as the use of warriors on horseback) from the continent and were thus able to overwhelm their rivals in central Honshu. At any rate, by the middle of the fourth century the ruling family that had established its authority in the Yamato region had more or less unified Japan except for the outlying areas to the north, which were not pacified until the ninth century, and southern Kyushu.

The period from about the third century A.D. to the early eighth century is known as the Yamato period. It is also referred to as the "age of ancient tombs" because important personages were interred in large burial mounds.

JAPAN'S NEIGHBOR: KOREA

Scholars investigating Japanese-Korean historical relations have cited numerous evidences—place names, shrine names, common myths and tales, archaeological evidence—to point out that Korean immigrants or invaders with close ties to the three Korean kingdoms of Koguryo, Paekche, and Silla played decisive roles in the formative period of Japanese history, not only materially and culturally but also politically. In fact, these historians believe that one of the early emperors, Ōjin, was a Korean chief, Homuda, a member of the Puyo ruling house of Paekche.[8]

In A.D. 400 Korea was divided into three kingdoms: Koguryo in the northern half, Paekche in the southwest, and Silla in the southeast, a division that occurred during the second half of the first century B.C. and lasted until the second half of the seventh century A.D. In the central part of the southern tip was Mimana, or Kaya, a small area with close ties to Japan.

Koguryo quite naturally was under strong Chinese influence and had adopted Confucianism and Chinese institutions and practices. Paekche also had close Chinese ties, mainly with South China. It was frequently beset by its larger and more powerful neighbors and was willing to accept Japanese aid against both Koguryo and Silla. Silla was the least Sinified of the three kingdoms, although later it too began to adopt Chinese culture. Earlier the southeastern region had maintained close contacts with Japan, but with the establishment of the kingdom of Silla relationships became strained.

In the middle of the seventh century Silla allied itself with T'ang China and put an end to the kingdoms of Paekche and Koguryo (in 660 and 668, respectively). Many people from these kingdoms fled to Japan. Some became influential figures in the Japanese court and played significant roles in implementing reforms, known as the Taika Reforms, in the late seventh and early eighth centuries.

Silla managed to free itself from T'ang political domination and extended its authority over the entire peninsula, unifying Korea for the first time. Thereafter Korea remained unified except for brief periods. From the end of the eighth century Silla was plagued with internal disturbances. In 935, order was restored under the Koryo dynasty, which remained in power until 1392. Korea, however, became tributary to the ruling powers of China. When the Mongols conquered China, they also made repeated military forays against Korea and in 1258 finally brought her to her knees. With the expulsion of the Mongols from China in 1368, Korea freed herself from the former's control but, under a new ruling family, the Yi, entered into tributary relationship with the new Chinese dynasty, the Ming. The Yi dynasty lasted from 1392 to 1910, when Japan annexed the peninsula.

EARLY YAMATO SOCIETY:
FOURTH AND FIFTH CENTURIES

The period from the unification of Japan by the imperial family to the time when the country came under the massive cultural, political, social, and economic influence from China and Korea is still a rather obscure era. The conditions that prevailed around the time of unification are matters of conjecture again. Pimiku, or Himiko, was a priestess who served as the medium conveying to the people the words and laws of the gods. Religious and political functions were regarded as being one and the same. Governmental functions were called *matsuri*— worship of or service to the gods. The act of being possessed by the gods when receiving their words was called *noru*. The noun of this word is *nori*, meaning law; laws, then, were divine decrees. Religion served as an instrument of political control. Ordinarily the shamans were females, so the rulers were usually women. The *History of Wei* states that after Pimiku's death a king was placed on the throne, but the people refused to obey him and civil strife ensued. To restore order, a girl of thirteen was placed on the throne.

After a period in which various clan groups contended for power, the clan that emerged as the founder of the imperial dynasty extended its authority to outlying areas. In administering the land it either appointed its own officials or allowed the conquered chieftains to continue as governors (*kuni-no-miyakko*). In areas not under the immediate control of the imperial clan, the head of the *uji* of each area was allowed to manage his own land.

The uji, customarily translated as clan, was a lineage group organized around the main family. Each uji had a patriarchal chief (*uji-no-kami*) and worshipped a guardian god (*uji-gami*). As a member of the ruling elite each uji controlled its own land and also had under its authority workers organized into associations or corporations (see below). The imperial family, before it gained ascendancy over the other uji, was one of the uji contending for land and power.

With the growth of imperial power, the number of kuni-no-miyakko increased. By the middle of the seventh century, just prior to the Taika Reforms, there were perhaps as many as 120 such officials. Around the fourth century the imperial government began to confer titles of nobility (*kabane*) upon the chiefs of the leading uji. Evidently these titles had been used prior to this, but the imperial family sought to assert its authority over the clan chieftains by assuming the right to confer them officially. With the titles went certain official functions and positions that were hereditary. Without a title one could not occupy a high government position. Among the patriarchal chieftains, those claiming direct descent from the legendary first emperor, Jimmu, or from the founding gods occupied the highest places in the political and social hierarchy. The former were given the title of *omi* and the latter *muraji*. The clans of the omi and muraji and the imperial family were the major landowners. Those chieftains who held the title "great omi" or "great muraji" were entitled to hold key government positions.

Another institution came into being about the same time as the kabane system, the hereditary associations or corporations called *be*. They were under the control of the imperial family and the leading uji. Members of these functional communities were required to perform fixed services for the uji to which they were attached or to supply them with certain commodities. They were not slaves, for they retained their personal freedom. The hereditary guilds of the later Roman Empire would be the closest Western analogy to these corporations.

As imperial power grew, the leading clans themselves were organized into functional corporations to serve the emperor. For instance, the head of the Mononobe family, holding the title of muraji, was responsible for the maintenance of weapons for the imperial family. The head of the Ōtomobe family, also a muraji, was responsible for the safety of the emperor. There were be for every category of occupation: those engaged in military and religious affairs, ricefield workers, fishermen, sake makers, weavers, grooms, smiths, potters, arrow makers, bow makers, mirror makers, lapidaries, cooks, scribes, and so forth. These classifications eventually came to denote family names, in the same way that words such as miller and smith came to be used as surnames in English. Immigrants from Korea and China, many of whom were skilled artisans, constituted important elements of the corporation system. For instance, toward the end of the third century A.D. a considerable number of weavers arrived in Japan from Paekche and were organized into a weavers' corporation. By the middle of the sixth century there were 7,053 households belonging to this community, numbering, it is estimated, over 30,000 members.

By subjugating the uji and making them serve as functional corporations, the imperial family was able to extend its control over the rest of the populace, because the be under the authority of the uji fell indirectly under imperial control. These institutions remained in existence until the Taika Reforms movement was initiated in the seventh century, although they had begun to deteriorate prior to that because of disputes over titles and positions among the leading uji.

SHINTO

As the imperial family extended its authority, its ancestral god, the Sun Goddess, became the chief deity of the entire land. She was enshrined at Ise, which is still today the sacred city of the native religion known as Shinto. Each uji had its own god, the uji-gami, who was usually the founder of the clan or a prominent ancestral figure. In addition it was believed that a whole host of gods or spirits were present in all things in nature. There were gods or spirits identified with the woods, streams, mountains, fields, rain, fire, water, stones, grass, trees, and so on. Some animals, such as snakes and foxes, were also believed to possess supernatural powers and were worshipped out of fear. Worship of the lingam, or phallus, was also practiced. All spirits and deities were referred to as *kami*, that is, superior beings.

In worshipping the kami, ritual purity was stressed, and purification rites constituted an important part of Shinto ceremonies. Even today the compounds of Shinto shrines are kept immaculate. Visitors to Shinto shrines usually wash their hands and rinse their mouths with water before entering the sacred grounds, and the Shinto priest waves his sacred wand over their heads to drive the evil spirits away and cleanse the worshippers spiritually.

The ancient imperial court employed an official whose function was to preserve the ceremonial purity of the entire community. It was his duty to observe the taboos and to conduct the rites of abstention. Another official was assigned the task of reciting the litany of purification twice a year to cleanse the people of pollution.

The ancient Japanese made no animal sacrifices to the gods because blood was considered to be defiling. Instead, grain, fruits, and vegetables were proffered to the kami in times of thanksgiving.

This preoccupation with cleanliness and purity was carried over into the moral outlook of the early Japanese. Instead of relying on abstract standards of good and evil, they judged everything in terms of purity and impurity: What was pure was good, what was soiled was bad. "To do good is to be pure; to commit evil is to be impure," states a thirteenth-century Shinto tract. Thus an "unclean" mind or heart was abhorred while a "clean" mind or heart was admired.

The early Japanese evidently did not possess a sense of guilt but were governed instead by a sense of shame. It was shameful to be polluted. When Izanami was followed by Izanagi into the land of darkness and was seen in her state of pollution, she was humiliated and became angry at him for seeing her in that condition.

Another fundamental moral characteristic of the people of Yamato was their pragmatic, utilitarian nature. To the early Japanese what was agreeable was good, what was disagreeable was bad. The pleasant, the beautiful, the auspicious, and the valuable were all regarded as being good.

Since early Shinto was centered upon the uji, the concept of clan solidarity, with its stress on submission to the authority of the patriarchal chieftain, was emphasized. Defense of clan interests required military valor. This is reflected in Shinto by the worship of swords, spears, and bows and arrows as symbols of militaristic gods.

Shinto has been judged by a Western scholar to be "perhaps the most rudimentary religious cult of which we have an adequate written record. It has not advanced beyond crude polytheism; its personifications are vague and feeble; there is little grasp of the conception of spirit; it has scarcely anything in the shape of a moral code."[9]

Joseph Campbell tells a story concerning a Western sociologist who said to a Shinto priest, "You know, I've now been to a number of these Shinto shrines and I've seen quite a few rites, and I've read about it, thought about it; but you know, I don't get the ideology. I don't get your theology." The Shinto priest reflected for a moment and replied smilingly, "We do not have ideology. We not have theology. We dance." This, according to

Campbell, goes to the heart of the matter. "For Shinto, at root, is a religion not of sermons but of awe: which is a sentiment that may or may not produce words, but in either case goes beyond them. Not a 'grasp of the conception of spirit,' but a sense of its ubiquity, is the proper end of Shinto."[10]

Shinto rite is designed to evoke the sense of awe that inspires gratitude to the source and nature of being. "As such, it is addressed as art to the sensibilities—not to faculties of definition. So that living Shinto is not the following of some set-down moral code, but a living in gratitude and awe amid the mystery of things."[11]

Each community and each uji worshipped its own kami in sanctified grounds marked off by trees or fences. Later these primitive sanctuaries were replaced by shrines whose entrances were marked by wooden or stone portals known as tori-i, consisting of two quadrangular beams placed upon two round columns. Shinto ceremonies are simple and austere, consisting of thanksgiving offerings, the recitation of liturgies by the priest, and dancing accompanied by singing and the playing of musical instruments.

SOCIAL PRACTICES AND CONDITIONS

The native religion of ancient Japan had no formalized theological or philosophical interpretation concerning the afterlife; apparently it was believed that after death one went to the land of darkness, where everything was polluted. Consequently, death was viewed as defiling. The *History of Wei* records that "mourning is observed for more than ten days, during which period they [the bereft] do not eat meat. The head mourners wail and lament, while friends sing, dance, and drink liquor. When the funeral is over, all members of the family go into the water to cleanse themselves in a bath of purification."[12]

Upon the death of emperors and great chieftains, huge sepulchral mounds were built to entomb them. This practice started around the end of the third century or the beginning of the fourth century. Some of the tombs were of immense dimensions; the keyhole-shaped barrow of Emperor Nintoku (early fifth century), emcompasses 80 acres and is 90 feet high and 400 yards long. In terms of the area it occupies it is the largest tomb in the world. With the dead was buried a mélange of personal belongings and ornaments, such as bronze mirrors, swords, knives, curved beads, arrowheads, armor, and helmets.

Swords found in the tombs indicate that the long single-edged sword of Han China had replaced the short sword of early Yamato in popularity by the second half of the fifth century. Also by this time the paraphernalia of the mounted warrior had begun to replace the foot soldier's armor.

In addition to these objects, which were buried with the dead, a large number of clay images—known as haniwa (circle of clay) were placed around the mound to strengthen the sides and prevent earth washouts. These terra-cotta figures, which represent human beings, horses, birds, armor, furnishings, utensils, houses, etc., have proven invaluable in enabling archaeologists to reconstruct the mode of life of that era. It is assumed

that these artifacts were designed to replace human beings—perhaps slaves—
who had formerly been buried alive with the dead emperor or chieftain.
"When Pimiku passed away," records the *History of Wei*, "a great mound
was raised, more than a hundred paces in diameter. Over a hundred male
and female attendants followed her to the grave." No archaeological evidence
has been unearthed, however, to confirm that mass retainer burial was in
fact practiced.

The *Nihongi* states that when the younger son of Emperor Suinin (who
is thought to have ruled in the third century) died and his personal
attendants were buried alive with him, "for several days they died not,
but wept and wailed day and night. At last they died and rotted. Dogs
and crows gathered and ate them." The emperor was grieved by all this,
and five years later when the empress died, he asked his ministers to
devise a way to avoid burying her attendants with her. One of his advisers
called together hundreds of clay workers and had them make figures of
men, horses, and other objects and told the emperor, "Henceforth let it
be a law for future ages to substitute things of clay for living men, and
to set them up at tumuli." The emperor thereupon issued a decree stating,
"Henceforth these clay figures must be set up at tumuli; let not men be
harmed."[13] This, it is generally agreed, is a purely legendary account of
the origin of the haniwa. Cylinder-shaped haniwa were used at least a
century before the time of this story. Sepulchral mounds ceased to be
constructed after the introduction of Buddhism because Buddhists favored
cremating the dead. By the beginning of the ninth century, cremation had
become prevalent throughout the land.

In early Yamato society human sacrifice was practiced to propitiate the
gods in order to ensure the successful construction of buildings, bridgeheads,
and dikes. This practice survived as late as the seventeenth century, although
it became increasingly uncommon.

Polygamy was common in this society, and marriages between close
members of the family circle—such as half-brothers and sisters, aunts and
nephews, and stepmothers and stepsons—took place. After marriage the
wife continued to live with her parents; the husband either visited her
periodically or came to reside with her family. This is an aspect of the
matriarchal nature of early Japanese society. The prominent place held by
female deities—after all, the chief deity of Japan is the Sun Goddess—
and female rulers attests to this fact. Until the late eighth century the
Japanese throne was frequently occupied by an empress. Even during the
Tokugawa period the imperial court was twice headed by women. Although
Japan eventually became a decidedly patriarchal society, remnants of
matriarchy persist to the present. For example, when there is no male heir,
the family line is continued through the female issue.

As in other primitive societies, trial by ordeal was practiced in early
Japan also. The *History of the Sui Dynasty*, written around A.D. 630, states,
"Sometimes pebbles are put in boiling water and both parties to a dispute
made to pick them out. The hand of the guilty one is said to become
inflamed. Sometimes a snake is kept in a jar, and the accused ordered to
catch it. If he is guilty, his hand will be bitten."[14]

The protection of the farmers' rice fields was one of the chief concerns of the society. Severe punishments were meted out to troublemakers who destroyed the banks of rice paddies, filled in irrigation ditches, removed water conduits, reseeded fields already seeded, and planted stakes in rice fields to cause harm to others.

Certain actions were considered to be unclean and polluting and were therefore condemned. Skinning an animal alive or skinning it hind-end first was such an offense. It was also believed that the gods viewed as unclean albinos and people with external tumors and warts.

The punishments meted out in ancient Japan were harsh. The *History of Sui* reports that "it is customary to punish murder, arson, and adultery with death. . . . Other offenses are punished according to their nature— sometimes by banishment and sometimes by flogging. In the prosecution of offenses by the court, the knees of those who plead not guilty are pressed together by placing them between pieces of wood, or their heads are sawed with the stretched string of a strong bow."[15]

ARCHITECTURE

During the early Yamato period the simple but striking style of architecture that we see in Japanese shrines had come into existence. These shrines, with their raised platforms, boxlike structures, bargeboards extending above the roofs like the upper half of the letter X, heavy billets set crosswise across the ridges of the roofs, and unpainted, undecorated woodwork, were designed to blend into their natural surroundings. The early shrines still standing at Izumo and Ise are good examples of the style of architecture that prevailed during this protohistoric period.[16]

At Ise there are two shrines four miles apart, the Inner and the Outer shrines. The Inner Shrine was founded, according to the early chronicles, by Emperor Suinin and is dedicated to the Sun Goddess. The Outer Shrine is dedicated to the goddess of agriculture and sericulture. These shrines are surrounded by cedar trees in a beautiful setting. They are supposed to have been reconstructed every twenty years. The fifty-ninth rebuilding since the beginning of this practice in the seventh century took place in 1954. The buildings are constructed without nails or complicated joints, and the plain, unadorned style of the original shrines has been retained.

The early aristocracy lived in houses built on raised platforms, a style of dwelling that came perhaps from the southwest Pacific. Haniwa replicas of houses indicate that relatively substantial abodes were being built by the fourth and fifth centuries, perhaps with the aid of immigrant Korean workmen. The Koreans apparently introduced the practice of using planks in walls and roofs and taught the Japanese how to construct houses on an exactly regular plan using evenly spaced rectangular windows. Models have been found of two-storied buildings with fancy gabled roofs with overhanging bargeboards.

The haniwa figures with their simple but bold geometrical shapes are thought by art historians to be among the most interesting ancient sculptures. A characteristic that distinguished Japanese from Chinese art—the fact that

Inner shrine of the Grand Shrines of Ise dedicated to Amaterasu, the Sun Goddess. Courtesy of the Consulate General of Japan, New York.

the Japanese artist let the material determine his technique rather than allow his designs to dominate the material—is seen in the use of clay by the haniwa makers. The Japanese artist's skill in using natural material effectively and his sensitivity to the natural environment have been distinctive features of Japanese art throughout history.

NOTES

1. Susano-o and his descendants were believed to have been in Izumo, based on the fact that there was a political entity there with ties to Korea, distinct from the Kyushu-Yamato group. The submission of Ōkuninushi is seen as the conquest of the Izumo forces by the Yamato forces.

2. The date 660 B.C. seems to have been arrived at by the compilers of the Nihongi in the following manner: The Chinese had a cyclical time system in which sixty years formed a small cycle, and 1,260 years a large one. An event of revolutionary significance was believed to occur every 1,260 years. The year 601 was such a year. The innovations introduced by Prince Shōtoku around that period could be interpreted as constituting a revolutionary event. Counting back 1,260 years from A.D. 601, 660 B.C. was arrived at as the year for the founding of the imperial government.

3. Recently scholars have analyzed the similarities between the Korean and Japanese myths and have presented persuasive arguments concerning the Korean origins of many Japanese myths about the early gods. Shiba Ryōtarō et al., Nihon no Chōsen Bunka (Korean Culture in Japan) (Tokyo: Chūō Kōronsha, 1972), pp. 292 ff.

4. Joseph Campbell, The Masks of God: Oriental Mythology (New York: Viking, 1962), pp. 465–66.

5. In the post–World War II era archaeological excavations have been conducted extensively, facilitated in part by the relaxation of restrictions on diggings in areas that the imperial government considered to be "sacred" grounds.

6. Recently anthropologists at the Smithsonian Institution have theorized that around 3000 B.C. a Japanese boat that had been blown off course landed in Ecuador, bringing with it Jōmon pots. These influenced the style of Valdivian pottery, which is nearly identical to Jōmon pottery. See the New York Times, January 3, 1966, p. 1.

7. Ryusaku Tsunoda, trans., and L. Carrington Goodrich, ed., Japan in the Chinese Dynastic Histories: Later Han Through Ming Dynasties (South Pasadena, Calif.: Perkins, 1951), p. 13.

8. Wada Atsumu, Taikei Nihon no Rekishi (General Survey of Japanese History), vol. 2 (Tokyo: Shōgakukan, 1988), pp. 119–20, 173–74. Also Gari Ledyard, "Galloping with the Horseriders," Journal of Japanese Studies, Spring 1975, pp. 217 ff.

9. W. G. Aston quoted in Campbell, op. cit., p. 475.

10. Ibid., p. 476.

11. Ibid., p. 477.

12. Tsunoda and Goodrich, op. cit., p. 11.

13. W. G. Aston, trans., Nihongi (New York: Paragon, 1956), part 1, pp. 178–81.

14. Tsunoda and Goodrich, op. cit., p. 30.

15. *Ibid.*, p. 30.

16. "One cannot but remark on the similarity of these buildings to those still used in Indonesia, notably by the Batak of Sumatra." Sherman E. Lee, *A History of Far Eastern Art* (Englewood Cliffs, N.J.: Prentice-Hall, and New York: Abrams, 1964), p. 74.

CHAPTER 2

THE ADVENT AND ASSIMILATION OF CHINESE CIVILIZATION

THE INTRODUCTION
OF CHINESE CIVILIZATION

The fifth and sixth centuries are truly significant from the point of view of Japanese cultural history because it was during those years that Japan was influenced by Chinese civilization on a massive scale, much in the manner in which she was subjected to the influence of Western civilization in the nineteenth century. With the introduction of the Chinese writing system and the infusion of Confucian and Buddhist thought and Chinese arts and crafts into the society, Japan became a "civilized" nation during this period. During the seventh and eighth centuries the continental culture and institutions were assimilated by the Japanese. Immigrants from Korea played a significant role in this process.

The recorded history of Japan starts with the fifth century, for writing was introduced from the continent around A.D. 400. The historical chronicles that are extant were not compiled, however, until the early part of the eighth century. Consequently not all of the Japanese accounts of events and conditions between A.D. 400 and the eighth century are reliable, but they augment other historical evidence to give us a fuller story of Japanese history than that which we have for the preceding period.

From the middle of the third century to the beginning of the fifth century there is no mention in the Chinese historical records of any contact with Japan (due, perhaps, to unstable conditions in China), but fifth century records mention a number of Japanese missions that arrived in China. The Japanese emperors whose names are recorded in these chronicles can be identified as historical figures. The first emperor (referred to as ō, or king, in this period) regarded by many historians as a historical personage is

Emperor Sujin, who ruled either circa A.D. 240 or circa 270–290. A number of historians considered him the real founder of the imperial government in Yamato, not the legendary Emperor Jimmu mentioned in the mythologies. But now some historians consider Sujin to have been a mythical figure too. Only the kings or emperors after the reign of Ōjin (Homuda, who came from Korea), who is believed to have ruled around A.D. 400, are seen as actual historical figures. Many historians believe that a number of "kingly" chieftains contended for power in the fourth and fifth centuries and that it was not until Emperor Keitai of the early sixth century, who overthrew the dynasty established by Ōjin, that the imperial dynasty, which extends to the present, was established on a firm foundation. It is likely then that there were three dynasties in the Yamato period: one established by Sujin; the second by Ōjin and his son Nintoku; and the last, which persists to the present, founded by Keitai. The imperial dynasty does not consist of an unbroken line from 660 B.C. (from the time of Emperor Jimmu) to the present as the official history books, which presented myths as history during the prewar years, claimed.[1]

Intercourse with the continent was carried on prior to the fifth century through Korea. Technical knowledge and material goods had previously entered Japan from the continent, but during the fourth and fifth centuries a large number of artisans and craftsmen immigrated to Japan. The Chinese who had fled their country after the fall of the Han government and had gone to Korea were again forced to escape the political turmoil there; they arrived in Japan in the early fifth century and were organized into functional communities (be) to serve the imperial family.

One of the most significant importations from the continent was the Chinese writing system. No doubt some knowledge of Chinese writing had filtered into Japan before its official introduction, but the story as stated in the chronicles is that during Emperor Ōjin's reign the King of Paekche in Korea sent an envoy, Wani, to Japan with a list of one thousand Chinese characters and a copy of the Confucian *Analects*. The introduction of the Chinese system of writing caused the Japanese vocabulary to be enlarged tremendously and new concepts to enter the Japanese intellectual world. A Japanese dictionary published in 1884 classified thirteen thousand words as of Chinese derivation, compared with twenty-two thousand words of purely Japanese origin. The introduction of the writing system was an epoch-making event that propelled Japan into a new stage in her history. Henceforth records were kept, chronicles were compiled, poetry was anthologized. Chinese literature and philosophy came to be studied, and Confucianism, one of the decisive forces in molding the Japanese character and mode of thought, started to establish its roots in Japanese soil.

Not long after the introduction of Chinese learning to Japan, Confucian values and ideals started to be mirrored in the proclamations and decrees of the Japanese emperors. Confucian virtues such as benevolence, righteousness, propriety, wisdom, and faithfulness were extolled, and the importance of maintaining proper relationships between ruler and subject and between father and son was emphasized. The idea that government should be founded upon the moral character of the ruler also entered

Japanese political thought. Confucianism did not become deeply embedded in the Japanese way of life and thought until the Tokugawa era, when the ruling family adopted Neo-Confucianism as its official philosophy and actively inculcated Confucian moral ideals into the minds of the people. From around the fifth and sixth centuries, Chinese learning and Buddhism constituted the basic ingredients from which Japanese learning and culture emerged and developed.

In the sixth and seventh centuries the second impact from the continent was felt. Again, a large number of Koreans, escaping the political turmoil of their homeland, immigrated to Japan. With them they brought knowledge of medicine, the art of divination, and the calendar.

A far more momentous event was the introduction of Buddhism to Japan during this period. Again there are indications that some segments of the Japanese society, particularly the immigrants from the continent, were already familiar with Buddhism, but the official introduction and formal adoption of this religion did not occur until the latter half of the sixth century. In either 538 or 552, the king of Paekche presented Buddhist images and scriptures to the Japanese court with, it is said, the following message: "This doctrine is amongst all doctrines the most excellent. But it is hard to explain, and hard to comprehend. . . . This doctrine can create religious merit and retribution without measure and without bounds, and so lead on to a full appreciation of the highest wisdom. . . . Every prayer is fulfilled and naught is wanting."[2]

Whether or not to adopt the new religion became a matter of major political controversy at the imperial court. There were at that time two powerful factions competing for power. One group was led by the Mononobe family, in charge of arms, and the Nakatomi family, in charge of religious affairs. The other faction was headed by the newly risen Soga family, which was responsible for financial affairs. The former, representing the conservative faction, opposed the adoption of the new religion, while the latter, representing the new power bloc, favored it. Following a series of intrigues and open clashes, the Soga faction crushed the Mononobe family in 587, and the adoption of Buddhism was officially sanctioned. Thus, even the religion that was to play a vital role in molding the Japanese culture and character was initially a pawn in the struggle for power and influence.

BUDDHISM

Buddhism was founded in the sixth century B.C. in northern India by Gautama Buddha, who, distressed by the human suffering and misery that he saw around him, set out to discover a way to free his fellowmen from their suffering. After years of searching for the answer to his quest, he attained "enlightenment" and formulated what he believed to be the true principles of life, known as the Buddha's Four Noble Truths. Life, he taught, is full of sorrow: birth, disease, old age, and death are misery. The second principle that the Buddha taught was that the cause of all this misery is desire. The craving of the self to satisfy its ego results in the perpetuation of the cycle of birth-death-rebirth and, therefore, in endless misery. Thirdly, the only way to break this cycle and end suffering is to free oneself from this craving, that is, to extinguish the ego. Finally, the way to accomplish this is through an eight-fold path that entails adhering to right views, right intentions, right speech, right conduct, right livelihood, right effort, right mindfulness, and right concentration.

Right views consist of understanding the nature of reality, that is, the truth that life is in a constant state of change and flux; nothing is permanent or absolute. The phenomenal world is only an illusion; there is no absolute reality behind it. Neither the soul nor the self is an absolute entity. The self is actually an ever-changing composite of psychological states, part of a stream of universal consciousness. What persists after death is not the soul but *karma*, the result of our deeds. It is our ignorance that leads us to believe that we are individual entities and causes us to crave satisfaction of our selfish impulses. By following the eight-fold path and gaining self-mastery and self-knowledge, the sense of the self is extinguished and the state of *nirvana* is attained.

Because the Buddha never clearly explained what the state of nirvana is and because the exact nature of the eight-fold path is open to varying interpretations, many different Buddhist sects came into existence. But Buddhism can be divided into two major branches: Mahayana, or the Greater Vehicle, and Hinayana, or the Lesser Vehicle. The adherents of the latter group prefer to be called Theravada Buddhists or the followers of the Way of the Elders. Although Buddhism eventually declined in India, it spread to other parts of Asia and flourished as one of the major religions of the world. Theravada Buddhism spread into Southeast Asia, while Mahayana Buddhism extended into China, Korea, and Japan. The former stresses the attainment of the state of nirvana through self-knowledge and self-mastery, whereas the latter offers salvation with the help of *bodhisattvas*, merciful Buddhist deities who have attained enlightenment but have postponed entrance into the state of nirvana in order to help those who are incapable of gaining salvation by themselves.

As we noted, Buddhism was adopted officially in Japan because of the triumph of the Soga family over its political rivals. Buddhism's beneficence, the chronicles record, was judged in terms of its ability to outdo the Shinto gods in controlling the forces of nature, but no doubt the ruling class was most impressed by the learned scriptures and beautiful artifacts that accompanied the religion. In the early period of its adoption, Buddhism appealed only to a small elite, who either took a scholastic interest in its scriptures or were interested in its more esoteric and ritualistic aspects. The masses were at first largely unaffected by the new religion, but as Buddhist temples and monasteries began to be constructed, not only in the seat of the imperial government but also in the outlying provinces, the impact of Buddhism upon the lower classes began to grow.

PRINCE SHŌTOKU

After Buddhism was officially adopted in Japan, it found a powerful and enthusiastic supporter in the person of a very able leader,

Prince Shōtoku (574–622), who exercised authority as regent to the empress from 593 until his death.

There was an urgent need to reorganize the government and strengthen the position of the imperial court. The leading clans had ensconced themselves in the central government and had begun to overshadow the imperial authority. Moreover, the rivalry among the leading families was undermining the stability of the government. In the provincial areas, also, the clan chieftains and the provincial governors appointed by the imperial court were beginning to act independently of the central government, usurping the right of taxation and extending their power by seizing the lands of their weaker neighbors. There is some evidence to indicate that the general disorder of the period was caused in part by the rise in population and the consequent struggle over existing resources.

In order to deal with this situation, Prince Shōtoku in cooperation with the Soga family initiated certain changes. Hoping to end the hereditary control of top government posts by the entrenched elite families and allow men of ability to rise to positions of importance, he established a table of ranks. There were to be twelve grades for government officials. Reflecting the Confucian influence, senior and junior ranks entitled "virtue," "benevolence," "propriety," "good faith," "righteousness," and "wisdom" were created. In theory, men of talent were to be appointed to these ranks and assigned appropriate government positions.

The prince also promulgated in 604 what is known as the "Constitution of Seventeen Articles."[3] It is not a constitution as we ordinarily understand the term, that is, a document that defines the structure, functions, and powers of the government. Rather, it is a set of moral injunctions that were intended to serve as guiding principles for government officials. These moral injunctions were meant to strengthen the authority of the imperial family. Article III states: "When you receive the imperial commands, fail not scrupulously to obey them. The lord is Heaven, the vassal is Earth. Heaven overspreads, and Earth upbears." Article XII decrees: "Let not the provincial authorities . . . levy exactions on the people. In a country there are not two lords; the people have not two masters. The sovereign is the master of the people of the whole country."[4]

Prince Shōtoku and the reformers who followed him not only adopted the Chinese view that the emperor was the supreme ruler possessing the sanction of Heaven but went further and equated him with Heavenly power itself. Being the direct descendant of the Sun Goddess, the emperor was not a mere mortal who received the Mandate of Heaven—a mandate that the Chinese emperor received because of his superior moral character—but was a living god. Around this period or soon after, the emperor came to be referred to as *Aketsu-mikami* (manifestation of kami, or god) or *Arahito-gami* (kami appearing as man). Thus, although Confucian concepts were imported into Japan, the Japanese did not speak of the Mandate of Heaven, a basic principle in Confucian political philosophy. In a way, the military rulers (*shōgun*) who emerged later were the ones who received the Mandate of Heaven, that is, the imperial mandate to govern on behalf of the emperor. Consequently, although they became the real wielders of power, they never eliminated the emperor; they continued to pay lip service to him as if he were the true sovereign. The emperor was necessary as the symbol of Heaven, and his outward approval, or even tacit consent, was indispensable to the shōgun.

It was also during Prince Shōtoku's time or slightly later that the term *tennō* (heavenly prince) came to be applied to the emperor, rather than the terms *ō* (king) or *ōgimi* (great lord) used until then. The term tennō was also imported from China; the first use of the word is found in the *Shih Chi, Historical Records,* written by the great Chinese historian Ssu Ma-ch'ien in the first century B.C.

That Confucian concepts influenced the framers of the Constitution is discernible throughout the entire Constitution. The Confucian ideals of propriety, good faith, harmony, etc., are upheld in different passages. The Legalist viewpoint is seen in this document in its emphasis on the necessity of properly meting out rewards and punishments.[5] As one might expect, Buddhist precepts are also embodied in the document. Article II, for example, reads, "Sincerely reverence the three treasures. The three treasures, *viz.* Buddha, the Law, and the Priesthood, are the final refuge of the four generated beings, and are the supreme objects of faith in all countries."[6]

Throughout most of Japanese history an aversion to dictatorial rule prevailed. This is reflected in Article XVII of the Constitution: "Decisions on important matters should not be made by one person alone. They should be discussed with many." This injunction did not immediately produce significant changes in the government, but it provided the basis for later attempts to centralize political power.

Efforts to broaden contact with China continued during Prince Shōtoku's regency and after. Embassies to the courts of Sui (581–618) and T'ang (618–907) were dispatched, and students and monks were encouraged to travel to China to study its religion and culture. Sixteen missions were sent to China during the T'ang period.

THE TAIKA REFORMS

The imperial court's efforts to strengthen the authority of the central government failed. The reformers' hope of weakening the position of the entrenched elite families through the implementation of the new table of ranks was not fulfilled because it failed to replace the old kabane system as the basis for power and status in the government. In the provinces, leading clans continued to extend their landholdings at the expense of weaker clans and to poach upon public lands and forests. At the center, the Soga family, which steadily gained in power after their victory over the Mononobe and Nakatomi families, had fastened a firm grip on the government and began behaving in an arbitrary fashion, controlling the succession to the imperial throne. It appeared as if they might even usurp the sovereignty of the imperial family. Consequently, their opponents awaited an opportunity to oust them and to effect a general reform to strengthen the authority of the imperial court.

The situation in Korea also caused the political leaders in Japan to feel the acute need to strengthen the powers of the central government. Korea, it appeared, might fall under the control of T'ang China. If this were to happen Japan's security would be endangered. The Sui dynasty had invaded Korea three times during the second decade of the seventh century in an attempt to bring the kingdom of Koguryo under its control. These invasions had failed, but in 644 the founder of the T'ang dynasty led a huge army against Koguryo. Japan's old antagonist, Silla, cooperated with the T'ang authorities and attacked Koguryo and Paekche, hoping to establish its hegemony over all of Korea with the aid of the T'ang forces. Japan sent an expeditionary force into the Korean peninsula to aid Paekche, but the Japanese forces were defeated in 663 at Paekch'on. This had an important impact on Japan's relations with the continent because it undercut the close political ties Japan had with Korea prior to this. It also affected internal politics significantly. The possibility that the T'ang government might invade Japan after bringing Korea under control alarmed the Japanese court and touched off a reform movement to strengthen its internal political foundation.

In 644 the foes of the Sogas rallied around Prince Naka-no-Ōe (626–671), who later became Emperor Tenchi, to liquidate the Soga family. A leading figure in this coup was Nakatomi-no-Kamatari (611–669), a descendant of the foes of the Soga family at the time of the Buddhist controversy. He founded the powerful Fujiwara family that was to dominate the imperial government for the succeeding four centuries or so.

With the removal of the Sogas the new ruling clique set about initiating political, social, and economic reforms. The object was to strengthen the imperial authority and weaken the influence of the powerful families entrenched in the outlying regions.

The series of reforms started by Prince Naka-no-Ōe and his supporters is referred to as the Taika Reforms, after the era name adopted by them. (The use of era names was one of the innovations introduced by the reformers.) An edict was issued in 646 calling for reforms, but not all changes were implemented immediately; they extended into the next century. In 702 the Taihō Code, a compendium of penal laws and administrative practices, was written. This was a codification of all the administrative and legal changes that had been implemented or had been under preparation since 646. The reformers looked to T'ang China for their models, though they did not, of course, introduce exact replicas of T'ang institutions and practices. For the sake of convenience we can consider the changes listed in the Taihō Code as the major aspects of the general reform movement labeled the Taika Reforms.

The initial step taken by Prince Naka-no-Ōe and the reformers was to reaffirm the supremacy of the imperial authority. "The imperial way," they asserted, "is but one. But in this last degenerate age, the order of Lord and Vassal was destroyed. . . . Now, from this time forward . . . the Lord will eschew double methods of government, and the vassal will avoid duplicity in his service of the sovereign."[7]

The central government was reorganized. The offices of the great omi and the great muraji were abolished and replaced with the minister of the left, the minister of the right, and the minister of the center. The last of these served as the personal adviser to the emperor and consequently was the most important government official. Initially Nakatomi-no-Kamatari held this post. Under the Taihō Code, the occupant of this post was made the highest administrative officer and was called the *dajō daijin* (chancellor). He presided over the *Dajōkan* (Grand Council of State), which included the minister of the left and the minister of the right. The former was in charge of all the administrative departments and the latter served as his deputy. The office of dajō daijin was frequently left open, in which case the minister of the left usually served as the chief administrative officer.

Under the Dajōkan there were eight ministries or departments: Central Administration, Ceremonial, Civil Affairs, People's Affairs, War, Justice, Treasury, and Imperial Household. An Office of Deities (*Jingikan*), having precedence over the Dajōkan, was created to manage Shinto rituals at the court.

In local administration, the country was divided into 66 provinces, which were subdivided into 592 counties, which were in turn broken down into townships consisting of 50 households each. Provincial governors appointed by the central government were instructed to prepare registers of all the free and unfree subjects of the land and to investigate the titles of the clan chieftains claiming landownership and authority in their districts. Armories were to be built, and all weapons in the possession of private persons were to be stored in them.

These local reforms did not, however, spell the end of the authority of the clan chieftains; many were appointed governors of the provinces where they were entrenched. Generally speaking, the county heads were also chosen from among former landowners and clan leaders. Despite its desire to do so, the imperial government was not in a position to uproot all the vested interests in the outlying areas.

The provincial governors were given the power to levy taxes, but initially they did not have judicial authority. This remained in the hands of the county heads. The people, however, had the right to appeal the decisions of the county heads to the central government. The provincial governors' term of office was limited to about six years, but the county heads held lifetime tenures and their sons frequently succeeded them. Consequently they were able to develop and protect their interests in their respective counties.

The be, or functional communities, were abolished as part of the effort to undercut the strength of the major clans. This did not mean that the members of the corporations were made free and independent. Instead of being under the direct control of the clan chieftains they were now under the authority of the imperial government.

In the economic realm a significant attempt was made to change the nature of land tenure. Again following a practice of T'ang China, where a policy of maintaining equal landholding prevailed, the Taika reformers sought to equalize landholding in order to weaken the power that the clan chieftains exercised over the land and people under their control. For this purpose all land in the country was to be nationalized. To set an example,

Naka-no-Ōe transferred his land and workers to the public domain in 646 and asked other property holders to follow suit. They did so without much resistance because they were usually appointed governors of the areas in which their interests lay. Thus, although in theory they derived their authority from the imperial government, in reality they managed to retain their former privileges and interests. Moreover, the plan to nationalize all land was not put fully into effect. Important clansmen were allowed to hold a certain amount of land, commensurate with their rank and position. By special fiat the emperor also created tax-free estates for privileged members of the court or aristocracy.

The nationalized land was to be redistributed among the people. For this purpose a census was taken, and population registers were compiled. Everyone except slaves,[8] who were given smaller allotments, was to be given an equal share of land: 2 *tan* (1 tan was 30 paces long by 12 paces wide) for each male over the age of six and two-thirds that figure for each female. Individual families, however, did not have independent control over their land allotments. The family allotments were incorporated into communal holdings under the jurisdiction of local leaders. Members of the imperial family and nobility were entitled to larger allotments, from 16 to 160 acres, depending upon rank. Every six years a general redistribution was to be effected in order to ensure continued equality in holding.

An additional inducement to effect the land-reform program was the government's desire to increase its revenue by bringing private estates into the public domain. Consequently, at the same time the new land policy was introduced taxation was systematized, and a tax of 2 to 3 percent of the harvest was instituted. Estates held by monasteries and shrines, however, were exempt.

Although the land tax was fairly light, there were other forms of taxation that added to this burden. Each adult male was required to contribute to the government a fixed amount of such goods as silk and hemp fabrics. Corvée had to be performed for both the central government and the local authorities. The amount of labor exacted by the former was normally ten days a year but could be extended up to forty more days. When labor services were not needed the government asked for contributions of produce instead. The provincial governors could demand up to sixty days' service each year. In addition to the regular corvée, construction work on special projects such as the temples, shrines, and public buildings was required.

The Taihō Code also instituted military conscription. One-third of all males between the ages of twenty-one and sixty were required to serve from one to three years in the army. While the recruits were in the army they were obliged to provide their own weapons, food, and other necessities. Because of its ineffectiveness, however, the conscript army was abandoned in 792.

In theory the Taika Reforms opened government posts to men of ability and merit, but high government positions were still closed to men who did not rank high in the newly established system of court ranks. A person's standing in this system depended upon his family background or upon his success in examinations taken after attending the government college.

The practice of choosing officials by means of examinations was also imported from T'ang China, but in Japan the college was open only to children of government officials, so government service was limited to family members of the governing clans. As a result, the new system did not in reality provide for "a career open to talent." The ruling class was determined to preserve the hereditary governing caste. In 682 the emperor issued an edict stating, "Let the lineage and character of all candidates for office be always inquired into before a selection is made. None whose lineage is insufficient are eligible for appointments, even though their character, conduct and capacity may be unexceptionable."[9]

Another practice borrowed from China was the establishment of barriers (sekisho), check points in strategic places to restrict the movement of people. It proved particularly useful in controlling peasants fleeing from the tax collectors.

The establishment of a permanent capital was another practice adopted from China. In 710 Nara was selected as the site for the new capital. Prior to this the seat of government varied with each emperor because his residence became the center of government. Because death was regarded as defiling, no emperor resided in the same house that the former emperor had lived in. As a result, no permanent seat of government came into existence.

Now for the first time there was to be a capital city. This had a double significance because prior to this time hardly any Japanese community could have been called a city or even a town. Now an elaborate city and capital—modeled after the T'ang capital of Ch'ang-an, although only half its size—was constructed. It was laid out in checkerboard fashion with the imperial court placed at the center of the northern end of the city. A major thoroughfare, about 280 feet wide, ran through the center from north to south, dividing the city into two parts. One aspect of the layout of the Chinese capital that the builders of Nara did not adopt was the practice of building a wall around the city. At this time the Japanese were evidently less security-conscious than the Chinese. Perhaps they also abhorred the idea of cutting the city off from its natural environment. Public buildings, residences for the aristocracy, and many Buddhist structures were built in Nara, which became the center of political and cultural life in Japan from 710 to 784. The population of Nara at its peak is estimated to have reached 200,000. The years in which Nara was the capital are known as the Nara period.

The objectives of the Taika reformers were not fully attained and the changes introduced were not thoroughly implemented, but the imperial institution was strengthened and the authority of the central government was fortified. The emperor was endowed with greater prestige and dignity. The central government's administrative organs were systematized, and its control over provincial and local areas was strengthened by eliminating the be and nationalizing the land. In theory, the people and the land were now in the public domain, not the private possessions of the clan chieftains. The systems of taxation and compulsory service and the penal code were all designed to strengthen the central government's control over the populace.

The power and prestige of the prominent clans, on the other hand, were not diminished. The uji leaders were now incorporated into the top rungs of the central government's new bureaucracy as high officials or as provincial and county governors. They retained the privilege of collecting the taxes from the areas to which they were assigned. Moreover, they were paid generous stipends, were exempt from taxation, and were given special considerations in the enforcement of penal laws against them. The status and privileges of the officials of the upper ranks were inherited by their children. Thus the leading families retained their special status. In addition they were acquiring a strong cultural tradition, which gave them a further advantage over the masses; they were becoming a cultural as well as a political aristocracy.

At the beginning of the eighth century the number of officials occupying the higher ranks of the bureaucracy is estimated to have been no more than 125 men. They held the highest offices in the central government and served as governors of the key provinces. In addition there were about ten court aristocrats who were involved in decision-making at the very top level. These two groups of men constituted the elite—politically, socially, economically, and culturally. The gap between the aristocracy and the masses was further widened by the fact that the aristocracy tended to remain in the capital and manifested a growing unwillingness to serve in the countryside.

CULTURE OF THE SEVENTH
AND EIGHTH CENTURIES

Chinese civilization had a more lasting impact on Japan in the cultural sphere than in the political and social realms. The art and architecture that came from China were primarily Buddhist in nature, and, as temples and monasteries were constructed throughout the land, the cultural level of the society was greatly enhanced. The shapely, well-balanced tile roofs, the many-storied pagodas, and the vermilion gateways of Buddhist precincts undoubtedly would have made a Chinese or a Korean visitor of this period feel very much at home.

The art of sculpture took root in Japan and flourished very rapidly, reaching a level of figural art "never surpassed in the Far East."[10] The Buddhist structures that were springing up throughout the countryside were embellished with expertly carved wooden images and glittering bronze figures of the Buddha, the Kannon (Bodhisattva Avalokitesvara), and other Buddhist deities. Paintings and frescoes with Buddhist motifs also added new dimensions to the culture of Japan.[11]

The most renowned of the Buddhist edifices was the Hōryūji. The original buildings, constructed in 607, were destroyed in a fire and were rebuilt at the end of the seventh century. Nonetheless, they are believed to be the oldest wooden buildings extant in the world today. The plan of the monastery was patterned after the style of building in the Chinese Six Dynasties (222–589), with a relatively asymmetrical arrangement of the buildings. The five-storied pagoda with its gently curving tile roof occupies

Hōryūji, a Buddhist monastery in Nara. Founded in 607 by Prince Shōtoku, the principal buildings were constructed over a period of several centuries. Courtesy of the Consulate General of Japan, New York.

a prominent place in the compound, as does the Golden Hall. The structures convey a sense of order, balance, and cohesion; the pagoda in particular has a stately dignity and grace. The buildings use the Chinese bay system, a modified version of post-and-lintel construction employing intricate bracketing designed to transfer the weight of the heavy tile roof down through the wooden parts into the main columns that support the structure. The interior of the buildings is adorned with Buddhist frescoes and wooden and bronze statues. In 1949 the Golden Hall caught fire and the priceless frescoes were destroyed.

The construction of Buddhist monasteries was given further impetus by Emperor Shōmu (701–756), who ordered them to be built in all the sixty-six provinces. In Nara itself, the Tōdaiji, where a great bronze Buddha over 50 feet tall is housed, was constructed in the middle of the eighth century. The Great Buddha sits on a lotus petal with his right hand signifying "fear not" and his left hand making a boon-bestowing gesture. The Tōdaiji complex is much larger than Hōryūji, occupying about 20 acres. The columns, bracketing, and other architectural parts are also more elaborate and massive. The several halls house innumerable Buddhist images—made of dry lacquer, clay, wood, and gilded bronze—patterned after early and middle T'ang styles.

THE ADVENT OF CHINESE CIVILIZATION

The Shōsōin, where more than six thousand objects from this era are housed, was also built in the Nara period. Among the treasures stored here are the oldest printed manuscript extant in the world, brocades, silk fabrics, screen panels, musical instruments, mirrors, bowls, ivory works, lacquerware, dance masks, and weapons. Many of these were imported from China. Some items show traces of Eastern Roman, Persian, and Indian influence. Evidently objects from distant areas had found their way to Japan. The articles stored in the Shōsōin are still in excellent condition because the log construction "breathes with the seasonal changes in humidity, keeping out the damp and allowing the dry air of late summer and fall to circulate freely."[12]

Buddhism was still restricted largely to the aristocracy during this period. The abstruse philosophy was beyond the comprehension of the masses. In fact, both upper and lower classes together were attracted more to the pomp and ceremony of the rituals, the glitter of the benevolent- and merciful-looking images and the special powers that they believed the Buddhist gods possessed than they were to Buddhist doctrine. In a way, Buddhism was regarded as a magical cult. The people prayed to the Buddhist deities to give them good fortune, good health, and prosperity and to ward off the evil spirits and help them escape the pains and miseries of life as well as the many hells whose existence popular Buddhism envisioned.

With the arrival of monks from the continent, however, a small circle of specialists began studying the religion seriously. Six Buddhist schools arose during the Nara period, but none became a major movement. Three became extinct, while three have survived to the present with only a small number of adherents. The largest of these, the Hossō school, aimed at discovering the ultimate reality of cosmic existence through the investigation of the specific nature of all existence and a mystical apprehension of the nature of the soul. The second, the Kegon sect, sought communion with the Buddha, who embodies the cosmic soul, and, through him, communion with all beings. The third, the Ritsu school, emphasized monastic discipline and the mystical concepts embodied in the mysteries of the initiation ceremonies.

Some Buddhist priests were not content merely to engage in scholastic or mystical activities but sought to spread the word among the people and to do good works by building roads and bridges into previously inaccessible areas. The most notable of these missionaries was a monk named Gyōki, who was first condemned as a rabble rouser and preacher of false doctrines but was later honored as a high priest.

The native religion, Shinto, retained the following of the masses but it began increasingly to pale next to Buddhism, because it had no priestly caste, no elaborate moral code, and no heaven or hell. Neither could it match the glitter and glamour of the Buddhist artifacts and rituals. Moreover, the wealth and profundity of Buddhist teachings greatly overshadowed Shinto. As a result, even at this early stage attempts were made by Shintoists to reconcile their traditional beliefs with Buddhist concepts so as to enhance Shinto's spiritual and intellectual standing. This kind of syncretism did not take concrete form until the following centuries, however. Like the Chinese, the Japanese did not demand exclusive loyalty to any one religion; a person could worship at both a Shinto shrine and a Buddhist temple. Thus Shinto and Buddhism coexisted peacefully.

Perhaps an even more significant cultural development of this period was the emergence of a native written literature. At the beginning of the eighth century, the mythologies and legends concerning the founding of Japan, which had been transmitted orally down through the ages, were transcribed in the *Kojiki* (*Records of Ancient Matters*) and *Nihongi* (*Chronicles of Japan*).[13] Both works were patterned after Chinese chronicles and contain a number of stories that are not part of the indigenous tradition.

The compilation of these histories was started in the 670s as a project to revise and expand two earlier accounts, one a genealogical record of the imperial family and the other a collection of old tales. These two histories, it is conjectured, were written in the sixth century, but neither has survived. Their existence is known only because they are mentioned in the *Kojiki*. It is believed that the *Kojiki* and the *Nihongi* were based on oral tradition, on the two earlier works, and on Chinese and Korean sources. Accounts of political events prior to the sixth century are considered to be unreliable because the historical record is that commissioned by Emperor Temmu (who reigned from 673 to 686) to justify and glorify his dynastic lineage. The truism that "it is axiomatic that history is written by the victor" applies here. Political rivals such as the Soga family are depicted in a negative fashion. The official accounts formulated in Temmu's reign were incorporated in the *Kojiki* and *Nihongi*. The *Kojiki* consists primarily of mythological and legendary tales and contains very little that might be regarded as historical. The *Nihongi*, however, focuses more on history proper, and its coverage extends to A.D. 697. As noted above, its accounts of earlier years are questionable, but accounts from about the sixth century are considered to be fairly accurate although they are still embellished with materials taken from Chinese and Korean, especially Paekche, sources.

Although they are not entirely reliable as historical documents, as records of myths and legends of early Japan the *Kojiki* and *Nihongi* are significant. For one thing, they aided in establishing the tradition that claimed a divine origin for the imperial family. Partly because of the sanctity and authority conferred upon it by these accounts, the imperial family was able to maintain its special status above the rest of the society. These records became authoritative "scriptures" in the modern age when the ultranationalists turned to them to prove the uniqueness of the Japanese national polity.

The *Kojiki* and *Nihongi* symbolized the growing sense of ethnocentrism that is discernible in the seventh century. Japan is viewed in these accounts as a unique land. In fact, it was depicted as being at the center of the universe, and the ancestral god of Japan, the Sun Goddess, was seen as the ruler of the entire world. From around the middle of the seventh century the term *Nihon*, the place where the sun rises, came to be used to identify Japan. Much of the cultural activity of this era sprang from the Japanese desire to rise to the level of China.

Another significant literary accomplishment of this period was the compilation of the *Man'yōshū*, a collection of over four thousand long and short poems from the earliest period—although the majority of the poems anthologized had been composed after the fifth century—to about 760. The collection is invaluable not only for its intrinsic literary merit, but because it reflects the moral and intellectual outlook of early Japan. It is noteworthy that it includes poems composed not just by emperors and court nobles but also by nameless plebians. The Korean influence is also present in the anthology. One of the three main poets of the *Man'yōshū*, Yamanoe Okura, it is now believed, was a Korean immigrant in Japan.[14]

Motoori Norinaga, an eighteenth-century authority on the subject, indicated that the outlook that prevails throughout the *Manyōshū* is one of spontaneous, unadorned expression of natural human sentiments—even excessive sentimentality. The Confucian ideals of order, control, and restraint had not yet begun to mold the attitudes of the Japanese. The anthology consists of poems about nature, the landscape, the four seasons, flowers, birds, moonlight, the sorrows and joys of life, and, above all, love.

The belief that a man must not lay bare his feelings regarding such "unmanly" sentiments as love for the opposite sex, particularly his spouse, had not yet become embedded in the Japanese mind, whereas by the Tokugawa period love of wife and children came to be condemned as self-indulgence. For example, the following poem probably would not have been composed later, after the military class had become dominant.

> My wife and I are one in heart:
>> However long we are side by side
> She is charming all the more;
> Though face to face we sit,
> She my cherished love,
> Is ever fresh as a new flower. . . .

What appear to be Buddhist and Confucian ideas are discernible here and there in the *Man'yōshū*. For example, the following poems seem to reflect the Buddhist view of the ephemeral nature of life.

> Brief is this mortal life—
>> Let me go and seek the Way,
> Contemplating the hills and streams undefiled.

>> How brief is this lease of life,
>> To think my days will end,
>> Lost in those falling flowers of spring.

There are frequent expressions of loyalty to the emperor, such as the following poem, which schoolchildren in prewar Japan knew by heart:

> At sea be my body water-soaked,
> On land be it with grass overgrown,

Let me die by the side of my Sovereign!
Never will I look back.

Faithful service to the emperor was essential for the preservation of the honor of the family and clan.

Our forefathers served the Imperial House
With all their hearts faithful and true. . . .
So cherished and clean is the name of our clan,
Neglect it never, lest even a false word
Should destroy this proud name of our father. . . .

The Spartan attitude of the warriors of later years had not come to the fore as yet. A warrior taking leave of his family at the command of his sovereign departs with a heavy heart:

My wife and children gathering about here and there,
Wailed like birds of spring,
Their sleeves all wet with weeping. . . .
Having left my dear ones far behind,
My mind knew no rest
While the pain of longing wrung my heart.[15]

Traditionalists claim that the *Man'yōshū* embodies the Japanese outlook before Japan was strongly affected by Chinese culture. The influence of Chinese poetry and literature could not be kept out of the literary realm for long, however. In the newly established college and in the provincial schools the Chinese classics formed the core of the curriculum. The educated soon became well versed in Chinese poetry and literature, and they came to admire and emulate the works of such great T'ang poets as Li Po and Tu Fu.

In addition to utilizing Confucian concepts to buttress their political authority, the ruling authorities sought to instill in the people other aspects of Confucian thought. For instance, in 757 the emperor advised every family to keep a copy of the *Hsiao Ching* (a Confucian discourse on filial piety) and learn its contents. The *Hsiao Ching* taught that filial piety forms the foundation of all virtues and that all other teachings must be based upon it.

In other cultural developments, musical instruments, including a variety of wind, percussion, and string instruments, as well as dances, including Indian-style dances, came from the continent.

SOCIAL AND ECONOMIC CONDITIONS

In the economic realm, too, the influence of the continent pervaded. Better tools were imported, improved methods of irrigation were introduced, and wheat came to be produced in dry fields. These measures, it has been said, increased productivity. Recently, however, some scholars have concluded that epidemics, poor distribution of technology, abandonment of farm land by the peasants, and widely scattered farm settlements led to economic backwardness in this period.[16]

From the middle of the seventh century, copper, gold, and silver mines came to be exploited more extensively. Prior to this most of the minerals used in Japan were imported from Korea. With the construction of better roads and the introduction of horse stations to facilitate travel for government officials, commerce expanded and markets began to spring up in the major cities. In 708 the government minted its own coins, but a money economy did not develop to any significant extent right away. Rice and fabrics remained the chief mediums of exchange during the Nara period.

Medical knowledge and drugs also came from China during this period, and the long tradition of Chinese medicine in Japan, which persisted into the twentieth century, was founded. This included the use of not only herbs but also acupuncture (treatment by needles) and moxacautery (cauterizing with moxa leaves). But medicine in this age, of course, was powerless in face of the periodic epidemics that broke out. The smallpox epidemic of 735–37 killed 25 to 35 percent of the population.[17]

The smallest administrative unit introduced under the Taika Reforms was the township or village, consisting of fifty households. The size of the households varied but usually they consisted of several small or nuclear families within an extended family. The census records show that one household in central Honshu had 96 members, 59 of whom were slaves. Another in northern Kyushu included 126 members, 37 of whom were slaves.

Although slaves had existed in earlier days, the Taiho Code mentions them as *senmin* (base people, which included other semi-indentured people) and distinguished them from free men (*ryōmin*, or good people). Slaves could be bought and sold, but the masters did not have judicial authority over them; if a slave committed a crime he was tried by the magistrates. They were expected to work around the house and in the fields and also to perform corvée in place of their masters. It is believed that they were not treated too harshly, and their lot was more or less akin to that of household servants of later ages.

Although the Taika reformers adopted the patriarchal concepts of China, in reality it appears that women continued to enjoy a status equal to that of men. The wife had property rights, and women were given court ranks independent of their male relatives. Family life still centered around the mother. In most instances husband and wife lived apart, and the latter kept and raised the children, but the practice of the father retaining the children was becoming more prevalent in the late seventh century.

Polygamy was still common among the upper class. The emperor had a number of wives and concubines. The Taihō Code made provisions for the emperor to have nine concubines. There were also over two hundred female attendants serving at the court. Empresses were usually chosen from the emperor's immediate family circle, so close consanguineous marriages frequently took place. The first wife was usually chosen by the parents with political considerations in mind. Otherwise the young people were allowed to choose their own mates.

By the Nara period the aristocracy lived in houses with wooden floors and wooden or tile roofs. The common people, however, still lived in hovels with dirt floors, thatched roofs, and only primitive household furnishings. They usually went about barefoot, while members of the upper class wore wooden shoes or clogs, which were in use as early as the Yayoi period. Meals were taken only twice a day. Although Buddhism forbade the killing of living creatures and the eating of meat, the proscription was ignored by most of the people, and meat and fish were consumed. Buddhism also introduced the practice of cremating the dead.

INTERNAL AND EXTERNAL FOES

From the latter part of the seventh century Japan followed a defensive policy in her relations with Korea, in contrast to her earlier attempts to extend her political influence into the peninsula. Korea was now under the control of China and Silla, Japan's traditional foe, a potentially dangerous situation for Japan. Fearing a possible invasion from the peninsula, the Japanese rulers began to fortify northern Kyushu and southeastern Honshu. A military defense command was established at Dazaifu in Kyushu. The threat from Korea persisted even after Silla drove the T'ang forces out of the peninsula only a few years after they had joined forces to conquer Paekche and Koguryo. The Japanese kept their fortifications in good repair and kept a close watch on political developments in Korea.

Toward the latter part of the eighth and beginning of the ninth centuries the relationship between Japan and Silla became tense when the latter sent vessels to raid the Japanese coastal regions. In 894 Silla attempted to invade the island of Tsushima but failed. The potential threat of Silla contributed to the consolidation of the military tradition in Japan by compelling the Japanese to maintain military vigilance for nearly four centuries following Silla's destruction of the Japanese outpost in Mimana in 562.

Internal forces—hostile domestic tribes—also kept the imperial government preoccupied with military preparedness. The tribes of Kumaso and Hayato in Kyushu and the Ezo in the north resisted the imperial forces for centuries. The racial origins of the Kumaso and Hayato are not known, but from the early years of the Yamato state the imperial government was compelled to send its warriors against them. The Kumaso tribe disappeared from historical accounts early, but it was not until the beginning of the eighth century that the Hayato were brought under control. By the middle of the seventh century the Ezo were driven out of the Kantō region and were pushed into northeastern Honshu.[18] They continued to defy the imperial government, however, which found it necessary to send expeditionary forces against them periodically. Advance outposts were established in the north, and constant vigilance was maintained. The general in charge of the expeditionary troops was given the title *seiitaishōgun*, generalissimo in charge of subduing the barbarians. (After the late twelfth century this office was used as a stepping stone to exercise military control over the entire land.) In the early eighth century the northern region was brought more or less under the imperial government's control, although a major campaign had to be launched against the Ezo again at the end of the century. Like Silla, these domestic opponents of imperial authority can be viewed as having contributed to the strengthening of military tradition early in Japanese history.

NOTES

1. See Carl Ledyard, "Galloping with the Horseriders," *Journal of Japanese Studies,* Spring 1975, p. 254. Also Wada Atsumu, *Taikei Nihon no Rekishi (General Survey of Japanese History),* vol. 2 (Tokyo: Shogakukan, 1988), p. 172.

2. W. G. Aston, trans., *Nihongi* (New York: Paragon, 1956), part 2, p. 66.

3. Prince Shōtoku's authorship of the Constitution as well as the other reforms ascribed to him has been questioned in recent years. Some historians credit the Soga family with these reforms. Kim Sok-hyong and Matsumoto Seichō, "Kodaishi no Naka no Chōsen to Nihon" ("Korea and Japan in Ancient History"), *Chūō Kōron,* December 1972, p. 285.

4. For the Seventeen Articles see Aston, *op. cit,* part 2, pp. 129–33.

5. The Legalists, opponents of Confucianism, believed that moral precepts were useless in governing the people. Rigorous enforcement of the law was the method they favored.

6. The four generated beings are beings "born from eggs, from a womb, moisture-bred, or formed by metamorphosis (as butterflies from caterpillars). Aston, *op. cit.,* part 2, p. 129.

7. Aston, *op. cit.,* part 2, pp. 197–98.

8. Estimates of the size of the population and number of slaves that existed during this time vary. Earlier estimates held that the overall population numbered between 3 and 3.5 million, with slaves constituting about 5 percent of this figure. More recently it has been estimated that the population was about 6 million, with the slave population running as high as 10 or 15 percent.

9. Aston, *op. cit.,* part 2, p. 357.

10. Sherman E. Lee, *A History of Far Eastern Art* (Englewood Cliffs, N.J.: Prentice-Hall, and New York: Abrams, 1964), p. 146.

11. In art history the period roughly from the middle of the sixth to the middle of the seventh century is known as the Asuka period, and the eighth century is called the Tempyō period.

12. Lee, *op. cit.,* p. 274.

13. The *Nihongi* is also known as *Nihon-shoki.*

14. See Roy Andrew Miller, "Plus Ca Change," *Journal of Asian Studies,* August 1980, p. 776.

15. All of the poems quoted here are from the *Manyōshū,* translated by the Nippon Gakujutsu Shinkōkai (The Japan Society for the Promotion of Scientific Research) (New York: Columbia University Press, 1965), pp. 139, 142, 151, 177, 179. Reprinted by permission of Columbia University Press.

16. William Wayne Farris, *Population, Disease and Land in Early Japan, 645–900* (Cambridge, Mass.: Harvard University Press, 1985), pp. 142–44.

17. *Ibid.,* p. 142.

18. Historians formerly believed that the Ezo were the ancestors of the Ainus, but considerable doubt has been cast upon this theory.

CHAPTER 3

THE HEIAN PERIOD
The Age of Court Aristocracy

In 784 Emperor Kammu (737–806) decided to move the capital in order to escape the influence of the powerful monasteries in Nara. He first moved to Nagaoka near Kyoto, but believing the new capital to be plagued with the spirit of the dead, he moved once again in 794 to Kyoto, which remained the seat of the imperial court until 1868.

The new capital was laid out in the same manner as Nara, that is, in a checkerboard pattern. It was built on a larger scale, however, extending about 3.5 miles from north to south and 2.5 miles from east to west. The imperial palace was located at the middle in the north and from it an avenue 300 feet in width ran south.

The city of Kyoto was then known as Heiankyō, so the period from 794 to the establishment of the military government in Kamakura in 1185 is labeled the Heian era. Several significant developments took place during this period, among them the deterioration of the institutions and practices established by the Taika Reforms, the decline of imperial authority, the ascendancy of the Fujiwara family, the rise of the court aristocracy and its culture, and, toward the end of the period, the emergence of tax-free manors and military supremacy in the provincial regions.

THE CENTRAL GOVERNMENT

The administrative system established by the Taika Reforms changed its character when two new governmental organs were created at the beginning of the ninth century. They were the *Kurōdo-dokoro* (Bureau of Archivists) and the *Kebiishi* (police commissioners). The former served as the private secretariat of the emperor, assisting in the drafting of imperial rescripts and decrees, the latter as the judicial and police agency. As personal advisors to the emperor, officials in these offices came to wield more authority than the ministers in the Dajōkan. The Grand Council's authority was weakened further as regents to the emperor emerged as powerful political figures in the latter part of the ninth century.

There were two types of regents, *sesshō* and *kampaku*. The sesshō served as regent during the minority of the emperor or during the reign of an empress. In 858 this post was occupied for the first time by a person not of royal blood, a member of the Fujiwara family who was a descendant of Nakatomi-no-Kamatari. The kampaku, whose post was first established in 884, governed on behalf of the emperor regardless of the latter's age. By the end of the ninth century political power was concentrated in the hands of the Fujiwara family, which had come to monopolize the regency. During the tenth and eleventh centuries the office of the kampaku was made a regular organ of the government, and Fujiwara family members occupying the office ruled as virtual dictators. The emperors during this period devoted their time mainly to ceremonial and cultural activities.

The rise of the Fujiwara family to the position of supremacy was a slow process, effected by gaining control of key government posts, acquiring large tax-free manors, and intermarrying with the imperial family. The apex of Fujiwara power, wealth, and glory was reached during the regency of Michinaga (966–1027), who dominated the court for thirty years. Two of his sisters were imperial consorts and two of their offspring became emperors. Four of his daughters became imperial consorts, and two of his grandsons and one great grandson mounted the throne.

In most instances during this period the wife and children remained with her family, while the husband visited or came to live with them; as a result the maternal grandfather and uncles exerted great influence over the children. For this reason the Fujiwaras wedded their daughters to emperors whenever possible. When a son was born out of such an arrangement, the emperor was persuaded to abdicate and the young heir was placed on the throne, enabling the Fujiwaras to exercise political authority on his behalf. The new emperor was apt to be provided with another Fujiwara girl as his consort, most likely his aunt or cousin. For example, the two emperors who were Michinaga's grandsons were both wedded to his daughters.

With all the power and wealth they desired at their disposal, the Fujiwaras in Michinaga's time wallowed in sumptuous luxury and extravagance while the common people lived in a state of abject poverty.

It is noteworthy, however, that although the Fujiwara family dominated and virtually overshadowed the imperial family, it made no attempt to liquidate it and establish a dynasty of its own. Respect for the emperor was deeply embedded in the Japanese mind by this time, and the Fujiwaras could exercise power only by utilizing the prestige of the imperial family.

As regents, members of the Fujiwara family conducted the affairs of government through their own house organs staffed by majordomos and stewards who were also government officials. At first the Fujiwara family sought to uphold the Taika land reform program and endeavored to discourage the growth of tax-free estates (*shōen*, see p. 54). It kept its own holdings down to a minimum, also. As the acquisition of tax-free estates became prevalent, however, it, too, began to accept estates from donors as payment for the immunity from government control and taxation that it could grant. By the time of Michinaga's regency the Fujiwara family had accumulated huge holdings. Its power, however, was not based upon landholding but upon its marital ties with the occupants of the throne.

The domination of the imperial government by the Fujiwaras was finally broken during the middle of the eleventh century when the actual powers of government passed into the hands of the retired emperor, who controlled political affairs from behind the throne.[1] This practice was initiated by Emperor Shirakawa (1053–1129). When he came to the throne there was no dominant figure among his Fujiwara relatives, so he was able to reassert the authority of the emperor. After his retirement, in order to curb the Fujiwara family, he continued to exercise political power as the guardian of his successor, who was only eight years old. This practice was continued in the succeeding years. Later historians labeled this practice "cloister government," because after retirement the emperors usually entered a monastery, forsaking the secular world. After Emperor Shirakawa's time the retired emperors ran the government from the cloister. This situation did not end political intrigues at the court because the rivalry between the Fujiwara family and the imperial family was merely replaced by a power struggle between the emperor on the throne and the retired emperor in the cloister.

Emperor Shirakawa also brought the newly emerging regional military forces into the central political scene by using them as imperial guards as well as agents to subdue those who defied the imperial authority. This development not only evinced the declining power of the central government but also portended other changes.

The decline in the central government's authority was caused by its neglect of provincial administration and its inability to prevent the emergence of tax-free estates as well as by the continuous power struggle and political intrigues. Moreover, political offices fell into the hands of incompetent, untrained, or immature officials. Important posts were treated as hereditary possessions of the privileged families and in some instances came to be occupied by youngsters barely in their teens.

In the eleventh-century novel *The Tale of Genji*, Prince Genji's son is given a court rank at the age of twelve but his father decides that he must be given "a good, solid fund of knowledge," unlike sons of other members of the court aristocracy. Prince Genji notes that "a boy of good family moves ahead in rank and office and basks in the honor they bring. Why, he asks, should he trouble himself to learn anything? He has his fun, he has his music and other pleasures, and rank and position seem to come of their own accord."[2]

CULTURE

The Heian culture was the culture of the court aristocracy, which manifested highly refined taste in art and literature and strongly developed customs and modes of behavior. This was an age when the court nobles placed heavy emphasis on form, appearance, and decorum. There were prescribed rules for all aspects of life. An art historian described the period thus: "Here was artifice rather than art. . . . What most occupied the thoughts of those courtiers were ceremonies, costumes, elegant pastimes like verse-making, and even love-making conducted according to rules."[3]

Composure was important at all times for a noble at the court, even if he were ill or inebriated. Laughing with one's mouth wide open or wailing out loud were considered to be in poor taste. It was a highly self-conscious age. How one appeared in the eyes of others was the never-ending concern of the members of the court circle. This extreme sensitivity to appearance and form became so deeply implanted in the Japanese mind that it seems to have become a prominent feature of the Japanese character.

Heian society was also a highly snobbish and status-conscious world, in which pedigree and birth determined everything. For instance, it fixed a person's place in the table of ranks, which in turn determined his position in the government, emoluments, power, and proximity to the emperor. Common people were looked upon as insensible subhuman creatures and constantly referred to as "strange" and "grotesque." Even nonplebeians, if not of the same social status, were held in contempt. Prince Genji's son "winces" at having to mingle with his "shabby and uncouth" classmates. Sei Shōnagon, a renowned literary figure of this era, indicates her contempt for the common people in her masterpiece, *The Pillow Book*. Once when she was at a temple she found that "a throng of commoners had settled themselves directly in front of me. . . . They looked like so many basket-worms as they crowded together in their hideous clothes, leaving hardly an inch of space between themselves and me. I really felt like pushing them all over sideways."[4] The aristocrats in the capital were also very contemptuous of the country "rustics." Characters in *The Tale of Genji* constantly refer to the provincial regions as "uncivilized," "barbarous," "wretched" places.

The Japanese language is characterized by the many different levels of politeness that can be expressed by the proper use of polite and honorific terms. By the Heian period this practice too had become firmly established. Referring to things that were hateful to her Sei Shōnagon remarked, "It is particularly unpleasant to hear some foolish man or woman omit the proper marks of respect when addressing a person of quality; and, when servants fail to use honorific forms of speech in referring to their masters, it is very bad indeed."[5]

During the height of Fujiwara dominion, extravagant luxury, ostentatious display, and decadent sensuality prevailed at the court. Showy splendor characterized the costumes, buildings, furnishings, ceremonies, festivals, and processions. The comforts and pleasures of this world were pursued assiduously even in religious life.

The Heian court circle was also a society with highly polished aesthetic taste. Prince Genji shows a keen sensitivity to beauty in nature. At one point he says: "But aside from house and family, it is nature that gives me the most pleasure, the changes through the seasons, the blossoms and leaves of autumn and spring, the shifting patterns of the skies."[6]

When love notes were passed back and forth among the lovers in *The Tale of Genji*, the touchstones for worthiness were a beautiful handwriting and refinement of poetic expression. A girl composing a reply to a missive she received from Prince Genji "was timid, sure that any answer from her would seem hopelessly countrified. She chose richly perfumed Chinese paper and wrote only this, in a faint, delicate hand:

> You speak of lines and rushes—and by what line
> Has this poor rush taken root in this sad world?

The hand was immature, but it showed character and breeding." Genji was more confident about having her move in to his mansion as his mistress.[7]

The court aristocrats' aesthetic taste was also reflected in their acute sensitivity to color and concern about combining proper colors in their dress. They regarded slight errors in matching colors as an embarrassing lapse in taste.

Heian society was also governed by what we may regard as superstitions. In a testament left by a tenth-century member of the Fujiwara family, the daily routine for a young nobleman was prescribed. Upon awakening he was to recite seven times in a low voice the name of the star under whose sway he was. Then he was to cleanse his teeth with a toothpick, wash his hands, turn west and invoke the name of Buddha and also pray to his Shinto god. After recording the events of the previous day in his diary, he was to eat some gruel and comb his hair. Being a male it was necessary to use the comb only once in three days. Then he was to trim his fingernails on the day of the Ox and his toenails on the day of the Tiger. Also choosing the proper day, he was to bathe once in five days. He was to avoid bathing on the first of the month since this would lead to an early death. If he were to bathe on the eighth day, he would live longer; if he bathed on the eighteenth, he would be victimized by a thief; if he did so on the day of the Horse, he would lose love and respect; and on the day of the Boar, he would be dishonored.

These notions were based upon the Chinese concept of *yin* and *yang* and the five elements. All things in the universe were believed to be governed by yang (male, or positive, force) and yin (female, or negative, force) and by the five elements, namely, wood, fire, earth, metal, and water. For purposes of divination a sexagenary cycle—consisting of the twelve signs of the zodiac (rat, ox, tiger, hare, dragon, serpent, horse, sheep, monkey, cock, dog, and boar) and the ten celestial stems (each of the five elements was divided into two parts, the elder and the younger)—was used. By consulting this, experts could comprehend the forces that affected the lives of all men and discover which days would be auspicious and inauspicious. These beliefs, intermixed with magical aspects of Buddhism and traditional beliefs in magic, sorcery, and evil spirits, gave the society a strong superstitious sense. Diviners played an important role. The court employed experts on the stars, the calendar, and the science of yin and yang. Fortunetellers, geomancers, and exorcists were relied upon heavily by the populace at large to help them select lucky days and avoid unlucky ones, observe the proper taboos, and exorcise the evil spirits. These beliefs and practices persisted into the modern era.

In the Heian period Japanese culture came into its own. To be sure, Chinese influence was still very pronounced in all areas of Heian culture. *The Tale of Genji*, which is hailed as the outstanding testimony to Japan's coming of age in the literary sphere, is honeycombed with allusions and references to Chinese poetry, literature, and history. But once we recognized the profound debt that Nara and Heian Japan owed to Chinese civilization, it would then not be a distortion of the situation to assert that in the Heian period, having assimilated and adapted what they had imported from China, the Japanese began to develop an art and literature uniquely their own.

Up to the ninth century the Japanese consciously imported the products of Chinese culture. Students and monks were sent to China to study, and Japan sought to emulate T'ang art, poetry, customs, patterns of behavior, and institutions. Toward the end of the ninth century, however, the long-standing practice of sending cultural missions to China was discontinued because of the internal difficulties confronting the T'ang government just prior to its downfall.

A conscious effort was made to free Japan from the excessive dependence on T'ang China, especially in literature, where the most significant developments had occurred. Although great emphasis was placed on the art of composing Chinese poetry during the early part of the Heian era, the composition of *waka*, a Japanese-style poem of thirty-one syllables, also gained in popularity at the Heian court. As early as the middle of the ninth century Fujiwara-no-Yoshifusa (804–872), the first member of his family to hold the position of regent, wrote, "the poems that we are dedicating [to the emperor] are written in Japanese, and not a word of the land of T'ang is used. There is a sacred and ancient saying that Japan is a land blessed by the muses. It is the custom of this country to compose elegant poems in Japanese when the subject matters are the gods and the imperial family."[8] At the beginning of the tenth century Ki-no-Tsurayuki and three other poets compiled an anthology of waka called *Kokinshū* (*Collection of Ancient and Modern Poems*). It included eleven hundred poems from the time of the *Man'yōshū*. In its preface Ki-no-Tsurayuki wrote: "The poetry of Japan has its roots in the human heart and flourishes in the countless leaves of words."[9]

The development of native literature was facilitated by the invention of two phonetic Japanese writing systems derived from the Chinese ideographs. It is not known exactly when the two systems were invented, but they were in use by the end of the ninth century. The phonetic alphabet known as *hiragana*, which is more cursive in form than the more formal *katakana*, became the vehicle for literary expression for the Heian court ladies. The ladies in attendance to the imperial consorts were usually selected for their intelligence. Consequently many displayed great interest in literature; in fact, they were largely responsible for the Golden Age of Japanese literature that flourished in the late tenth and early eleventh centuries. The literary masterpieces they produced not only became classics in Japanese literature, but at least one, *The Tale of Genji*, came to be included among the great works of world literature.

The Tale of Genji was the creation of Murasaki Shikibu (978–1016?), a lady-in-waiting to Empress Akiko, one of Fujiwara-no-Michinaga's daughters. At one point in the novel the author has Prince Genji explain why a novelist feels compelled to write. Comparing historical chronicles and novels he says:

> We are not told of things that happened to specific people exactly as they happened; but the beginning [of novels] is when there are good things and bad things, things that happen in this life which one never tires of seeing and hearing about, things which one cannot bear not to tell of and must pass on for all generations. If the storyteller wishes to speak well, then he chooses the good things; and if he wishes to hold the reader's attention he chooses bad things, extraordinarily bad things. Good things and bad things alike, they are things of this world and no other.[10]

The story that Lady Murasaki recorded was set in the court life of her era and centered upon the love life of the central character, Prince Genji, and on other members of his family circle. The picture that Lady Murasaki paints has a decidedly feminine point of view. The novel focuses upon the thoughts and feelings of the various characters as they brood and fret about their relationships with members of the opposite sex. The author is not concerned about the physical relations between the various couples. What interests her is the emotional and psychological interplay.

Why, one may ask, has this work come to be ranked as a world masterpiece? It is certainly not intricacy of plot nor profoundness of theme that has sustained the interest of the Japanese readers for nearly a thousand years. What accounts for this is the author's graceful poetic style, her realistic description of scenes and events, her profound understanding of human nature, her sensitive treatment of subtle psychological moods, her ability to create delicate nuances and atmospheres. Above all, it is the overall aesthetic effect that the author successfully created that has drawn the Japanese reader to the novel down through the ages. Although it is one of the world's longest novels, the poetic effect is sustained throughout the work, and the Japanese approach it as a work of poetry rather than prose.

If one were to select the one mood that permeates the entire novel, it might be what Motoori Norinaga characterized as the sense of *mono-no-aware*, a sense of pathos. A melancholy sense of futility and despair occurs again and again, and a Buddhist awareness of the impermanence of all things permeates the entire work. "Nothing in this world is permanent," Genji says. "Life is uncertain for all of us."[11]

Lady Murasaki displays a wealth of knowledge about Chinese literature in her constant allusions to Chinese literary and historical figures and events. Women, Lady Murasaki realized, were viewed as inferior creatures in her age. Genji muses, "The conclusion was inescapable. Women were creatures of sin. He wanted to be done with them." A royal personage remarks, "I have heard . . . that women are shallow, careless creatures who are not always treated with complete respect."[12]

In painting, also, a distinctive Japanese style, known as *Yamato-e*, emerged toward the end of the Heian era. Although initially Yamato-e dealt with Buddhist subjects, it began increasingly to depict secular scenes and tales based on the everyday lives of the Japanese. The objects depicted in this style are outlined with thin lines and filled in with bright colors. Sliding-door panels and screens were painted in the new style, but the most noteworthy medium where Yamato-e found expression was in the horizontal narrative-picture scrolls called *e-makimono*.

Among the most famous e-makimono is *The Tale of Genji*. It is not as strictly narrative as the scrolls that appeared in the next era, the Kamakura period. Each scene is followed by a text and can be regarded as a separate framed picture; their function is more decorative than narrative. Concerning the style of *The Tale of Genji*, one authority writes, "This is not a bold splashing about, but a carefully calculated art of placement, of juxtaposition of color and texture, but particularly of placement. Placement is almost everything, along with the interrelationships of elaborate patterns of angle and line, of triangle and square, and of the large over-all patterns found on the costumes worn by the participants."[13]

There were also notable paintings of Buddhist deities during the Heian period. Among them are a number of renowned paintings of the Fudō, a manifestation of the cosmic Buddha Vairocana. He is depicted as a deity with fangs, fierce protruding eyes, thick eyebrows, and a powerful, muscular body. He holds a sword and a rope in his hands to combat the forces of evil and is framed by a raging fire. There were also representations of more serene Buddhist deities such as the *Fugen Bosatsu*, the Bodhisattva of wisdom and virtue, who is depicted as a graceful, elegant Heian beauty.

The art of calligraphy also flourished during this period, and a number of master calligraphers emerged. With the invention of the hiragana writing system, brush-writing in the cursive style became a highly polished and graceful art. The ability to write poetry in an elegant style was prized just as much as the content of the poem itself. A superior handwriting was a mark of learning and good breeding.

In the realm of architecture, too, a distinctly Japanese style began to appear in the construction of Buddhist temples in the early Heian era. The ground plans for the temples of this period were arranged in irregular, asymmetrical patterns to fit in with the lay of the land. One of the best-known structures of this era is the Phoenix Hall of the Byōdōin, which was built around the middle of the eleventh century in Uji near Kyoto. The Phoenix Hall is situated beside a pond, and its reflection in the water enhances the beauty of the total image. It is so named because its design suggests the mythical phoenix descending to the ground. It represents the Buddhist paradise on earth. In accordance with the developing Japanese style, the whole structure is fitted into the natural setting, but the building itself resembles the buildings depicted in ninth- and tenth-century Buddhist wall paintings in Chinese caves. The T'ang influence is also seen in the exact symmetry, lavish decoration, and bright red and white colors of the temple. The Phoenix Hall was used as an imperial villa as well as a Buddhist temple.

A style of architecture known as *shinden zukuri* characterized the dwellings built by the Heian aristocrats. It emphasized simplicity and lightness of construction. The wooden floors were raised, and the roof consisted of unpainted bark or reed. The pillars were also unpainted, and the walls were made of plain removable panels. Large rooms were partitioned by screens. These features foreshadowed the architectural style of the houses that emerged in later periods.

BUDDHISM

During the Nara period scholarship in Buddhist scriptures had been pursued by learned monks, but Buddhism did not extend its influence broadly among the masses. As we noted, there were monks such as Gyōki who went out among the people initiating a variety of projects for their benefit. Most of the powerful monasteries of Nara, however, concentrated on strengthening their political and economic position and made little effort to reach the masses.

Besides moving the capital away from Nara, partly to escape the political pressures of the monasteries, Emperor Kammu also encouraged the growth of new sects that might rival the older orders. These new Buddhist movements were led by two energetic leaders, Saichō (767–822) and Kūkai (774–835), who is also known as Kōbō Daishi. Saichō went to China in 804 and came under the influence of T'ien Tai (Tendai) and Ch'an (Zen) Buddhism. After his return he founded the Tendai sect in Japan. This sect based its teaching on the Lotus Sutra and contended that the Lotus Sutra was identical with the Living Buddha. The Nara sects had generally derived their doctrines from secondary sources instead of from the sutras. Saichō asserted the superiority of his position because he claimed that his doctrines were based on the actual words of Buddha. He upheld Mahayana Buddhism over Hinayana Buddhism and laid the foundation for its diffusion. He also broadened the basis of Buddhism in Japan by teaching that salvation was possible for all living creatures. All living things, he preached, are endowed with Buddha-nature. The way to salvation was moral perfection and contemplation.

Kūkai also went abroad to T'ang China and studied there for three years. He came under the influence of esoteric Buddhism, and returning to Japan, founded the Shingon (True Word) sect. The central deity in the Shingon sect is the Dainichi Nyorai. He was called Maha-Vairocana (the Great Illuminator) and was regarded as the primordial Buddha from whom all other Buddhas—which included deities and demons, saints and goblins from all religions–emanated. The Great Illuminator, Kūkai taught, is in all things in the universe. The body, speech, and thought of the Dainichi Nyorai constitute the life of the universe. The aim of the Shingon sect was to evoke the vitality of the "three mysteries" in the body, speech, and thought of everyone. In effect, each individual was to be divinely transubstantiated. To achieve this end special chants, spells, motions, and symbols were to be employed in the rituals; especially important were the mystic formulas, the "true word." When the mysterious powers of the Great Illuminator were evoked, salvation as well as mundane benefits could be realized.

The Tendai sect also employed certain esoteric practices. At the end of the Heian period the excessive reliance on magical formulae contributed to the outbreak of dissident groups that rejected esoteric Buddhism, offering a "purer" way to salvation.

Kūkai is also known for his artistic, literary, and linguistic achievements. He was one of the three outstanding calligraphers of his age and is credited with having invented the kana syllabary, although the authenticity of this attribution is questionable.

Both Saichō and Kūkai, like their predecessors, considered the protection of Japan as one of the chief functions of Buddhism. Saichō indicated that his incantations, prayers, and sermons were intended to serve the interests of the nation. Kūkai, too, professed his interest in serving the nation and offered this as the reason for his desire to establish his monastery on Mt. Kōya.

Another aspect of this growing strain of national consciousness in Buddhism is seen in the attempt to reconcile Buddhism with the native religion, Shinto. Some such attempts had been made earlier, but in the tenth century this movement, under the leadership of the Shingon sect, became more pronounced although it was not until later in the Heian period that it developed fully. This effort to syncretize Buddhism and Shinto is known as Dual Shinto. Its advocates explained that all deities on earth were merely manifestations or emanations of the primordial Buddha. Thus Shinto gods were not distinct and separate divinities but were merely emanations of the primordial Buddha under different names.

In spite of these new developments in Buddhism in the Heian era, it did not spread widely among the people until the end of this age, when the doctrine of the Pure Land with its worship of Amida Buddha came into existence. There were, however, some monks who went among the people to bring the blessings of Buddhism to them. Such a monk was Kūya (903–972), who traveled throughout the country constructing roads and bridges, repairing old temples, building wells, cremating corpses abandoned on the roadside, and reciting the name of Amida Buddha.

There is little doubt that Buddhism had begun to affect the thinking of the aristocracy in a very significant manner. Buddhist concepts run through all the major literary works of this period. References to Buddha and Buddhist doctrines and practices occur repeatedly in *The Tale of Genji*, and the concept of karma is ever present in the minds of the central characters.

Buddhism, however, like everything else, was becoming increasingly formalistic during the Heian period. Appearance rather than true piety, form rather than substance were stressed among the court aristocrats. The Buddhist temples and images were designed to appeal to the aesthetic taste of the observers rather than to their deep religious feelings. People often went to the temples for pleasure and entertainment rather than for devout religious worship. They were just as likely to pray for worldly success and ease as to pray for religious salvation.

Salvation was to be achieved through mechanical means, such as the routine recitation of spells and magical formulae. The esoteric sects fortified this tendency. It was believed that quantity was more important than quality. The more a person recited the formulae the better his chances of salvation were. Thus, people kept track of the number of times they recited the incantations by setting aside one bean for each time an invocation was made. One person, it was said, accumulated 3,600,119,500 beans in thirty years. It was also believed that the more images of Buddha a person dedicated, the better his chances of entering the Buddhist paradise were. One retired emperor had one thousand images of Kannon made and housed them in a structure 384 feet long. Although this occurred in the thirteenth century it typifies the spirit of Heian Buddhism.

Despite all its defects the Heian period was a remarkable age. It was one of the few periods in Japanese history when the accent was placed heavily upon peaceful pursuits. Arts and letters were the primary preoccupation of the court aristocrats in Kyoto. Force and violence seemed to have counted for little among them. Symbolic of this was the abolition, at the beginning of the ninth century, of capital punishment for government officials. This policy remained in effect until the middle of the twelfth century, when the military men came to the forefront. During the Heian period political foes were sent into exile, not executed. The literature of this era seldom mentions bloodshed and violence. A man was admired for his literary and artistic talents, not for his military exploits.

But while the court aristocrats were pursuing aesthetic values and amorous pleasures, a revolution was brewing in the countryside, and a new age was about to emerge. The makers of the new era will be of an entirely different breed and temperament—less concerned with propriety and decorum, less sensitive to the refinements of arts and letters, less squeamish about spilling blood. They will be more ruthless, more brutal, more coldblooded. They will present the other face of Japan. The polite Japan, the gentle Japan, the sentimental Japan will fade into the background for the time being. The age of "sweetness and light" will be replaced by an age of "blood and iron." The effeminate, placid age will be superseded by a more masculine, dynamic one.

RISE OF THE SHŌEN

While political intrigues and a poorly staffed administrative system were weakening the imperial government, significant changes were taking place in the countryside: the land reforms and legal institutions introduced by the Taika Reforms were slowly deteriorating. One of the objectives of the reformers had been to eliminate the local forces that had entrenched themselves between the central government and the people in the countryside. The authority of the central government was to have been extended throughout the nation, and taxation brought under its direct control. In actuality this plan was never fully realized, because some of the local magnates managed to maintain private control over their estates through special dispensations. Those local leaders who remained in power as governors of provinces and counties were also able to retain their prestige and influence in their traditional strongholds.

In areas where land reforms were put into effect, the plan to divide the land equitably among the people failed. The scheme to redistribute the land once every six years to prevent land concentration was not enforced vigorously. In 834 the cycle of periodic redistribution was extended to twelve years, but even then redistribution was not effected as scheduled.

As a result, land tended to become concentrated in the hands of the local magnates, Buddhist monasteries, court aristocrats, and high government officials. Another factor that contributed to the concentration of landholding was the reclamation of wastelands. In order to encourage this practice the government permitted all lands that were reclaimed to be held as private property with reduced rates of taxation. Originally the reclaimed land was to be retained as private property for one to three generations, depending upon the time and effort expended upon the project, but as the time for the reclaimed fields to be transferred to the public domain approached, the owners tended to neglect or abandon them. Moreover the drop in population caused by the epidemic of 735–737 compelled the government to seek measures to encourage the peasants to remain on the land and farm it. As a result, in 743 the government agreed to permit permanent ownership. This resulted in a significant increase in private estates. The monasteries were especially active in sponsoring reclamation projects. In addition, they purchased lands illegally from other landowners and also acquired additional plots as gifts. In many instances these were gifts in name only. Since the monastic lands were free from taxation, some land-holders arranged to have the monasteries become the legal owners of their estates to escape taxation. Then by paying nominal rents to the monasteries they were able to retain their now tax-free lands. As a result, the larger monasteries, such as Tōdaiji and Hōryūji, became huge landholding in-stitutions. The holdings of a monastery (*cum* "donors") might range from 1,000 to as many as 10,000 acres.

The court nobles, such as the Fujiwaras, eventually accumulated enormous landholdings because they could offer protection to the local landowners against the provincial governors, who had the authority to levy taxes. As a result, local landholders made the same kind of arrangement with the court nobles as they did with the monasteries. They would donate or offer the land in commendation to a powerful court noble and then be given back the land as a benefice and pay a nominal rent. Thus they gained freedom from taxation and from the legal control of the government and its agent, the provincial governor. The imperial court also granted thousands of acres of tax-free land to members of the imperial family and court favorites. Consequently, the number and size of tax-free estates began to grow. These estates, under civil proprietorship, were called shōen.[14]

The government granted two privileges to the shōen owners: freedom from taxation and the right to deny government officials or agents entrance to their estates. These privileges had to be granted officially by the government in each particular instance, and initially they were limited to monastic and shrine lands. Later, in some cases, the provincial governors took it upon themselves to grant these immunities. Eventually many owners of estates came to claim these privileges without any official sanction. For example, those landholders who had ties with powerful officials, court nobles, or monasteries could claim these privileges without official permission because their patrons could gain for them de facto exemptions from taxation and freedom from the authority of the magistrates. Free from official supervision, the shōen owners came to exercise complete police and judicial authority over their own estates. The government repeatedly issued decrees prohibiting the establishment of shōen without official approval. In 902, for example, a comprehensive ban on illegal possession of land, woods, and streams was decreed. Such prohibitions were futile, however, because the violators included members of the imperial court itself as well as high government officials and nobles upon whom the government had to rely for the enforcement of its decrees. The imperial family and the Fujiwara family, the two authorities that showed some interest in curbing the growth of the shōen, ended as major proprietors of tax-free estates themselves. By the beginning of the tenth century shōen existed throughout the country.

A local shōen holder might be free of all outside control or influence, or he might be under the nominal jurisdiction of powerful monasteries and court nobles in Kyoto, who would be his legal guardians. Some shōen were under the direct management of the monasteries and court aristocrats. These tended to be larger than the shōen held by local magnates, but some local chieftains also became owners of large shōen by extending their protection and control over lesser shōen owners.

Usually a certain portion of shōen land was reserved for the owner to cultivate, and the rest was rented out to tenant farmers who paid rent and provided labor services in return. In some instances there were small and medium-sized independent farmers who owned land in the shōen, but they were subjected to the political jurisdiction of the shōen owner. These independent farmers were known as *myōshu*, that is, owners of *myōden* (name fields) that had originally been acquired by reclaiming wasteland. The fields were named after the reclaimers of the land in order to protect their property rights. Some tillers of the soil also acquired proprietary rights over the fields they worked and gained possession of them as myōden. In the twelfth century the myōden was made the basic unit of organization in the shōen. An effort was made to equalize the size of the myōden to about 1 acre in the provinces near the capital, but they varied greatly in size in the outlying regions.

The shōen owners employed agents or managers to handle the affairs of the estates. Those managers whose employers lived in Kyoto, far removed from the shōen, tended to acquire considerable authority. Some gained hereditary rights to their position as well as the right to collect a fixed amount of income from the shōen. In fact, everybody connected with the shōen—the tillers of the soil, the manager, the proprietor, and the patron— had specific rights in the shōen. This system of rights, which also included the right of officials such as county heads to maintain hereditary possession of their positions, was known as *shiki*.

With the increase in the number and size of the shōen, the area under the jurisdiction of the provincial governors decreased proportionately. Several attempts made in the eleventh century to ferret out shōen owners who had gained possession of their estates illegally failed to reduce the number of tax-free manors. By the twelfth century it was estimated that only about one-tenth of the land remained in the public domain under the authority of the provincial governors.

THE EMERGENCE OF THE WARRIOR CLASS (SAMURAI)

The rise of the shōen meant a steady decline in the authority of the central government. Taxes collected by the government decreased, and police and military power in the provinces fell increasingly into the hands of the local magnates. After the military conscription instituted under the Taihō Code was abandoned in 792, the local governors were required to maintain the necessary military forces. In order to fulfill their military tasks, the governors relied upon the local chieftains for assistance. As the authority of the central government declined, the shōen proprietors and managers had to rely upon their own resources to protect their property and preserve peace and order in the shōen. Thus they found it necessary to maintain their own private militias, which were manned initially by shōen workers as part of their corvée. The influence and power of the local chieftains increased as the inhabitants began to submit to their leadership in order to receive protection.

The size of the local armies grew as unemployed or displaced farmers, reduced to being vagrants or brigands, joined their ranks. The deterioration of the peasantry resulted in part from the fact that, as tax-free estates proliferated, the tax burden grew heavier upon those who worked the little-remaining taxable land. The exploitation of the peasantry by the local governors became more intense also. Many of the farmers fell into debt to the government or to moneylenders. Unable to pay their debts and unable to bear the burden of heavy taxes, they left the land and joined the ranks of the vagrants. The land they abandoned was taken over by the rising local landowning magnates.

As the local chieftains—usually shōen owners, managers of shōen whose owners resided in Kyoto, county heads, and, in some cases, provincial governors who had established their roots in the countryside—grew more powerful, they began to establish lord-and-vassal relationships with their followers. The hard core of their following consisted of vassals who had some sort of blood ties with them. This was, in a way, the clan or uji system of old—a tightly knit unit based on kinship ties. In addition, among the followers of a local chieftain were those who had entered into a master-vassal relationship with him because of the circumstances discussed above. This relationship was formalized with the presentation of a name plate from the vassal to the lord. In return for the vassal's loyal services, the lord was expected to provide him with a piece of land or the right to collect taxes or rents from the land. Thus what was essentially a feudal relationship was established between the local lord and his followers. Unlike European feudalism, however, the peasants on the shōen were generally not serfs but either free tenants or independent, landowning farmers. The local lords and their followers constituted the ascending samurai class, which was to play a dominant role in Japanese political history from this time until the middle of the nineteenth century.

There was a hierarchy of lord-vassal relationships, since the lord himself might be a vassal of a more powerful chieftain, while the vassal might have followers of his own. Something like the system of sub-infeudation that existed in Europe in the Middle Ages began to emerge in Heian Japan.

Gradually larger and larger nuclei of power began to develop. The more powerful local military chieftains—those who were descendants of the imperial family or those who were related to powerful court aristocrats— tended to attract a larger following and succeeded in extending their control over an increasingly wider area. Thus, while the central government was neglecting to maintain its military strength, local lords were building formidable private armies to fight for economically productive and strategically important areas.

As the powers of the local military men grew, they began to defy openly the authority of the central government. Having allowed its military strength to decline, the central government was forced to call upon other local leaders to help curb the more recalcitrant military chieftains. In this way it inadvertently strengthened the position of certain local leaders over others and at the same time provided these military men with an excuse to interfere in its affairs.

As early as the tenth century, the government was confronted with two major uprisings that could not be suppressed without the aid of loyal local chieftains. One rebellion was led by Fujiwara-no-Sumitomo (?–941), who had been assigned by the government the task of subduing the pirates in the Inland Sea. After bringing the pirates under control he in turn defied the central government and plundered the western region between 936 and 941. Sumitomo was subdued, however, with the aid of a local military chieftain bearing the name Minamoto, a name that would have to be reckoned with later.

The other rebellion occurred in the east, in the Kantō region. In 939 Taira-no-Masakado (?–940), who had been extending his power in that area, declared himself the emperor of Kantō and established his own government, modeling it after the Heian government. His rebellion was crushed in 940 when another member of the Taira clan turned on him. In quashing both of these uprisings, the central government had to rely upon the support of other provincial magnates, and it had to continue relying upon the help of the emerging military chieftains to maintain its authority in the countryside. This tended to strengthen those military families that cooperated with the imperial government, and power came to be concentrated in the hands of fewer and fewer families.

By the twelfth century the Taira and Minamoto families, two major military houses both claiming direct descent from emperors of the Heian period, came to dominate the outlying regions. They both came to power first in the Kantō region where, because of the long history of conflict with the Ezo in the north, the military tradition was the strongest. The Minamotos distinguished themselves by subduing rebellious military chieftains in the Kantō region and in the north. They had also established close ties in Kyoto by catering to the interests of the Fujiwara family. Their power and prestige grew under Yoshiie (1041–1108), who attracted a large following not only because of his military exploits but also because of his generosity. When the imperial government refused to reward the troops under him for subduing the northern rebels, Yoshiie compensated them out of his own property. His popularity caused a large number of farmers and warriors to commend their lands to him. This alarmed the imperial government, and it felt compelled to prohibit further donations to him.

The Tairas first emerged in the Kantō region also but lost their base of power there as a result of Masakado's rebellion. A Western branch of this clan located in Ise emerged as the nucleus of Taira power. The Ise Tairas first gained prominence by helping the imperial government subdue rebels and pirates in the western regions. They strengthened their economic position by engaging in trade with Sung China and also by cultivating close ties with the cloister government.

In addition to these two major families, there was another power to the north, the Fujiwaras—unrelated to the Fujiwaras in Kyoto—who posed a potential threat to the other military families until the end of the twelfth century.

The struggle for power and land in the provinces resulted in the emergence of powerful military forces that eventually were in a position to dominate the central government.

NOTES

1. The decline of the Fujiwara regency resulted partly from the fact that the paternal side of the family was growing in importance. Wives were beginning to leave their families to establish independent households with their husbands.

2. Murasaki Shikibu, *The Tale of Genji*, trans. Edward C. Seidensticker (New York: Alfred A. Knopf, 1976), p. 363.

3. Langdon Warner, *The Enduring Art of Japan* (New York: Grove, 1952), p. 32.

4. Ivan Morris, ed. and trans., *The Pillow Book of Sei Shōnagon*, 2 vols. (New York: Columbia University Press, 1967), vol. 1, p. 258.

5. *Ibid.*, p. 28.

6. Murasaki Shikibu, *op. cit.*, p. 345.

7. *Ibid.*, p. 402.

8. Quoted in Inoue Mitsusada, ed., *Kodai Shakai (Ancient Society)*, vol. 2 of *Shin Nihonshi Taikei (A New Outline History of Japan)*, 6 vols. (Tokyo: Asakura Shoten, 1952–1954), p. 294.

9. Quoted in Earl Miner, *An Introduction to Japanese Court Poetry* (Stanford, Calif.: Stanford University Press, 1968), p. 18.

10. Murasaki Shikibu, *op. cit.*, p. 437.

11. *Ibid.*, pp. 530, 581.

12. *Ibid.*, pp. 529, 620.

13. Sherman E. Lee, *A History of Far Eastern Art* (Englewood Cliffs, N.J.: Prentice-Hall, and New York: Abrams, 1964), p. 307.

14. *Shō* means village and *en* means farmland.

CHAPTER 4

THE KAMAKURA PERIOD
The Triumph of the Samurai

We saw in the previous chapter how the authority of the central government steadily declined as the shōen dominated by local military chieftains grew in size and number throughout the land. It not only virtually lost control over the outlying areas, but its authority was undermined in Kyoto itself where there was a continuous power struggle between various imperial factions. In addition, the imperial government was challenged by the powerful monasteries in and around the capital, which had recruited inmates who were monks in name but warriors in reality. Most of these warrior-monks were farmers who wished to escape the heavy tax burdens and unemployed vagrants who sought a place of refuge. They were used by the monasteries to protect their shōen and also to coerce the government to grant special privileges and ecclesiastical posts to their members. In time the number of warrior-monks increased—some monasteries retained as many as several thousand men—and from time to time they poured into the streets of Kyoto to intimidate the government authorities. They contributed further to the political disorder by engaging in disputes among themselves. Particularly troublesome were the Kōfukuji of Nara, which was patronized by the Fujiwara family, and the Enryakuji of Mt. Hiei, an "order" founded by Saichō.

THE RIVALRY OF THE TAIRA
AND MINAMOTO CLANS

As noted earlier, two major military families rose to power in the countryside, the Taira (Heike) and the Minamoto (Genji). In 1156 a dispute at the court provided the Taira family with an opportunity to emerge as a significant force in Kyoto. A power struggle between the reigning emperor and the retired emperor broke out, and both factions

61

appealed to the provincial military leaders for support. The Taira family, led by the able and ambitious Kiyomori (1118–1181), came to the aid of the reigning emperor and defeated the rival faction, which was supported by Minamoto-no-Tameyoshi (1096–1156), the grandson of Yoshiie. This was not an outright confrontation between the Tairas and the Minamotos, however, because some members of the Taira clan fought on the side of the retired emperor, while some Minamoto clansmen supported the emperor. The most prominent of the latter was Tameyoshi's own son, Yoshitomo (1123–1160), who, after victory, was ordered by the emperor to execute his own father. This power struggle is known as the Hogen Insurrection, Hogen being the era name for the years 1156–1158.

After the Hogen Insurrection both Kiyomori and Yoshitomo became influential at the court, but in 1159 Kiyomori managed to eliminate Yoshitomo when the latter, jealous of Kiyomori's growing popularity and power, supported dissident elements at the court and attempted to stage a coup, known as the Heiji Insurrection. Having failed, he was executed, together with those of his sons who had participated in the uprising. One son, Yoritomo (1147–1199), who was only twelve years old at that time, was saved from execution by the intercession of Kiyomori's stepmother. He was exiled to an island off Izu Peninsula instead. Yoshitomo's three younger sons by a concubine were also spared on the condition that their mother become Kiyomori's mistress. One of these boys, Yoshitsune, later emerged as the leading general of the Minamoto forces.

It now appeared that the Minamotos had been eliminated from the national scene and the paramountcy of the Taira family established. Kiyomori became virtually a dictator. He rose rapidly in court rank and in 1167 became dajō daijin (chancellor). His family members became high-ranking court officials. He married his daughter to the emperor and his grandson thus became heir to the throne. His possessions were immense; in addition to controlling the governorships of thirty provinces, the Taira family owned over five hundred shōen. They gained such power and prestige that people came to say, "If one is not a Taira, one is not a human being."

Like all dictatorships, the Tairas tolerated no adverse criticism. The *Tale of the Heike*, a historical romance written in the early Kamakura period, relates, "If there was anyone who spoke evil against the Taira and one of these [youths employed by the Tairas to patrol the streets of Kyoto] chanced to hear it, straightway summoning to him his fellows, they would violently enter that man's house, seize his treasures and household goods and bring him bound to Rokuhara [the Taira residence]. So that none were found to open their mouth about things they saw or knew."[1] But they could not control the secret feelings of the people. "The provinces are oppressed by the governors and the fiefs are abused by the commissioners; people are harried in all matters and there is no peace. . . . Outwardly all submit but inwardly there are none who do not dislike the Heike rule."[2]

Besides focusing upon the consolidation of his political position, Kiyomori endeavored to develop commerce with Sung China. He built the port of Hyōgo and excavated the Straits of Ondo near the city of Kure to facilitate this trade.

Unlike Yoritomo, his successor, Kiyomori did not seek to establish his own government. Instead he chose to rule through the imperial court in cooperation with the cloistered emperor. As the balance of power shifted in favor of the Tairas, however, the imperial faction began to engage in intrigues to reduce the power of the clan. But the several conspiracies directed against the Tairas failed.

In 1180, however, anti-Taira uprisings broke out in the Kantō region and spread to the provinces near the capital. The leadership for this anti-Taira movement was provided, ironically enough, by Minamoto-no-Yoritomo who, while in exile, managed to build his military strength by joining forces with the Hōjō family, a local power in the Izu area. Yoritomo had, in fact, married a member of the Hōjō family, Masako. Heeding the imperial call to overthrow the Tairas, Yoritomo led his forces against them, and the two rival families confronted each other again. The struggle continued for five years. Tales of heroism and treachery, valor and cowardice, chivalry and cruelty fill the chronicles of this conflict.

The closing years of Taira supremacy were plagued by disastrous natural calamities, causing severe famines. A contemporary account describing the terrible famine of 1181–1182 describes conditions in Kyoto thus:

> Beggars swarmed by the roadsides, and our ears were filled with the sound of their lamentations. . . . Everybody was dying of hunger. . . . By garden walls or on the roadsides countless persons died of famine, and as their bodies were not removed, the world was filled with evil odours. . . . The numbers of those who died in central Kiōto during the fourth and fifth months alone were 42,300. To this must be added many who died before and after; while if we also reckon those who perished in the various outlying quarters, the number has no limits.[3]

These conditions no doubt helped to undermine the position of the Tairas. They had also incurred the opposition of the powerful monasteries and many local leaders. Eventually, the Minamoto faction emerged victorious as Yoritomo consolidated his position in the east and broadened his base of support by welcoming all comers into the Minamoto faction regardless of family or historical ties. Although the Tairas were superior in number, the Minamotos had the advantage of superior leaders, among them Yoritomo's younger brother, Yoshitsune (1159–1189), whose daring tactics led to many victories, and his cousin Yoshinaka (1154–1184), who drove the Tairas out of the capital. Before the Tairas were completely crushed, however, Yoritomo and Yoshinaka found their ambitions to be incompatible. Yoshinaka was defeated and killed by Yoritomo's men.

In the early stage of the conflict Kiyomori fell ill and died in the spring of 1181, and the fortune of the Tairas, deprived of their able leader, steadily declined. They were forced to retreat to the west and were finally annihilated in 1185 by the Minamoto forces under the brilliant generalship of Yoshitsune, who was at that time only twenty-four years old. Determined not to repeat the mistake that the Tairas had made, Yoritomo had all the important members of the main Taira family executed. Even little children were not spared; all were drowned or buried alive.

Yoritomo now set about consolidating his power. If Yoshitsune was the military genius who made the Minamoto triumph possible, Yoritomo was the political genius. It was said that the Tairas had failed to maintain their position because they had imitated the flaccid ways of the court, neglecting to maintain a firm grip on the real source of their power, their provincial strongholds. Yoritomo was determined not to make the same mistake. Throughout the conflict with the Tairas, Minamoto military headquarters were at Kamakura. Even after his victory, Yoritomo chose to remain in Kamakura, refusing to move to Kyoto. Thus the real seat of government was transferred to Kamakura, although the imperial government in Kyoto was still regarded as the legal government and was treated as such by Yoritomo.

With the establishment of Minamoto hegemony in 1185 we enter the period in Japanese history in which the military class dominated the country, a situation that prevailed for almost seven centuries. From 1200 on the imperial court and the emperor were increasingly relegated to the background and played no role of real significance in the political life of the nation until the middle of the nineteenth century. Not only were the political, social, and economic patterns of the land set by the military, but the cultural, moral, and intellectual tone was also molded largely by the military outlook. Military domination would have a decisive and lasting effect in forming the Japanese mind, character, and temperament; in this sense the political triumph of Minamoto-no-Yoritomo was of paramount significance in Japanese history.

THE KAMAKURA SHOGUNATE (1185–1333)

After the defeat of the Tairas, Yoritomo, a jealous and ruthless man, set out to remove all potential rivals, including his brother Yoshitsune, who had gained renown because of his military exploits. Yoritomo suspected his brother of harboring political ambitions and sought to repress him. In anger Yoshitsune rebelled against his brother but failed to gain sufficient support. Yoritomo had him hunted down relentlessly and executed. When Yoshitsune's wife gave birth to a baby boy, Yoritomo had the child killed. Earlier he had had his son-in-law killed because he suspected him of disloyalty. He also did away with his half-brother Noriyori. Using the excuse that they had provided help to Yoshitsune, Yoritomo seized the opportunity to destroy the northern Fujiwara clan. By 1189 he had removed all potential military threats to his position.

Although there no longer remained anyone who might challenge his supremacy, Yoritomo did not attempt to bring the entire country under his direct control. He deferred to the imperial court as the legal government and obtained imperial sanctions for all his policies and decrees. At the same time he went about strengthening his political position. In 1185 he assumed the position of supreme constable and supreme land steward of all sixty-six provinces.[4] The former office gave him military and police power over the entire country, and the latter the right to collect taxes from all public domains and the shōen. He also acquired the right to appoint provincial constables and land stewards at all levels—in provinces, counties, and townships. The right of Yoritomo and his successors to appoint and control these officials eventually eliminated the immunity from taxation and from official intervention that the shōen had heretofore enjoyed.

Yoritomo was also given proprietary rights over the lands he formerly held in the Kantō region, amounting to nine provinces. The governors of these provinces were appointed by Yoritomo from among his followers. Yoritomo also acquired the lands formerly held by the Tairas. This meant an additional five hundred shōen scattered throughout the country. Over these areas Yoritomo exercised direct control, just as the imperial court, the court nobles, the monasteries, and some of Yoritomo's own followers exercised proprietary rights over their shōen. To supervise his estates he appointed vassals whom he wished to reward as land stewards and managers of his holdings.

Yoritomo's authority was also felt in the public domains and in the shōen owned by the court aristocrats and the monasteries because the constables and land stewards appointed by him exercised authority over the lower officials in both sectors. His control over Kyushu and western Honshu was weaker than in eastern Honshu, where his direct holdings were located. He did not insist upon appointing land stewards to those areas where his influence was weak.

In effect a dual authority prevailed during the early Kamakura period. Yoritomo exercised direct control over the Kantō provinces and his own shōen scattered throughout the land. The governors of the eastern provinces were his appointees. He also held supreme military and police power over the entire country. On the other hand, the imperial faction still controlled a large number of shōen, and the provincial governors in the areas outside of eastern Japan were appointed from Kyoto. Nonetheless, these governors had to share their authority with the constables and land stewards appointed from Kamakura.

Although Yoritomo had to share the administration of the country with the imperial court, he was supreme in the military realm. In 1192 he was appointed seiitaishōgun, which made him officially the military commander-in-chief of the land. In order to exercise his military authority and manage the lands under his proprietorship, he established an administrative system in Kamakura known as the Bakufu (tent government). This was not intended to replace the imperial government in Kyoto but was designed to manage his "family" affairs. The system established by Yoritomo was a relatively simple one. There were three offices: the Office of the Samurai, the Administrative Office, and the Court of Appeals. The first organ dealt with promotions and demotions of the samurai and generally supervised their conduct. The second managed administrative, legislative, and legal affairs. The third functioned as a judicial board to settle civil disputes, particularly those involving land, among those samurai under Yoritomo's jurisdiction. To staff these offices Yoritomo employed members of the Kyoto aristocracy who, unlike many of his vassals, were well educated. The three offices were under the close supervision of Yoritomo, who made all the important decisions.

In local administration, as we have noted, Yoritomo appointed provincial constables and land stewards from among his followers. The constable had military and police authority. It was his duty to apprehend criminals, suppress rebellions, and, when summoned by the shōgun, to come to his aid with his warriors. He also served as the local liaison and administrative officer for the shōgun.

The land stewards were at first authorized to collect taxes from all the estates in the provinces to which they were assigned, whether public or private. This policy was opposed by the shōen owners in Kyoto, however, so the land stewards' tax-collecting power was limited to the public domains. The extent to which land stewards exercised their influence in the provinces varied from place to place, but they usually held considerable power. At the lower levels they exercised police power. Their authority was extended greatly after ex-emperor Gotoba sought to overthrow the Kamakura forces in 1221. This attempt was crushed, and the estates of the nobles and monasteries who had supported the move were confiscated and placed under the jurisdiction of the land stewards. Throughout the Kamakura period the land stewards steadily increased their authority over the shōen not owned by the Bakufu. One of their duties was to collect the rent for the shōen owners, but in time they tended to ignore their responsibilities to the proprietors, concentrating instead on increasing their own incomes and control over the peasants on the land. By the end of the Kamakura period many stewards had acquired proprietary rights over the shōen and emerged as a new landholding class.

In discussing Kamakura society we should consider whether we can properly label it a "feudal" society. Although hitherto it has been customary to consider the Kamakura society feudal, recently a more cautious viewpoint has begun to emerge. Some authorities now feel that to call the Kamakura system of land administration feudalism would be an oversimplification, because the vassal was usually appointed to some office such as that of land steward or shōen manager and was not given a piece of land to control as his own fief. With the office went the right to extract some income from the land, but the actual proprietary rights were retained by the Bakufu or the shōen owner. Moreover, the feudal elements centering upon Yoritomo were still not the dominant forces in the political and social systems. Although the real power was in the hands of the shōgun, the administration operating out of Kyoto still controlled large parts of the country. Thus, we have something like a dual administration, with the Bakufu, or shogunate, operating—at least on the surface—under the jurisdiction of the imperial government. For convenience, the term feudal can be used to designate the hegemony of the military chieftains, but it should be clearly understood that this term does not denote the same kind of system that prevailed in medieval Europe.

During the Kamakura period, the earlier practice of submitting a name plate at the ceremony of investiture was abolished, and the vassal merely presented himself to his lord at the ceremony. As noted above, the benefice granted by the lord to the vassal was usually some office. In return the vassal performed military duties in time of both war and peace and helped defray the cost of his lord's expenses. For example, he had to present gifts to the lord's household on such important occasions as births, coming of age ceremonies, and weddings.

Although the tillers of the soil varied greatly in status, no peasants in Kamakura society could be characterized as serfs. The most well-off were the myōshu, who held title to land under the jurisdiction of the shōen proprietors. The myōshu in outlying regions tended to have larger holdings and often used semi-slave workers to till the soil. Although the practice was illegal, impoverished peasants were often driven to selling their wives and children as slaves to be used as household or farm workers. In addition there were a variety of tenant farmers and hired workers.

THE HŌJŌ REGENCY

Yoritomo died in 1199 and was succeeded by his son Yoriie (1182–1204), but the real power of the Bakufu passed into the hands of Hōjō Tokimasa (1138–1215), the father of Yoritomo's wife, Masako. When Yoriie became ill in 1203, Tokimasa forced him to resign and made Yoriie's younger brother, Sanetomo, the shōgun. He later had Yoriie and his eldest son assassinated. Since Sanetomo was a minor, Tokimasa made himself regent and exercised power as the actual head of the Kamakura government. We now have a situation in which the nominal government in Kyoto was run by a regent, while the de facto government in Kamakura, which was governing on behalf of the imperial court, was also controlled by a regent.

In 1205 Tokimasa sought to eliminate Sanetomo also. Instead he was ousted by his daughter Masako, Yoritomo's wife, and his son Yoshitoki, who exiled him. Thereupon Yoshitoki became regent. In 1219 the figurehead shōgun, Sanetomo, was assassinated by Yoriie's other son. This ended the brief era of the Minamoto shogunate. Following Sanetomo's death the position of the shōgun was filled by court nobles from Kyoto. The shōgun remained a mere figurehead, and the Hōjōs controlled the Kamakura government as regents until its downfall in 1333. Thus, the Minamoto rule was almost as brief as the Taira.

After Yoritomo's death the imperial court intensified its intrigues against the Bakufu. When the Minamoto shogunate ended with the death of Sanetomo, ex-emperor Gotoba decided to take advantage of this situation and move against the Kamakura Bakufu. In May, 1221, he issued a call for all loyal military leaders to come to the support of the imperial family and overthrow the shogunate. The imperial court had gained the friendship of the military chieftains and constables in the Kyoto vicinity, and over ten thousand men responded to Gotoba's call. Faced with this threat and with the possibility that other military magnates might defect to the imperial faction, Masako rallied the Bakufu forces, reminding the vassals of the many favors that had been bestowed upon them by Yoritomo. She managed to marshal a huge force under the Kamakura flag and overwhelmed the imperial forces with ease.

This incident, known as the Jōkyū Insurrection, produced two significant results: (1) the supremacy of the Bakufu over the imperial court was clearly established; and (2) the Hōjō family gained absolute control of the Bakufu. The Kamakura government confiscated all the shōen of those who had taken part in the uprising—over three thousand estates—and established regional headquarters in Kyoto to maintain a check on the activities of the imperial court and to administer the western provinces.

Throughout the thirteenth century the Hōjō regents governed the land effectively without any major disturbances. The Bakufu's domains were scattered throughout the entire country, although there were some provinces in which it held no land. It held virtually all the land in the Kantō region, and in most of the other provinces its holdings were more extensive than estates owned by proprietors free from immediate Hōjō control.

One noteworthy innovation occurred in 1226, when the third regent, Yasutoki (1183–1242), established a council of state. The council consisted of eleven important military chieftains. They deliberated upon important questions and advised the regent, who was obliged to accept their decisions. Yasutoki also codified the customary practices that governed the relationships among the military elements.

In 1232 Yasutoki issued the Jōei Code, which was not strictly speaking a code of laws but rather a set of guidelines for jurists. Yasutoki explained that the object of the code was "to establish standards so that fair trials without regard to the disputants' social status can be held, and eliminate the unjust practice in which the disputants' power determines the outcome." Consisting of fifty-one articles, the code was based on customary law and dealt with property rights, land tenure, inheritance, duties and functions of officials, criminal punishments, and so on. It established a basis for the feudal laws and practices of subsequent periods. One noteworthy provision of the code was the right of women to inherit property and serve as vassals. This was not an innovation, however, but merely a codification of the practice in existence during the Kamakura period.

In other respects, too, women were accorded fairer treatment in this period than in the later Tokugawa era (1600–1867). Women who committed adultery were not punished very much more severely than adulterous men. (In the Tokugawa period such women were executed, while no stigma was attached to wanton behavior by men.) During the Kamakura period women played a much more active role than in subsequent eras. Some even led warriors into the field of battle; others proved their worth as able administrators. One of the ablest women of this era was Masako, who acted as one of the powers behind the shōgun after her husband Yoritomo's death and is sometimes referred to as the "nun-shōgun."

The Jōei Code classified people into three categories: samurai, commoners, and slaves. Unlike the Taihō Code, the Jōei Code did not give the upper classes privileged treatment. On the contrary, in some instances they were punished more severely than the common people for the same offense.

In the trials of this period documentary evidence and testimony by witnesses were weighed carefully by the magistrate in arriving at his verdict, but when such evidence or witnesses did not exist, the disputants were required to swear to the gods that their claims were true. The outcome was then determined by whether some ill omen or event befell a disputant in the following seven days. Among such signs were nosebleeding, sickness, choking while eating, the occurrence of misfortune among relatives, and being wet by a crow or a kite. Vestiges of the ancient trial by ordeal were still present.

THE MONGOL INVASIONS AND THE
DECLINE OF THE KAMAKURA BAKUFU

During the early years of the Kamakura period, the friendly relations with Sung China that had been established during the Heian period were maintained. Sung influence was manifested in the Japanese economic realm in the form of imported copper coins, and, more significantly, in the cultural sphere in the form of Zen Buddhism and Sung-style painting and literature.

The most momentous political event in Sino-Japanese relations during the Kamakura period was the attempt of Kublai Khan (1216–1294) to bring Japan into the fold of the vast Mongol empire. The first Mongol invasion occurred in 1274 against northern Kyushu, but before the Mongols could successfully launch their attack, a typhoon struck and destroyed a large portion of their fleet. Expecting a second foray, the Japanese fortified northern Kyushu, and in 1281, when the Mongols did initiate a second attack with a force of about 140,000 men, they were turned back after seven weeks of fighting in northern Kyushu by the efforts of the Japanese warriors and yet another typhoon. These typhoons were interpreted as interventions by the gods and were later referred to as *kamikaze* (divine wind).

This grave threat to their independence aroused a greater sense of unity among the Japanese than the nation had ever before experienced, and a concerted effort to defend the country was made under the able leadership of Hōjō Tokimune (1251–1284), who had become regent at the age of eighteen and was only twenty-three when the Mongols launched their first attack.

Although the Mongol invasions were successfully repelled, the defensive efforts sapped the strength of the Kamakura Bakufu, especially its financial resources. Those who had taken part in the campaign expected to be rewarded for their services, but the Bakufu did not have any fruits of victory to distribute among the warriors. The samurai, disappointed and frustrated, began to grow increasingly disaffected from the Bakufu.

Changes in the economy were undermining the Kamakura society also. The military class was beginning to feel the pressures of the rising money economy. The samurai had fallen under the influence of the more elegant life of the court aristocracy, and were no longer satisfied with leading simple and frugal lives. While their expenses mounted, their income remained stationary because the amount of land they held remained more or less fixed or even decreased when divided among the children, a practice that prevailed during most of the Kamakura period.

Many of the landholding samurai were forced to sell or mortgage their estates in order to meet rising expenses. They also fell into debt to the emergent moneylenders. In order to cope with this situation, the Bakufu issued in 1297 an edict (*Tokusei,* or Act of Grace) canceling all debts and calling for the return to the samurai of all lands they had lost or sold. But this action only created quarrels and legal disputes and did little to alleviate the situation. At the same time land and power were being concentrated in the hands of the more powerful military leaders, especially the provincial constables, who were beginning to overwhelm the land stewards and the lesser samurai.

Thus political disorder began to increase in the provinces as the struggle for land and power continued among the Bakufu's vassals, constables, land stewards, and shōen owners. This also created disturbances and unrest among the peasantry, who were not only being oppressed more severely by the local authorities but were also beginning to be plagued by the growing number of brigands and thieves who raided and pillaged the countryside.

By the end of the Kamakura period there were many provincial military leaders who were powerful enough to challenge the Bakufu. The sense of loyalty that prevailed during the early years of the Bakufu had weakened with the passing of several generations. The original benefactors of the Kamakura samurai, the Minamotos, had long since passed from the scene. Meanwhile, the imperial court was constantly on the alert, waiting for an opportunity to recapture political power.

An imperial uprising against the Bakufu was attempted in 1324 but failed. Another insurrection was attempted in 1331; this one proved more successful. The military chieftains and constables around Kyoto and western Japan rallied to the support of the imperial court under the leadership of Emperor Godaigo (1288–1339). The most able and determined of these military chiefs was Kusunoki Masashige (?–1336), who carried on a struggle akin to guerrilla warfare against the Hōjō forces. For a while, however, it appeared as if this insurrection would fail, too, but the imperial faction was ultimately rescued by two powerful leaders, Nitta Yoshisada (1301–1338) and Ashikaga Takauji (1305–1358). Takauji was one of the generals whom the Hōjō family had counted on to crush the insurgents. With his defection the Hōjō family could no longer stem the tide and fell in 1333. This terminated the Kamakura era and ushered in a brief return to imperial rule, a period known as the Kemmu Restoration (1333–1336).

THE ETHOS OF THE SAMURAI

The cultural and intellectual outlook of the Kamakura period is identified closely with the military outlook and way of life. Although the term *Bushidō* (Way of the Warriors) was not yet used during this period, the ideals of the *bushi,* or warriors, that emerged with the rise of the military eventually developed into the concept of Bushidō in the Tokugawa period. In the Kamakura period the samurai spoke of "*yumiya no narai,*" or "the way of the bow and arrow."

The ethos of the samurai demanded that the warrior live by the principles of duty, loyalty, integrity, honor, justice, and courage. Japanese history abounds with tales of warriors who acted nobly, chivalrously, and selflessly, but they were not always motivated by noble ideals. Underneath the high-sounding ideals lay an equally if not more powerful motivation: self interest. The world of the samurai, particularly in time of disorder when no strong controlling force existed, was a society in which the law of the jungle prevailed.

Expediency and opportunism guided the actions of many warriors who were ready to shift with the changing tide of fortune. "The past is the past, the present is the present," was the attitude that prevailed in the years when the fortunes of the Tairas and Minamotos were shifting rapidly. There are numerous examples of local chieftains switching sides when the prevailing political winds shifted. During periods of disorder and strife the inconstancy of the warriors became particularly noticeable. The years between 1337 and 1392, when the country was split into two factions, "might not inaptly be characterized as the Great Age of Turncoats."[5] The latter part of the sixteenth century is also noted for the absence of loyalty among warriors; then, too, they transferred their allegiance freely depending upon the rewards that were forthcoming.

For the sake of expediency, family loyalty and sentiments were sometimes sacrificed. Basically, however, family interests played an important part in the samurai's system of values. The family was the essential unit upon which the feudal relationship was constructed. The samurai built his power structure by extending his family ties to all his blood relations, enlarging it further by martial connections, and encompassing followers. Such a follower was virtually regarded as a family member and called "a man of the house" (gokenin) or "a child of the house" (ie-no-ko). The lord-vassal relationship was viewed as a father-son relationship. The individual warrior usually served his lord in the hope of extending the interests of his family. In general, individual interest and family interest coincided. When they clashed, however, personal interests often superseded family interests. Examples of a warrior spilling his brother's blood in disputes over land and inheritance occurred with distressing frequency.

Once a master-vassal relationship was entered into, ideally the vassal was expected to dedicate his entire life to the service of his master. In return for his loyalty and services, the master was expected to reward him. The entire samurai system was founded upon reciprocal relationships of services and rewards. The reward usually took the form of land or an office that entailed a certain income. The protection and security offered the vassal was also part of the benefit that he derived from his contract with his lord. The benefits that a vassal obtained from his master placed him under the latter's obligation, that is, on. Even a display of good will and benevolence by the master to his vassal would place the latter under the on of the former.

A close emotional and psychological bond between master and vassal could lead the vassal to serve his master selflessly without any anticipation of immediate rewards, but more often than not tangible rewards were expected. After serving in battle, vassals openly asked for compensations. When no rewards were forthcoming after the Mongol invasion, some warriors implied that unless they were properly remunerated, the Bakufu could not expect them to remain loyal. One of the reasons why the Kemmu Restoration failed was because the imperial faction could not properly compensate its supporters.

On the other hand, when a strong sense of on did develop, the followers of the lord would join him in death. When the Hōjōs faced their downfall, thousands of loyal samurai committed suicide to share the fate of their masters. A samurai who enjoyed the special favor of his master was expected to accompany him to the next world, a tradition that continued even into modern times, dramatically demonstrated by General Nogi's suicide upon the death of Emperor Meiji in 1912. Even during the peaceful rule of the Tokugawa shōgun, the samurai were expected to join their dead lords by committing suicide. The Bakufu found it necessary to ban this practice in 1663.

The practice of committing suicide by disemboweling oneself with the sword (known as *seppuku* or *hara-kiri*) emerged around the end of the twelfth century and became a highly ritualized affair, particularly in the Tokugawa period. A warrior might be ordered to commit seppuku for violation of the samurai code of conduct, or he might voluntarily commit seppuku if he felt disgraced in any way. Warriors also committed suicide to expiate mistakes or transgressions, to protest against unjust actions, and to persuade superiors to refrain from following a certain course of action. Gruesome as this practice might seem it brings into focus one positive aspect of the code of the warrior, namely, the warrior's willingness to play the game strictly by the rules and assume total responsibility, paying the full price for whatever action he takes.

In order to be properly rewarded for heroic exploits in battle, witnesses were necessary. So it was said that "to cut into the enemy all alone, and die unseen by any witnesses is a futile action. This is called 'a dog's death.' Only when a warrior charges into the enemy and sacrifices his life while his friends are nearby would he gain fame, and his descendants be properly rewarded."[6] So honor and reputation were valued not only for idealistic reasons but for the tangible results that would accrue. The descendants who benefited from the heroic achievements of an ancestor were expected to be aware of the on owed him and to honor and revere him.

To gain fame and honor for himself and the family, the samurai, of course, had to excel in military exploits and be fortified with the Spartan virtues of courage, strength, discipline, and endurance. He was not to waste his time in aesthetic or cultural pursuits. "A person born into a military family," one warrior is purported to have said, "must pursue the way of the military. Of what use is it to allow the mind to concentrate on the moon and flowers, compose poems, and learn how to play musical instruments? What good would it do to play the *koto* [a Japanese harp] and flute in the battlefield? Members of my household, including women, must learn to ride wild horses, and shoot powerful bows and arrows."[7]

Above all the warrior had to be indifferent to considerations of life and death. Regardless of how one may romanticize the exploits of the samurai, his chief function was to kill his foe. Life had to be held cheaply, and a callousness necessarily characterized the samurai outlook. Thus not only were the warriors ruthless and cold-blooded about killing their enemies on the battlefield, they were also frequently as heartless in their treatment of the aged, women, and children, although the code of the warrior required the samurai to protect and aid the weak, the injured, and the defeated. For example, when Yoritomo was in exile in Izu he had a love affair with the daughter of the official who was assigned the task of keeping him under surveillance. A baby girl was born of this relationship. When the official, who had been away in Kyoto for several years, returned and found out about this affair, fearing the reaction of the Tairas, he threw the innocent little girl down a waterfall.

The Spartan virtues of the samurai were also demanded of women. Young girls were trained to repress their feelings, to harden their nerves, and even to use weapons. The samurai's treatment of women in the Kamakura period was quite different from the relationships of aristocratic couples during the Heian era. The samurai's wife was expected to go and reside with her husband. She was to aid him in advancing his family interests and to manage the affairs of the household. Upon his death she inherited his property and was expected to take charge of the family and perform the duties of a vassal. As the practice of equal inheritance was abandoned in favor of single inheritance, however, women's property rights declined as they were increasingly relegated to an inferior position.

The method of warfare during this period deserves some comment. The chief weapons used were the bow and arrow and the long sword. It is said that some Minamoto warriors used such powerful bows that it required three to five people to stretch the bow and shoot the arrow. The arrows for such bows were almost four feet long. Contending warriors usually faced each other on horseback. They wore suits of armor that did not provide full protection from the flying missiles, which might have a range of 45 to 110 yards. Each knight was armed with twenty to thirty arrows, which he usually shot while mounted. Once the arrows were depleted the warriors turned to single combat. Each warrior called out his name to identify himself and seek out a worthy opponent. As the two combatants approached each other on horseback, each warrior tried to cut down his opponent with his long sword. This was rather difficult to accomplish, however, since the knights usually charged swiftly past each other. Hence each sought to knock his opponent off his horse, wrestle him to the ground, get on top of him, and use the dirk to slit his throat. The victor usually cut off his opponent's head to prove that he had finished him off or, if the victim happened to be an important foe, to be properly rewarded for it.

A certain code of combat was followed before the Minamoto-Taira conflict. For instance, both sides would agree on the site of combat and avoid using treacherous means to take unfair advantage of the enemy. But the Minamotos and Tairas were not playing a game; they were involved in a bitter struggle to the end. As a result, sneak attacks were frequently resorted to and came to be an accepted mode of combat. Also while at the beginning of the Kamakura era it was considered unfair to shoot the horse from under the opponent, later in the period warriors deliberately aimed at the underbelly of the opponents' horses. Warfare was becoming a much more ruthless and sanguinary affair.

BUDDHISM

During the Heian period Buddhism was a religion restricted primarily to the upper segment of the society, but in the Kamakura era it spread rapidly among the common people. There are several reasons why the Kamakura period became an era of religious ferment. For one thing it followed an age of disorder and chaos—the time of troubles at the end of the Heian and beginning of the Kamakura eras. Civil strife was widespread and continuous; great powers rose and fell. Moreover, man-made disasters were aggravated by natural calamities—earthquakes, floods, and droughts. Famines and epidemics followed. The Buddhist concept of the decline of the law and the end of the world (*mappō*) seemed to be becoming a reality. People turned to religion for consolation and security, but the older religious sects failed to satisfy their spiritual needs. The monks, who lived in worldly splendor and stressed the mechanical and ritualistic aspects of the religion, had removed themselves from the common people. Thus, to meet the spiritual needs of the people, several new sects came into existence.

The movement that won widespread adherence was Amida Buddhism, which had been introduced into Japan during the middle of the Heian period. It belonged to the Mahayana branch of Buddhism that—unlike Theravada Buddhism, which equated salvation primarily with the attainment of enlightenment through self-effort and the extinction of the erroneous sense of the self we possess—envisioned a rebirth into another world, a Buddhist paradise, a land of bliss. This was to be achieved through the aid of merciful Buddhas and Bodhisattvas who, after having attained enlightenment themselves, delayed their entrance into paradise in order to help those remaining behind gain salvation too. The Buddhist paradise is not the ultimate goal but rather a place where the individual incapable of attaining enlightenment by his own merit will be aided in doing so and will thus be able to achieve the ultimate goal of nirvana, self-extinction. For the common people, however, entrance into the Buddhist paradise became a goal in itself.

Theravada Buddhism did not envision the existence of Buddhist deities, whereas Mahayana Buddhism conceived of a multitude of divine Buddhas and Bodhisattvas. The tendency to idolize and even worship the Buddha had developed early in history, however. By the first century A.D. he was represented in images that were venerated by the believers. Then Bodhisattvas—Enlightened Beings—came to be revered by some members of the Buddhist community. Next the doctrine of the Three Buddhas came into existence. The Buddha, it was taught, had three bodies—the Body of Essence, the Body of Bliss, and the Created Body. The Body of Essence was the primordial Buddha, permeating the universe. The historical Gautama Buddha was the Created Body. The Body of Bliss takes the form of many Buddhas, but for the development of Mahayana Buddhism in Japan the most significant of these was Amida Buddha, or Amitabha (Immeasurable Glory), who dwells in the Western Paradise where all the faithful can enter.

In the Heian period a monk called Genshin (942–1017) sought to propagate Amida Buddhism in Japan. He wrote the *Essentials of Salvation* and prepared the grounds for the emergence of the Pure Land Sect during the Kamakura period. Genshin was concerned with making salvation, that is, entry into the Western Paradise, possible for everyone, regardless of class status or sex. In his day, the path to salvation involved the understanding of difficult scriptures, metaphysical training, participation in complex rituals, adherence to rigorous spiritual discipline and purity of conduct, and the doing of good works, such as dedication of images and temples to Buddha. These things were not possible for everyone. How then could the common man gain salvation? It could be achieved through devotion to Amida Buddha and the recitation of his name, said Genshin.

Other monks preached this doctrine also, and the movement gained some following among the aristocracy. But the powerful monasteries were still concerned primarily with the furtherance of their economic and political interests. As noted earlier, they even maintained their own armies to protect their interests. Initially, Amidism had little effect on the traditional religious practices of the major sects. It was still believed that the invocation of Amida's name had to involve an understanding of the profound meaning of that name and a mental visualization of the Land of Bliss to be truly effective. The blessings to be derived from the recitation of Amida Buddha's name by itself were slight. The troubles and disorder of the late Heian period, however, turned the people toward a religion that offered them a place in the Land of Bliss and an escape from the miseries of this world.

The monk who popularized Amidism and founded an independent sect was Hōnen (1133–1212). Hōnen offered those who could not save themselves by their own efforts an easy path to salvation. He taught that faith in the compassionate mercy of Amida Buddha and the sincere repetition of his name were sufficient for salvation and entrance into the Land of Bliss. Metaphysical training, spiritual discipline, and personal effort were not essential for salvation. It could be achieved by total reliance on the saving power of Amida Buddha.

In order to become independent of the older sects that emphasized traditional practices, Hōnen founded his own sect known as the Jōdo (Pure Land) Sect. His unorthodox views disturbed the existing sects, and he was subjected to constant persecution and was finally exiled from Kyoto late in his life. His sect flourished, however, and he won a wide following among the aristocracy as well as the common people. Yoritomo's wife, Masako, was one of his devoted followers.

Hōnen's disciple Shinran (1173–1262) simplified his master's teachings even further and made Pure Land Buddhism truly a religion of the masses. Hōnen and his other disciples believed that the more one recited the Amida

Buddha's name, the better one's chances of salvation were. It was even asserted that Amida Buddha's name should be invoked 70,000 times a day. Shinran, however, taught that one sincere invocation of Amida's name was sufficient for a believer to gain salvation and entry into the Western Paradise. A person might, if he so desired, continue to repeat Amida's name in order to honor him, but it was not necessary for salvation. If repeated invocations of the name were necessary, Shinran reasoned, it would mean that salvation was still dependent upon individual effort. The believer would not be throwing himself completely upon the mercy and compassion of Amida Buddha. It would indicate a lack of faith in his saving power. Shinran even discontinued chanting the sutras, which until then was believed to contribute to the salvation of others. This too, Shinran held, would be contrary to the belief that only the invocation of Amida's name was necessary for salvation.

Shinran went further than his master in another aspect. He concluded that all external conduct was irrelevant to salvation. Whether one was moral or immoral made no difference in one's eligibility for entry into the Land of Bliss. Amida was not a stern judge but rather a compassionate savior. All men, good or bad, rich or poor, learned or ignorant, clerical or secular, would be saved by the merciful Amida. In fact, Shinran taught that a wicked person might have a better chance of being saved because he had to rely wholly on the mercy of Amida Buddha while a good man might be inclined to feel that he could rely on his own good conduct to gain salvation. What was necessary was complete reliance on "the other power." The *Tannishō*, a collection of Shinran's sayings, records that Shinran said, "If the good can gain salvation, there is all the more reason to believe that the wicked can win salvation."

Because external conduct was irrelevant to salvation, Shinran concluded that traditional injunctions against eating meat, drinking alcoholic beverages, and so on were unimportant. He also rejected all forms of ritualism and ascetic practices. Furthermore, he repudiated monasticism and clerical celibacy; there was no need for the clergy to maintain a different mode of life than the laity. He himself married and had a number of children. This does not mean, of course, that Shinran and his followers were unconcerned about moral conduct. Shinran believed that by giving oneself over completely to Amida Buddha one automatically became moral. As Shinran developed his own interpretation of Amida Buddhism, he and his disciples came to consider themselves the "True" adherents of the Pure Land Sect (Jōdo Shinshū).

The Pure Land Buddhists emphasized the significance of Amida Buddha over all other Buddhas and Bodhisattvas. The founder of Buddhism, Gautama Buddha, or Shakyamuni, was looked upon as only a teacher and transmitter of the faith, not a divinity to be worshipped. Amida Buddhist sects were truly egalitarian, in that they made salvation possible for the most humble and ignorant person. Shinran consciously sought to spread his teachings to the common people, and he gained a wide following, particularly among the peasants. It soon became the most popular of the Buddhist sects and even today has one of the largest body of followers.[8]

The second important Buddhist sect that arose during the Kamakura period was the Nichiren Sect (or the Lotus Sect) established by Nichiren (1222–1282). Nichiren was born into a lowly fisherman's family but founded a powerful Buddhist sect and became prominent enough even to defy the Bakufu. Some students of Buddhism question whether Nichiren can be classified as a Buddhist because of his narrow ethnocentric sentiments. It would be more appropriate to consider the Nichiren Sect as an offshoot of nationalistic Shintoism, asserts one authority on Buddhism. "Nichiren suffered from self-assertiveness and bad temper, and he manifested a degree of personal and tribal egotism which disqualify him as a Buddhist teacher," he writes.[9]

Yet the source of Nichiren's religious faith was Buddhism. He preached that salvation was to be achieved by the repeated invocation of the Lotus Sutra, which contains the true teachings of Shakyamuni Buddha. The Lotus Sutra emphasizes the importance of the three bodies of Buddha, that is, the universal Buddha (*Dainichi Nyorai*, or the Body of Essence), Amida Buddha (the Body of Bliss), and the historical Buddha (the Created Body). Nichiren taught that all three should be regarded as a unity and equal in importance, unlike other sects that stressed only one of the three. Insofar as Nichiren taught that salvation can be gained by the simple recitation of the name of the Lotus Sutra, he paralleled the teachings of the Pure Land sects.

Unlike the other Buddhist masters, Nichiren was extremely dogmatic, intolerant, and aggressive. He violently condemned all other sects for what he considered to be their erroneous beliefs, and he looked upon himself as a reincarnation of the Bodhisattva of action mentioned in the Lotus Sutra. He embarked upon the task of eliminating the false teachings of the other sects and replacing them with his own "true" interpretation of the Buddhist scriptures. Unlike the other Buddhist sects, the Lotus Sect was militant, activist, and zealous, reflecting the personality of the founder.

In criticizing the other sects, Nichiren argued that the natural calamities, famines, and epidemics of his day were caused by the prevalence of false religions. He was particularly critical of Hōnen and the Pure Land Sect, but he did not spare the other sects either. In his criticisms of other religious leaders, he resorted to bitter invectives. He attacked all those who did not submit to his views and even turned his wrath upon Ninshō, a monk renowned for his charitable activities.

Nichiren emerges as one of Japan's earliest super-patriots. He did not limit himself to the task of saving the souls of individuals; he considered himself the savior of Japan. "I will be," he proclaimed, "the Pillar of Japan. I will be the Eyes of Japan. I will be the Great Vessel of Japan."[10] He predicted the invasion of Japan by the Mongols and insisted that the only way the country could be saved from this calamity was to adopt his religion. His aim was to make his the official state religion.

Nichiren emphasized the concept of requiting one's obligation (on) to the sovereign. This was to be achieved through faith and devotion to the Nichiren Sect. Service to the Lotus Sect was to be identified with service to the country. Conversely, he taught that Buddhism could not prevail without the country. Thus national security had to be the primary concern of all true Buddhists. The way to strengthen the country was through the propagation of the true faith. His teachings, he said, "are not designed to further my own interests, but the interests of the gods [kami], the ruler, the country, and all the people." He came to concern himself more with the salvation of the country than the individual. Japan to him was the land of the gods and was destined to become the center of the universal religion, that is, the Nichiren Sect.

Nichiren, like a good Shintoist, considered Japan to be a unique land. He compared India, where Buddhism was born, to the moon and Japan to the sun. The moon moves west to east, thus Buddhism moved from India to Japan. The sun moves from east to west, so, according to Nichiren's line of thinking, Japanese Buddhism would spread westward, back to India. He was happy, he said, to be born in a land that was protected by the Sun Goddess, Amaterasu.

His uncompromising, aggressive attacks on the other sects and his scathing criticisms of the Bakufu for supporting them repeatedly led Nichiren into difficulties, but he won a wide following among the samurai, who were attracted to his positive, dynamic point of view as well as to his emphasis on fulfilling one's obligations to the country through service.

The Nichiren Sect continued its growth and became one of the major Buddhist sects. It retained the unique character stamped upon it by its founder and continued to represent an unusual combination of Buddhism and militant ethnocentrism. In the modern era it contributed to the rise of ultranationalism and was used to support the imperialistic policies of the militarists. Today it is regaining its influence in the political sphere with activist programs spearheaded by its secular organ, the *Sōka Gakkai* (Value-creating Society), which in the late 1960s had a membership of more than eleven million.[11]

Zen Buddhism was the third significant Buddhist movement to emerge in the Kamakura period. Each of the three new Buddhist sects that arose during this era contributed something unique and significant to Japanese history and culture. Zen Buddhism had its greatest impact in the cultural sphere, in molding the aesthetic taste of the Japanese.

Zen, or Ch'an, Buddhism was, it was said, introduced to China by an Indian monk, Bodhidharma, about A.D. 520, although it is now believed that the doctrine of meditation had entered China much earlier. Some aspects of Ch'an Buddhism had entered Japan prior to the Kamakura period and were adopted by the older sects, but it was not until the Kamakura era that it emerged as an influential, independent movement. Zen Buddhism differed from the Pure Land and Nichiren sects in that it emphasized self-reliance, while they emphasized reliance upon external powers. The ultimate goal of the Zen Buddhists was not entrance into the Buddhist paradise but the attainment of "enlightenment" (satori), which involved the acquisition of insight into one's true or original nature and the comprehension of the nature of reality. Buddhists believe that beneath the surface manifestations that lead us to distinguish between the subject and the object, between this and that, there is an underlying unity or reality which, when the surface illusions are removed, can be perceived as a "great void," a reality that is infinite. The object of the Zen Buddhists is to enter this reality itself, not simply to come into contact with it as a Christian seeks to come into contact with God. When a person attains satori he becomes immersed in reality just as naturally as a fish finds itself in water.

Satori, according to the Zen Buddhists, is to be achieved through an intuitive grasp of the nature of reality by means of meditation and concentration, not by relying on the intellect or reasoned knowledge. Just as the hand that grasps cannot grasp itself, the reason that seeks to comprehend cannot comprehend itself. Satori occurs as a sudden and direct perception of reality. Study of the scriptures, metaphysical speculation, and performance of rituals are useless in this quest for enlightenment. All the embellishments and trimmings of the religion must be eliminated if man is to probe directly into his soul to grasp his Buddha-nature. When a person attains enlightenment and comprehends reality he cannot transmit it to others by use of words because it is a completely subjective process. The message that Bodhidharma brought to China was:

> A special transmission outside the scriptures;
> No dependence upon words and letters;
> Direct pointing at the soul of man;
> Seeing into one's nature and the attainment of Buddhahood.[12]

Zen Buddhism emerged in Kamakura Japan as a major force largely through the efforts of two monks, Eisai (1141–1215) and Dōgen (1200–1253). Both had traveled to China and studied under Ch'an masters. Returning to Japan they embarked upon the propagation of Zen Buddhism. Eisai founded the Rinzai Sect, and Dōgen the Sōtō Sect. No fundamental differences divided the two sects. The former, however, tended to emphasize the importance of kōan, enigmatic, paradoxical themes to be concentrated upon by the acolyte.

The kōan was designed to break the mind's customary habit of thinking in rational, logical terms and to force it to attain sudden, intuitive insights into reality. They simply serve as means of derailing the mind from the path of ratiocination.

One of the kōan given to an initiate to contemplate is "Listen to the sound of the Single Hand!" Another is "Thinking neither of good nor of evil, at this very moment what was the original aspect before your father and mother were born?"[13]

The kōan results in the liberation of the unconscious.

> Evoked by the enormous psychological strain of trying to force a solution of the insoluble kōan problem, enlightenment is experienced as the dawn of a new reality, in which the boundaries between the conscious and the unconscious disappear, and conscious and unconscious alike are openly revealed. The Zen disciple realizes the totality of human nature in its primal unity, prior to all discrimination and division.[14]

Although the Sōtō Sect did not reject the kōan, it emphasized *zazen*, or sitting in meditation, above all. While one is sitting in meditation the kōan is not employed, because the object of zazen is to free the mind from all mundane things. The kōan, the Sōtō adherents said, insofar as it is motivated by the desire to gain sudden insight into reality, is a manifestation of the self.

Zazen entails a prescribed posture, regulation of the breath, and special concentration to still the mind in order to control the emotions and strengthen the will. Then one looks into the "heart-mind" to discover the true nature of existence. The end of zazen was not only satori-awakening but also the spiritual and moral development of the practitioner, who, hopefully, will emerge a man of virtue and of all-embracing compassion and wisdom. In the process of sitting in meditation, Dōgen asserted, one's Buddha-nature is being realized.

Although the practice of kōan might induce sudden enlightenment, zazen ordinarily does not result in sudden expansion of consciousness or the onset of a sudden sense of buoyancy and exhilaration. Even though a profound inner transformation takes place when satori is achieved, the person himself, it is contended, may not even be aware of it initially. In some instances, however, a sense of elation and buoyancy evidently do occur. A Zen monk of the Meiji era (1868–1912) said of his experience of satori:

> I found myself, as it were, on the ground of the Great Death, and no awareness of the being of all things and of the ego remained. I felt only how in my body a spirit extended itself to ten thousand worlds, and an infinite splendor of light arose. . . . In a flash seeing and hearing, speech and motion, were different from every day. As I sought the supreme truth . . . my own self was clear and things appeared bright. In the excess of delight I forgot that my hands were moving in the air and that my feet were dancing.[15]

Because the Zen masters did not preach the easy way to salvation as did the masters of the Pure Land sects, Zen did not become a mass movement. Instead it tended to be a religion of the elite, those who had the strength of character and willpower to work out their own salvation. It gained a strong following among the samurai and the ruling class. It was said that "the Tendai is for the royal family, the Shingon for the nobility, the Zen for the warrior classes, and the Jōdo for the masses."[16]

Zen's emphasis on discipline, single-minded concentration, simplicity, and a direct and decisive approach to life and reality appealed to the samurai, who had to face the moment of truth constantly in the field of battle and act with singleness of purpose and firmness of will. Suzuki Daisetsu points out that Zen appealed to the samurai "because it teaches us not to look backward once the course is decided upon . . . because it treats life and death indifferently."[17] Thus Zen became the moral and philosophical mainstay of many military men in Japan from the Kamakura period to the modern age. Even in prewar Japan many military officers entered Zen monasteries to discipline themselves in order to face the enemy on the battlefield.

The Zen point of view played an important role in the formation of the Way of the Warriors, which required the samurai to conduct himself with honor, courage, and dignity in face of ever-present death. To live up to these ideals the samurai had to come to terms with the problem of death and conquer his fear of it. A seventeenth-century samurai wrote, "The idea most vital and essential to the samurai is that of death, which he ought to have before his mind day and night."[18] Zen helped the samurai to cope with this problem. Takeda Shingen (1521–1573), a warlord of the sixteenth century and a student of Zen, advised his warriors, "devote yourselves to the study of Zen. Zen has no secrets other than seriously thinking about birth and death."[19]

Thus a close connection was established between Zen Buddhism and the warrior class. Zen certainly played a positive role in disciplining the samurai and training him to deal with the problem of death. But rising above considerations of one's own life and death could also entail a general indifference to the life and death of other people. In the words of an authority on Japanese thought, "to get accustomed to the idea of death is to treat death lightly."[20] Suzuki asserts that the Zen master does not use the sword to kill but that the sword itself performs its function automatically to eliminate the enemy that appears to injure the Zen swordsman. This explanation does not resolve the unpleasant paradox. To prepare the swordsman to kill efficiently is a far cry from the profound mercy and compassion that led Gautama Buddha to embark on his search for a way to relieve the suffering of his fellowmen.

This aspect of Zen Buddhism is, of course, only one phase of its varied contributions to Japanese life and culture. It contributed to the development and refinement of the tea ceremony, the art of gardening and flower arrangement, sword-making, the Nō drama, painting, ceramics, and haiku, as we shall see in later chapters.

Moreover, the Zen masters were certainly not indifferent to human suffering. There has been a long tradition of charitable activities on the part of Buddhist monks in Japan. There is a story that Eisai gave to the poor a piece of copper that was to be used to make a halo for an image of Buddha. When he was criticized for this, he replied, "You are right, but just consider the will of the Buddha. He sacrificed his very flesh and limbs for the sake of all mankind. If some men are about to die of starvation, would he not want us to give the whole Buddha figure to save them?"[21] Dōgen, too, sought to instill the spirit of charity among his disciples. A monk of the Tokugawa period, Ryōkan (1758–1831), who was known for his simple and humble way of life as well as his love of all living things, was a member of the Sōtō Sect. He extended his selfless love to his fellow men, aiding the poor, even showing compassion to thieves.

The two monks most renowned for their charitable social work during the Kamakura period, however, belonged to the Ritsu Sect, which emerged in the Nara period and enjoyed a revival during the Kamakura era. The two monks were Eison (1201–1290) and his disciple, Ninshō (1217–1303).

Eison devoted his life to helping thousands of outcasts, beggars, the homeless, the sick, and lepers. Ninshō followed in his master's footsteps and built hospitals and homes for orphans, beggars, and outcasts and cared for the lepers. Every other day for several years he carried a young leper back and forth on his back 5 miles to the outskirts of Nara to enable him to beg in the streets.

During this period the practice of monks traveling throughout the countryside to extend the blessings of Amida Buddha became widespread. The most popular of these wandering saints was Ippen (1239–1289), whose followers eventually merged with the True Pure Land Sect. Ippen danced about while chanting the name of Amida Buddha and is credited by some with having originated the Bon dances performed to console the souls of the departed.

CULTURE

The pragmatic, realistic outlook of the samurai is reflected in the art of the Kamakura period. Portraits of actual personalities rather than idealistic images of Buddhist deities are a prominent feature of Kamakura art. The most famous such painting is one of Yoritomo. The artist presumably portrays him as he actually appeared, with relatively close-set eyes, a large curving nose, and a face wider at the bottom than at the top. The art of painting narrative scrolls (e-makimono) also continued to flourish. These picture scrolls were long, often more than 40 feet in length, and were unrolled from right to left. They depicted scenes from renowned battles or episodes from the lives of religious personalities such as Ippen. A scroll depicting the Heiji Insurrection is the most representative of the narrative picture scrolls. The paintings in this scroll are characterized by forcefulness, animation, and realistic details. The landscapes depicted in the scroll paintings of this era have also become more realistic, serving not simply as decorative settings but as representations of local scenes.

Another noteworthy feature of the scroll paintings of this period was the introduction of a satirical element into the medium. Comic-strip-like drawings of animals satirizing the human world—attributed formerly to a Buddhist monk, Toba Sōjō (1053–1140), but now believed to be works of the thirteenth century—are especially unique. Such animals as frogs, monkeys, and hares are used to make fun of the rituals of the Buddhist priests and the devotions of the pilgrims.

In sculpture, too, the spirit of the samurai is discernible. We have the vigorous, powerful, and somewhat grotesque—because of the exaggerated muscles and tendons—works of Unkei and Kaikei. They carved the 26 foot high Deva kings that guard the gateway of the Tōdaiji Temple in Nara, which was rebuilt at the end of the twelfth century after being destroyed by fire during the struggle between the Taira and Minamoto families. These huge statues successfully convey a sense of tactile value, movement, and force.

In architecture the major effort was still expended in the construction of Buddhist temples. Reflecting the Zen influence, clarity of line and simplicity of decor were increasingly stressed. In domestic dwellings, also, the stress was on simplicity. In the middle of the thirteenth century the 42 foot tall Great Buddha of Kamakura was built. Representing the serene majesty of the Amida Buddha, the figure is in the yogi position, with legs crossed and hands in the gesture of meditation.

Being the age of the samurai, the art of sword making reached new heights of excellence, and many great master swordsmiths emerged, the greatest being Masamune (1264–1344), whose creations are valued today as rare treasures. It is said that no sword of any age or country can surpass the Kamakura swords. The samurai sword had to have a "blade keen enough to hack through armor but resilient enough not to snap on impact." In order to produce such a sword, the swordsmith forged a compound blade with carbon steel or white cast iron on the cutting edge, a mild metal in the center, and a fairly soft but unbrittle iron on the back. When steel alone was used, the process of welding and folding was repeated until a blade consisting of more than four million layers of steel was forged. Armor making also became a fine art. The grand armor of this era was especially rich in decoration: gilt-bronze, patterned leather, and figured textile.

The art of ceramics came into its own also, thanks to the influence of Sung China. The town of Seto, near Nagoya, became the center for pottery manufacture and has remained the leading ceramics center to the present. The term Setoware became a generic term for pottery in general. This art acquired greater significance in the next era (the Ashikaga period), when the tea ceremony became popular among the ruling class.

In literature the great romantic war stories, such as the *Tale of the Heike*, the *Rise and Fall of the Genji and Heike*, the *Tale of Hogen*, and the *Tale of Heiji*, were written during this period. They were not composed by the samurai themselves but by noblemen and priests, so the sentiments described in them do not directly represent those of the samurai. They do reflect the general outlook of the age, however, as well as the ethos of the samurai: martial valor, courage, loyalty, and integrity. The Buddhist outlook on life, with its emphasis on the ephemeral and transitory nature of all things and its belief in the inevitable fall of those who have risen, sets the tone of these works. Thus a sense of melancholy and sorrow pervades many of the tales, notably the *Tale of the Heike*, which depicts the heroic exploits of the samurai in the course of the rise and fall of the Taira clan. The tale starts with the lines:

> In the sound of the bell of the Gion Temple echoes the impermanence of all things. The pale hue of the flowers of the teak-tree shows the truth that they who prosper must fall. The proud ones do not last long, but vanish like a spring-night's dream. And the mighty ones too will perish in the end, like dust before the wind.[22]

This sense of the ephemeral nature of all things runs through the entire tale and is stated over and over. " 'Those who are born must die; those that meet must part,' is the way of the world. 'The last dew or the first drop,' one must go before the other, and whether one dies first or last, all must leave this world at last."[23] The only consolation in this life was to be found in a Buddhist renunciation of the mundane world and the hope of being reborn into the Western Paradise.

The *Hōjōki*, a collection of personal observations by Kamo-no-Chōmei (1151–1213) written in 1212, embodies the same sense of the ethereal nature of life. It starts with the statement:

> The current of a running stream flows on unceasingly, but the water is not the same: the foam floating on the pool where it lingers, now vanishes and now forms again, but is never lasting. Such are mankind and their habitations. . . . In the morning some die, in the evening some are born. Such is life. It may be compared to foam upon the water. Whether they are born or whether they die, we know not whence they come nor whither they go.[24]

During this period the composing of waka, a poem of thirty-one syllables—a pastime that flourished at the Heian court—continued to be pursued by the courtiers. At the beginning of the thirteenth century an anthology of waka was compiled under the auspices of a retired emperor. This was the *Shinkokinshū* (*New Collection of Ancient and Modern Poems*), which, with the *Man'yōshū* and the *Kokinshū*, constitutes one of the three most prominent collections of early Japanese poems.

Several histories or chronicles were also written in this era. Of particular interest is the *Gukanshō* (*Jottings of a Fool*), written by a monk named Jien (1155–1225). Its significance lies in the fact that Jien viewed the course of Japanese history as a process governed by a general principle. It was the first attempt at a philosophical interpretation of history in Japan. Jien characterized Japanese history in terms of the Buddhist theory of the periodic decline of the Law of Buddha. His age, he said, was an era when the Law had already deteriorated. This view, as we noted earlier, was common at the end of the twelfth and the beginning of the thirteenth centuries. Jien divided Japanese history into seven stages and identified the decline of the Law of Buddha with the decline in the authority of the imperial family. Governed by this principle of decline and degeneration, history moved forward inexorably in accordance with the Law. The rise of the military, which had deprived the imperial house of all political power, could not be challenged because this was brought about by the general principle of history and was inevitable. One had to accept the existing situation and await the return of the Law after the period of the absence of the Law had spent itself.

NOTES

1. A. L. Sadler, trans., *The Heike Monogatari*, in *Transactions of the Asiatic Society of Japan*, vol. 46, part 2, p. 10.
   2. *Ibid.*, p. 48.

3. W. G. Aston, *A History of Japanese Literature* (New York: Appleton, 1899), pp. 149–51.

4. The position of the constable (*shugo*) was "an 1190s Yoritomo invention essentially to aid the bakufu in keeping the latter's own vassals in check," and the land stewards (*jitō*) were "war-period outlaws with whom Yoritomo, as emergency police chief, became unavoidably identified." Jeffrey P. Mass, *Warrior Government in Early Medieval Japan* (New Haven, Conn.: Yale University Press, 1974), p. 10.

5. James Murdoch, *A History of Japan*, 3 vols. (New York: Ungar, 1964 [1st edition 1902–1926]), vol. 1, p. 564.

6. Quoted in Ienaga Saburō, *Nihon Dōtokushisōshi* (*History of Japanese Moral Thought*) (Tokyo: Iwanami, 1951), p. 78.

7. Quoted in Okada Akio et al., *Nihon no Rekishi* (*A History of Japan*), 12 vols. (Tokyo: Yomiuri Shimbunsha, 1959–1960), vol. 4, p. 186.

8. The total number of followers of the Pure Land and True Pure Land sects was 20.4 million in 1968. Of these about 14 million belonged to the various branches of the True Pure Land Sect.

9. Edward Conze, *Buddhism: Its Essence and Development* (New York: Harper, 1959), p. 206.

10. Quoted in Masaharu Anesaki, *History of Japanese Religion* (Tokyo and Rutland, Vt.: Tuttle, 1963), p. 198.

11. The total number of people affiliated with the many branches of the Nichiren Sect came to over thirty-one million in 1968.

12. William Barrett, ed., *Zen Buddhism: Selected Writings of D. T. Suzuki* (Garden City, N.Y.: Doubleday, 1956), p. 61.

13. I. Miura and R. F. Sasaki, *The Zen Koan* (New York: Harcourt, 1965), p. 44.

14. Heinrich Dumoulin, *A History of Zen Buddhism* (New York: Random House, 1963), p. 132.

15. *Ibid.*, p. 273.

16. Daisetsu T. Suzuki, *Zen and Japanese Culture* (New York: Pantheon, 1959), p. 63.

17. *Ibid.*, p. 61.

18. Quoted in *ibid.*, p. 72.

19. *Ibid.*, p. 78.

20. Tsuda Sōkichi, *Bungaku ni Arawaretaru Kokuminshisō no Kenkyū* (*A Study of Japanese Thought as Manifested in Literature*), 4 vols. (Tokyo: Iwanami, 1951–1955), vol. 1, p. 617.

21. Ryusaku Tsunoda, W. T. de Bary, and Donald Keene, eds., *Sources of Japanese Tradition* (New York: Columbia University Press, 1958), p. 248.

22. Donald Keene, ed., *Japanese Literature: An Introduction for Western Readers* (New York: Grove, 1955), p. 78.

23. Sadler, *op. cit.*, part 1, p. 207.

24. Aston, *op. cit.*, p. 146.

CHAPTER 5

THE ASHIKAGA PERIOD
The Emergence of the Daimyō

POLITICAL DEVELOPMENTS

When the imperial faction, aided by the discontented military chieftains and warriors, succeeded in overthrowing the Hōjō family, Emperor Godaigo took personal charge of the government, hoping to set a precedent for direct rule by the emperor and to centralize power in the court. The emperor was not powerful enough, however, to keep the military under control. What actually ensued was a government composed of both imperial and military elements.

The new government retained some features of the Bakufu. Samurai were appointed as high officials in the central government and as provincial governors and constables at the local level. The office of constable was a holdover from the Bakufu, but the imperial government was unable to abolish it and empower the governors with full authority in local affairs. In many instances powerful military chiefs held both the offices of governor and constable.

For various reasons the new government failed to win the support and confidence of the samurai. Emperor Godaigo first concentrated on making secure the holdings of the imperial court, the court nobles, and the monasteries. He also claimed most of the Hōjō holdings for the imperial court. The samurai who had aided the imperial cause expected to be rewarded generously and flocked to the capital to present their claims, but the imperial government failed to satisfy their demands. Furthermore, as the new government was being established disputes over boundaries and proprietary rights broke out frequently. The imperial government had to arbitrate these quarrels, but the settlements it made naturally failed to please all the disputants and added fuel to the fires of discontent with the emperor. In addition, as soon as it gained power the imperial court began to renovate the imperial palace and taxed the samurai for this project.

86

From the outset, then, there was considerable dissatisfaction with the new government.

The imperial family itself was weakened internally by a cleavage between the emperor and his son, Prince Morinaga, who had led the imperial forces against the Hōjōs. The prince was accused of plotting to capture the throne and was assassinated while in custody of the Ashikaga family. At the same time local uprisings by forces antagonistic to the new government continued to break out in various areas.

Realizing that the new regime was on a weak footing, Ashikaga Takauji, who had played a decisive role in the victory of the imperial forces over the Hōjō family, decided to gain control of the government himself. The Ashikaga family had descended from Minamoto-no-Yoshiie and had held constabulary posts in two provinces, controlling a considerable amount of land in the Kantō region. When the Kamakura Bakufu fell, Takauji occupied Kamakura and became the leader of the Kantō warriors. Evidently Takauji was not completely trusted by the imperial faction and was not allowed to play any major role in the new government.

In 1335 Takauji led a military expedition to the Kantō region to crush a rebellion led by the remnants of the Hōjō clan. He then refused to return to Kyoto and remained in Kamakura. Thereupon the imperial government dispatched Nitta Yoshisada to subdue Takauji. Takauji, however, succeeded in defeating Yoshisada and moved on to Kyoto and occupied it temporarily. The imperial forces rallied to drive him out of the capital, however, and he was ultimately forced to flee westward. He then rebuilt his forces with the support of the Kyushu warriors and other military men who were discontented with the decline in their fortunes since the restoration of imperial rule. Takauji then marched back to the capital and defeated the imperial forces led by Kusunoki Masashige, who died in the course of the conflict.

Emperor Godaigo surrendered to Takauji and recognized the sovereignty of the new emperor whom Takauji chose from a collateral line of the imperial family and had enthroned. However, when his supporters rallied the pro-imperial forces together, Emperor Godaigo fled south to Yoshino in the Kii Peninsula and established a rival government there in 1336. Until 1392 there were two imperial courts, both claiming to be the legitimate dynasty. The imperial court in Yoshino was known as the southern court, and the one in Kyoto the northern court.

Takauji became shōgun in 1338, but he was preoccupied with the task of subduing his foes and therefore delegated his political functions to his younger brother, Tadayoshi. Even after Nitta Yoshisada, Godaigo's military chief, died in battle in 1338, the supporters of the southern court continued to resist the Ashikaga government. They were especially strong in the north and in Kyushu. In addition, the Ashikaga forces were weakened by armed conflict between Takauji and Tadayoshi. After the latter's death his adopted son continued the struggle against Takauji. Thus, in effect, the country was engaged in a triangular power struggle.

By the time of the third Ashikaga shōgun, Yoshimitsu (1358–1408), however, his clan had managed to extend its control over a large portion

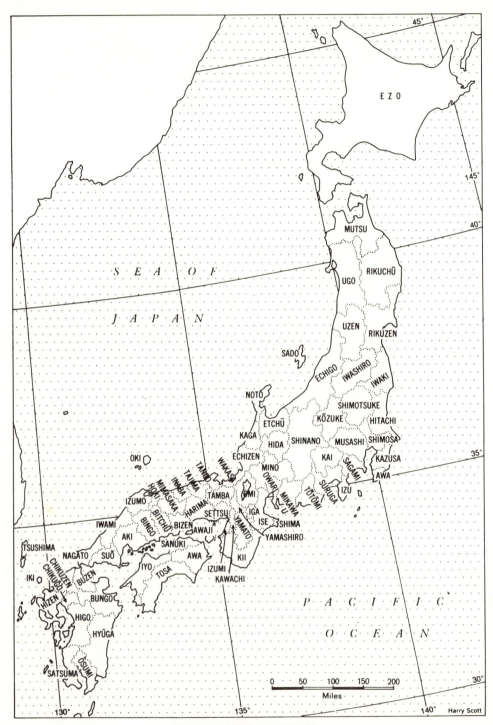

EZO

SEA OF

JAPAN

MUTSU

RIKUCHŪ

UGO

UZEN

RIKUZEN

SADO

ECHIGO

IWASHIRO

IWAKI

NOTO

SHIMOTSUKE

ETCHŪ

KŌZUKE

HITACHI

KAGA

HIDA

SHINANO

MUSASHI

SHIMOSA

OKI

ECHIZEN

MINO

KAI

KAZUSA

TANGO

WAKASA

AWA

TAJIMA

OMI

SAGAMI

INABA

OWARI

MIKAWA

IZU

TOTOMI

SURUGA

HOKI

MIMASAKA

IZUMO

TAMBA

OMI

SHIMA

IWAMI

HARIMA

IGA

AKI

BITCHŪ

BIZEN

SETTSU

ISE

YAMATO

YAMASHIRO

BINGO

AWAJI

TSUSHIMA

NAGATO

SUŌ

SANUKI

AWA

KII

IKI

CHIKUZEN

BUZEN

IYO

TOSA

IZUMI

CHIKUGO

KAWACHI

HIZEN

BUNGO

HIGO

HYŪGA

ŌSUMI

SATSUMA

PACIFIC

OCEAN

0   50   100   150   200
Miles

Harry Scott

THE PRE-MEIJI PROVINCES.

of the country. As a result, the southern court was persuaded in 1392 to return to Kyoto and to merge with the northern court, with the understanding that the imperial throne would be occupied alternately by the descendants of the two courts. This promise, however, was not kept by the northern court, and since that time only its descendants have occupied the throne.

ASHIKAGA RULE

Although Takauji did not make Kamakura his headquarters, he retained the governmental machinery of the Kamakura Bakufu when he established the shogunate in Kyoto.[1] He selected loyal vassals to serve as constables in provinces under his control. In 1367 the post of deputy to the shōgun was created, and the heads of three leading military families served alternately in this capacity. A governor-general was also appointed to oversee the administration of the Kantō region. The holder of this office resided in Kamakura and functioned as a semi-independent ruler of Kantō. Shōgun's agents were also appointed to oversee the northern provinces and Kyushu, but the Ashikaga government's control over these areas remained fairly precarious.

Because the Ashikaga rulers were challenged by rival forces throughout most of the fourteenth century, they were compelled to work closely with the leading military houses. Three major families (Shiba, Hosokawa, and Hatakeyama) alternately served as the shōgun's deputy. Yoshimitsu, the third Ashikaga shōgun, selected his department heads as well from leading military families. By gaining the cooperation of the major military houses, Yoshimitsu stabilized and strengthened his government. The foundations of the Ashikaga Bakufu were strengthened even further after rebellions by two major houses—the Yamana family, which held constabulary posts in eleven provinces, and the Ōuchi clan—were crushed in 1391 and 1399, respectively. It was under Yoshimitsu's shogunate that the southern court finally agreed to end its struggle and merge with the northern court. Thus the Ashikaga Bakufu reached its apex of power and prestige during Yoshimitsu's rule. In 1394 Yoshimitsu transferred the title of shōgun to his son and became dajō daijin (chancellor), the first samurai to hold that position since Taira-no-Kiyomori. He soon resigned this post as well and became a monk, but he remained the real wielder of power.

Yoshimitsu not only enjoyed supremacy of power but indulged himself by expending huge sums of money on lavish architectural projects. The most famous of his undertakings was the construction of the Golden Pavilion, whose interior and exterior were covered with gold leaf, a dazzling symbol of the power and glory of the shōgun.

The demesne of the Ashikaga Bakufu was far less than what had been retained by the Kamakura Bakufu and its hold over the constables, particularly those in the outlying regions, was weak. It could not adequately finance its expenditures with income and taxes from the land and was consequently forced to rely heavily upon taxes imposed on the merchants in Kyoto, particularly the sake brewers and the moneylenders.[2] Emergency taxes on houses and rice fields were also frequently imposed.

After Yoshimitsu's death in 1408 the authority of the Bakufu began to decline, and the Ashikaga government experienced increasing difficulty controlling the major constabulary houses. The power of the constables in general had been growing steadily during the period of conflict between the southern and northern courts.

THE DECLINE OF THE SHŌEN

At the beginning of the Ashikaga period, the land throughout the country was held by a variety of proprietors. There were, of course, the direct holdings of the Bakufu. Then there were the shōen (estates) held by the imperial household, the court nobles, major monasteries, and shrines. Important military houses, many holding constabulary posts, possessed shōen in their home provinces as well as in other provinces. Local military leaders, many of whom were land stewards, and local warriors who had ties of vassalage with the Bakufu or with a military chieftain also owned property. In addition there were independent farmers, the myōshu, who in some instances held a considerable amount of land and were influential leaders in their communities.

Because the central government was involved in a power struggle with rival elements during most of the fourteenth century, it was unable to extend its authority effectively to the outlying provinces. The power vacuum in those provinces was filled immediately by the leading military chieftains, particularly those in constabulary posts. These provincial constables steadily extended their control over the shōen held by absentee proprietors and even over the estates held by the local military men. Initially the Ashikaga rulers transferred the constables from province to province, but this practice was soon discontinued and they became entrenched in the provinces to which they were assigned. By the middle of the fifteenth century a majority of the constables had acquired hereditary possession of their posts. Some constabulary houses held jurisdiction over more than a single province.

In order to enable them to defray the cost of maintaining military forces, Takauji granted the constables the right to collect one half of the rents collected in the shōen. This was intended to be merely an emergency measure, but the practice persisted. Moreover, many constables began to claim half the land of the shōen rather than simply to collect one half the rent. In some instances they persuaded the shōen owners to grant them the authority to collect the rents on the owners' behalf as well, thus gaining de facto control over the shōen. The constables also had the authority to impose corvée on the people in the shōen and to extract various dues and gifts as well.

In addition to these economic encroachments, the constables extended their political influence over the manors by converting many shōen officials and myōshu into their own "housemen" or vassals. In the fifteenth century many constables began to expropriate the shōen outright. For instance, in the beginning of the fifteenth century one court family reported that it had been divested of fourteen of its twenty-three shōen by the constables and their vassals. One monastery complained that four of its shōen had been seized by the constable. By the outbreak of the Ōnin War in 1467, the shōen owners had virtually lost control of their manors.

The local military men, such as the land stewards and the samurai, sought to remain independent of the constabulary families by maintaining direct ties with the Ashikaga family by becoming its retainers. As the power of the provincial constabulary houses grew, however, many local military men found it necessary or more advantageous to become vassals of the constable. If the local military leader was powerful, the constable appointed him as a deputy constable and secured his support in return. By the fifteenth century a considerable number of constabulary magnates controlled much of the country.

THE ONSET OF THE TIME OF TROUBLES

After Yoshimitsu died, the Ashikaga shogunate's authority began to decline. The constabulary chieftains began increasingly to assert their independence from the Bakufu. In 1416 a rebellion against the governor-general in Kantō broke out. Although this uprising was subdued, other political disturbances led by Kantō military chieftains followed. In addition, uprisings of local samurai began to occur with increasing frequency. In 1441 the sixth Ashikaga shōgun was assassinated by one of the leading constables. A young child was installed as the successor, but the real power came to be exercised by four major constabulary houses. Rivalry among these major families, as well as frequent power struggles within them, undermined the stability of the central government, however. The feuding culminated in a conflict, the Ōnin War, that split the entire nation into two contending military factions, one led by the Yamana family and the other by the Hosokawa.

The struggle was touched off by disputes over succession—both to the shogunate and to the family leadership of several major constabulary houses. (The two issues were intertwined because the Ashikaga shōgun had a voice in the selection of successors to the major constabulary families, while the major constabulary houses participated in choosing the successor to the shogunate whenever there was no obvious heir to the post.) The trouble started when a son was born to the eighth shōgun, Yoshimasa, after he had already named his brother as his heir. Yoshimasa's wife, supported by the Yamana family, sought to have her newly born son designated as the successor. The shōgun's brother, however, advanced his claim to the shogunate with the support of the Hosokawa family.

The quarrel over the succession to the shogunate, however, was not the basic cause of the outbreak of the conflict. It was merely a by-product of the power struggle among the leading constabulary houses. In the course of the civil war the dispute over the shogunate was lost sight of, and the rival claimants even switched sides: Yoshimasa's brother turned to the Yamana faction for help, and the Hosokawa family transferred its support to the shōgun's son.

The civil war, known as the Ōnin War, raged from 1467 to 1477. It ushered in the time of troubles known as the Age of the Warring States (*sengoku jidai*), which lasted for about a century. Initially some 250,000 men joined in the fighting in and around Kyoto. As the conflict became protracted, the struggle spread to other areas, and the entire country was devastated and desolated. Places were plundered, and many valuable treasures were destroyed; the people were subjected to atrocities, and the residents of the capital were compelled to flee to the countryside. During the war the authority of the Bakufu deteriorated rapidly. Even though the leaders of the rival factions in the Ōnin War finally settled their differences in 1477, the truce had little bearing upon the general political situation. By then the authority of the Bakufu was virtually nonexistent, and the struggle for land and power continued unabated not only in Kyoto, where contending factions sought to control the shogunate by supporting rival claimants to the post, but throughout the countryside as well.

THE RISE OF THE DAIMYŌ
AND THE WARRING STATES

The Ōnin War changed the entire political complexion of the country. With the Ashikaga Bakufu wholly incapable of asserting its authority over the land, a period of decentralized rule came into existence. Many of the constabulary houses that had dominated outlying provinces lost control over their home bases as they expended their energy and attention on the Ōnin War, which was fought mainly around Kyoto. New local leaders began to emerge. Many constabulary families were overthrown by their subordinates, adventurers, or local military chieftains. These new regional military leaders began establishing independent principalities in different sections of the country, using force and guile to enlarge their territories at the expense of their former masters and neighbors. This was an era when control of regional territory changed very rapidly. Rank and position counted for nothing. Lowly warriors challenged the authority of the mighty warlords, and peasants defied shōen officials and proprietors. Consequently this period came to be known as the era of *ge-koku-jō*, those below subjugating those above. The only thing that counted was power. The people of this period recognized that the old order was being overturned and that a new era free from the fetters of tradition was coming into existence. Yamana Sōzen, the leader of one of the contending forces in the Ōnin War, admonished a court noble, "I disapprove of the constant references you make to 'precedents.' In the future you must replace the word 'precedent' with the word 'the times.' "[3]

The new military leaders who emerged during these changing times are known as *daimyō*. The constabulary chieftains are also referred to as daimyō or *shugo* (constabulary) *daimyō*, but they were not quite like the freewheeling warlords who emerged after the Ōnin War. The daimyō of the period of the Warring States were in effect fully independent regional rulers. Although their backgrounds were diverse, they can be roughly classified into three types.

One group consisted of the constabulary families that survived the political upheavals and emerged even more powerful than before. An example would be the Shimazu family of Satsuma, which remained a formidable regional power until the Meiji Restoration. Another was the Takeda family of Kai; under Shingen, who drove out his father to take power, the Takedas became a major force in central Japan. Of the 142 major daimyō in existence in 1563, however, only 32 families could claim to have been constabulary houses.

The second type of daimyō was the local military leader who prior to the Ōnin War had played a subordinate role as a deputy or vassal of a constabulary family. A notable example would be Asakura Toshikage, who replaced his master as constable of Echizen by taking advantage of the troubled times of the Ōnin War. His effectiveness in wielding power was recognized by the Hosokawa faction, which persuaded him to defect from the Yamana forces by offering him the constableship of Echizen. He was heartily detested by the court nobles for his ruthless expropriation of their shōen. Takeda Shingen's rival, Uesugi Kenshin, also came from a family that had served as deputy constable. Kenshin's father killed the constable to gain control of Echigo. Other examples of daimyō who rose to power from subordinate posts are the Mōri clan of western Honshu, the Oda family of Owari, and the Tokugawa family.

The third category of daimyō consisted of men who had been lowly samurai, frequently warrior-farmers, but had managed to rise rapidly to the top by taking advantage of the civil disorder and breakdown of authority. A striking example of this type of daimyō is Hōjō Sōun (1432–1519).[4]

Sōun was an unemployed warrior, but his younger sister was the concubine of Imagawa Yoshitada, a powerful constable in the region around present-day Shizuoka, so Sōun stayed with the Imagawa family as a guest. While he was there the samurai in the service of the Imagawa family rebelled and assassinated Yoshitada. With the Imagawa family confronted with an insurrection, other local chieftains, hoping to fish in troubled waters, intervened. At this point Sōun stepped in and succeeded in negotiating a settlement, placing the son of his sister and Yoshitada at the head of the Imagawa family. As a reward he was given a fief and was made the chief of a castle. With this as his base, Sōun used cunning and treachery to extend his power and territory. He made a surprise attack on the province of Izu while its leaders were engaged in a power struggle. After conquering the province of Izu, Sōun intervened in a family quarrel of the Uesugi family, a major power in the Kantō region, and gained control of the provinces of Musashi and Sagami. In order to extend his control over the entire Kantō region, he made another surprise attack on the fortress at Odawara, a strategic stronghold whose occupant controlled the main road that led into the Kantō region. Then by concluding alliances and by engaging in intrigues and acts of treachery, he managed to enlarge his base of power sufficiently so that his descendants were able to control the entire Kantō region. Some historians view Sōun's campaign to conquer the Kantō region as the beginning of the Age of the Warring States. The new Hōjō empire remained intact until 1590, when Toyotomi Hideyoshi sent 200,000 men to capture the stronghold at Odawara.

Despite his ruthlessness in his drive for power, Sōun was a benevolent ruler and concerned himself with the betterment of the lot of the common people. In fact his successful rise to power was based partly upon his policy of benevolent rule, which won him the support of the common people, the peasants, and the artisans. He told his retainers, "For the lord of the domain the people are his children. For the people, the lord of the domain is their father."[5] Whenever his warriors conquered new territory, he forbade them to touch a single item belonging to the people. He provided aid when necessary and reduced taxes from 50 percent of the crop to 40 percent.

Sōun's spectacular rise to power was not unique. The same story was repeated throughout the land. Lowly but ambitious and shrewd warriors connived and clawed their way to the top, replacing the established constabulary houses, perhaps to be overthrown by others even more resourceful and ruthlessly ambitious. The rapid turnover in regional political leadership is reflected in the fact that of the 142 major daimyō in existence in 1563, only 45 were still around thirty years later, when Toyotomi Hideyoshi established his hegemony over the entire country. In the era of the Warring States, then, the concept of loyalty that was supposed to govern the conduct of the samurai was hardly discernible. Self-interest and tough-minded realism seemed rather to guide the conduct of the ambitious warriors.

Unlike the constabulary lords, who had been responsible to the shōgun, the new military chieftains were responsible to no one. They were in effect independent warlords who had complete control over the land and the people on it. Their power depended upon the number of loyal vassals they retained. There were several categories of vassals: those who were blood relations of the daimyō, those whose family had served in the house for several generations or had become vassals early in the political ascendancy of the daimyō, and those who had been subjugated by force but still retained a degree of independence. The last category of vassals were regarded as potential foes and were treated as outsiders (tozama), in contrast to the others, who were regarded as hereditary (fudai) vassals. In addition to those vassals who were given fiefs to manage as their own, the daimyō maintained immediate retainers to serve as his attendants, personal guards, and managers of his demesne.

During the Kamakura and Ashikaga periods the vassal's authority over his "fief" had accrued from the post to which he was appointed, such as the office of land steward or shōen manager. With the office went certain rights and privileges (shiki, see p. 57), including the right to an income from the land, but the lord retained the right to collect rent from the peasants. The office rather than the land was central to the benefice. During the era of daimyō rule, on the other hand, the vassal was given full control over the land granted to him as his fief.

In order to prevent the fiefs from being subdivided into small, submarginal plots, the principle of primogeniture came to be enforced. This weakened the position of women, depriving them of the right of inheritance that they had heretofore traditionally held. In an age in which only naked power counted, women could no longer retain the rights they formerly possessed. They became mere pawns for military alliances and were forced to marry whoever their fathers or brothers believed would serve useful political ends.

In return for their fiefs the vassals not only owed personal military service to their lord but also had to provide him with a fixed number of men on horseback and foot soldiers. The number depended on the size of the fief the vassal was given. In the middle of the sixteenth century Uesugi Kenshin had 5,514 men at his disposal. They included 566 knights on horseback, 321 musketeers, and 3,609 peasants armed with pikes.

Muskets were introduced to Japan by the Portuguese in 1543. Japanese smiths quickly learned how to make them, and within a decade they were widely used by the contending daimyō.[6] As the size of the warring armies grew and the use of firearms became more widespread, an increasingly larger number of peasants were mobilized to fight for the warlords. In Uesugi Kenshin's army the ratio of peasants to samurai was three to one.

The daimyō usually maintained one castle that served as his home base and several auxiliary castles or fortresses in strategic spots. The auxiliary castles were guarded by his trusted vassals. The site of the main castle usually became a fairly lively and populous town, since merchants and artisans as well as the daimyō's retainers congregated there. Each daimyō encouraged merchants and skilled artisans to settle in his town to assist in the production and distribution of weapons, food, and other necessities. In order to strengthen the economic foundations of their domains, many daimyō initiated public works projects, particularly in water control and irrigation.

For the purpose of governing their territories and guiding their retainers most daimyō issued "house laws." These laws were in effect moral injunctions and rules of conduct. The house laws of Sōun contained such articles as:

1. Rise early in the morning. If you rise late, the servants too will become lethargic and cease to be industrious, and private and public tasks will be neglected.
2. Do not seek to acquire swords and apparel as splendid as those owned by others. As long as they are not shoddy, do not fall into debt to obtain better ones.
3. Keep a book with you constantly and use every spare moment to read it when unseen by others.[7]

The daimyō kept a close check on his vassals, trusting very few men. He employed spies to make certain that his followers, particularly the latecomers to his camp, were not plotting against him. He also had a voice in determining his vassal's place of residence, choice of wife, and succession to the family headship.

To determine taxes and to maintain close surveillance over his domain, the lord took censuses and checked land titles, acreage, and yield. He exercised judicial control over all the people on his land, usually punishing both parties in a dispute. When a person committed a serious crime, the entire household—including servants and retainers—or community was also held responsible. Punishments were extremely cruel and inhuman. Impaling, crucifying, tearing apart, boiling, burning, and sawing the offender to death were common means of execution. The peasants had little protection against the samurai, who were permitted to cut them down with impunity.

THE PEASANTRY

During the period of civil strife following the establishment of the Ashikaga Bakufu, control over the peasants slackened, and they were able to assert themselves, acquiring more freedom by taking advantage of the rival claims of the constables and the proprietors of the shōen. The element among the peasantry that provided the leadership in their ascendancy were the independent farmers, the myōshu. Those peasants who were not myōshu either owned a small plot of land or worked for the myōshu or the proprietors of the manor. There were also warrior-farmers who stood socially between the myōshu and ordinary peasantry. They, unlike the peasants, were entitled to use surnames.

During the Ashikaga period the villagers were able to exercise a certain degree of autonomy in managing the irrigation system, utilizing the woodlands and meadows, and maintaining peace and order within the community. When the local authorities failed to offer them protection from plunderers they banded together to form their own defense forces. The residents of a shōen belonging to the Tōdaiji in Nara, in requesting that rental payments be suspended, complained about the difficulties inflicted upon them by the contending forces of the northern and southern courts as follows:

The forces of the two factions came to the shōen day and night and expropriated our cattle, horses, resources, rice, soybean, etc. Realizing that we would starve to death unless some action were taken we, the shōen residents, met and decided to band together to defend the shōen with our own lives. As a result we were able to put an end to the pillaging. But our burden has remained heavy. After the constable and governor arrived we expected to enjoy peace and tranquillity but they continuously make demands upon us, first asking for recruits for their armies, and then demanding food, horses and equipments. If we refuse they threaten to arrest us as supporters of their enemies and to burn our houses down.[8]

Taxes under the Ashikaga Bakufu grew steadily more burdensome, until about 70 percent of the peasants' produce was being collected by tax and rent collectors. Under normal circumstances the lot of the peasants was a difficult one, but in times of famine they were reduced to starvation. Daughters were sold to brothels, and sons were sold to priests who indulged in pederasty. Many peasants left the villages to become beggars and vagrants. A particularly serious famine occurred in the middle of the fifteenth century. Between 1459 and 1461 the country was plagued by a series of meteorological catastrophes, including droughts, floods, and typhoons. In addition, a plague of locusts destroyed the rice crop. These successive calamities resulted in serious food shortages, and a great number of people began to starve. The consequences were disastrous for large cities like Kyoto. In two months during the winter of 1460–1461 it was estimated that 82,000 persons starved to death in the capital. Yet there is no evidence that the Bakufu under Yoshimasa—the eighth Ashikaga shōgun, who was interested primarily in the construction of attractive villas and gardens and in amusing himself with Nō plays and flower-viewing—took any measures to alleviate the suffering of the people except to have prayers intoned on behalf of the dead.

With the growing burden of taxation, mounting debts, periodic crop failures, and the ruling class's general indifference to the well-being of the peasantry, it is not surprising that the peasants began to riot in protest. In the fifteenth century peasant uprisings began to occur with increasing frequency. In 1428, when the entire nation suffered from crop failure and famine and mass starvation occurred, a major uprising broke out in the Kyoto region. The peasants in the province of Ōmi staged an insurrection demanding tokusei (acts of grace), that is, the cancellation of all debts. They were soon joined by peasants from adjoining regions as well as by the townspeople of Kyoto. They attacked temples and monasteries, sake merchants, pawnbrokers, moneylenders—destroying, looting, and tearing up certificates of loan. Similar uprisings followed in other areas, especially in the central and western provinces. Such disturbances continued to break out until the following year. They were directed not only against the Bakufu and shōen owners but against a new force in the countryside, the urban moneylenders who had become more active in the rural areas as commerce and a money economy grew in importance. The peasants in the Kantō region were kept under firmer control by the local authorities and were unable to register their complaints effectively, but isolated instances of peasant uprisings did occur there also.

In 1441, while the Bakufu was in a state of uncertainty following the assassination of the sixth shōgun, the peasants in the provinces around Kyoto staged an uprising, again demanding the cancellation of all debts. During the thirty-year rule of the eighth shōgun, Yoshimasa, eighteen peasant uprisings occurred. Yoshimasa issued thirteen decrees cancelling debts. That he issued these decrees so readily may have been related in part to the fact that the debtors were required to pay 10 percent of their debts to the Bakufu in return for having the other 90 percent cancelled.

The peasant uprisings contributed to the emergence of the local samurai as an important political force. The leaders of these uprisings were frequently shōen officials, lower-class samurai, or myōshu, who utilized peasant discontent to weaken the authority of the constabulary families and further their own political fortunes, a trend that was particularly strong following the Ōnin War. This meant that in the long run the interests of the samurai rather than those of the peasants were advanced. Eventually the lower-level samurai became retainers of some rising military chieftain and then, as members of the new ruling class, helped to keep the peasants under control. As the daimyō came to dominate the country they suppressed the autonomous tendencies that had been developing among the peasantry. They held the peasants collectively responsible for rents, taxes, and crimes. Generally speaking the samurai were more ruthless than the constables in collecting rents and taxes and in exacting corvée and military service from the peasantry.

Although the peasants' lot worsened as the daimyō became powerful, until a strong central authority was reestablished in the late sixteenth century there was always an opportunity for a peasant to take advantage of the unsettled conditions to climb up the social hierarchy. As we noted, they were brought into the daimyō's armies as foot soldiers in increasing numbers in the Age of the Warring States. If they served with distinction they were able to join the ranks of the samurai because no rigid caste system existed in this period. The most dramatic example of an individual's rise up the social and political ladder is the life of Toyotomi Hideyoshi, who rose from the peasantry to become the dictator of the entire country. Only rarely were groups of peasants able to acquire political power, however. The most notable exception was the peasants of Yamashiro Province, near Kyoto, who gained control of the province in 1485 and held it for eight years.

ECONOMIC GROWTH

During the Ashikaga period a significant change in the economic life of the country took place. Agricultural production increased, and commerce and industry began to expand. The reason for this change cannot be ascribed to any dramatic shift or innovation. Agricultural production had increased through the years as a result of gradual changes in the methods of farming. Increased production in agriculture stimulated commerce and then industry. There were also technical improvements in the industrial sphere—in salt making, mining, textile production, metalwork, pottery, sake brewing, and paper making. Furthermore, economic growth was stimulated by the peace and order that prevailed after the country was unified under the Kamakura Bakufu. Even when the central government was weakened during the latter part of Ashikaga rule, the damages done by military conflicts were evidently minor. Indeed, there is some reason to believe that the constant movement of warriors and the emergence of many population centers in the form of castle towns tended to quicken the pace of economic activities. At the same time, the renewal and intensification of contact with China, Korea, and the Ryukyus greatly stimulated economic growth.

In the densely populated area around Kyoto, Osaka, and Nara, known as the Kinki region, agricultural production was conducted on a small scale, but arable land was utilized intensively by terracing the hillsides. With the rise of the military families, new land was opened for farming in the Kantō and Kyushu regions. At the same time better tools and improved methods of farming came to be employed. Metal plows and hoes, which were not readily available for use by the common peasants before the Kamakura era, were now used by them. Draft animals also came to be utilized by a larger number of peasants. Better methods of irrigation through the extensive use of waterwheels were introduced. In the production of rice, the introduction of a new strain better suited to the climate and the use of the seedbed resulted in greater yields. In addition, two crops, rice and another grain or a vegetable, came to be grown in many areas during the latter part of the Kamakura period. With the increased use of draft animals, manure was used as fertilizer; human waste was also used for this purpose. The practice of burning trees and grass to enrich the soil had been followed since the end of the Heian period. In addition to rice and other grains, the production of fruits and vegetables for the newly established towns as well as the production of tea and silk increased during this period.

This increase in agricultural production inevitably stimulated commerce. Toward the end of the Kamakura era market towns came into existence. As early as the Nara period markets had been set up periodically under the auspices of local authorities, monasteries, and shrines. By the end of the Kamakura period they came to have fixed locations, although they were still open only several times a month. Not until the middle of the fifteenth century were they held as often as six times a month. Out of the markets grew new towns near, not surprisingly, monasteries, shrines, and seats of local political power and at crossroads and forks of rivers.

To sell one's product at such markets a merchant had to pay a fee to the local lord, monastery, or shrine that offered him protection. Initially the people who operated these markets were local peasants who came to sell their farm produce and handicrafts. Eventually, however, regular merchants came to dominate the marketplaces. As these markets grew in importance, merchant and craft guilds, designed to acquire and preserve monopolistic rights for the members, came into existence.

These guilds, or *za*, originated in the early twelfth century as associations designed to serve the needs of the court and the monasteries. With the rise in commerce the number of guilds increased, and during the Ashikaga period they existed throughout the country. Some guilds managed to acquire monopolistic rights that extended over the entire country. Most guilds, however, usually held a commercial monopoly in a single town or other limited area, with each guild specializing in a single commodity. The Kinki region had the greatest number of strong guilds.

There were guilds for practically every commodity in use at that time. For example, there were za for vegetable oil, rice, sake, salt, paper, straw mats, sliding doors, sedge hats, braziers, metal goods, candy, rice-cakes, noodles, fish, textiles, lumber, charcoal, and medicine. The za varied in size from as few as two members to more than fifty members; the average size, however, was about ten.

Although the primary object of the guilds was to establish and maintain a commercial monopoly, they also sought to acquire for their members such privileges as exemption from taxation and protection from outside competitors and lawless elements. In return a guild paid the protecting authority, either the local lord or monastery, a fixed fee. There were also artisans' and workers' guilds for blacksmiths, silversmiths, swordsmiths, carpenters, dyers, carriers, etc.

Another consequence of the rise in commerce was the emergence of a money economy. Although money existed during the Nara and early Heian periods, it was not widely used, and coins were not minted after the early part of the tenth century. In the eleventh century rice and silk were used as the chief media of exchange. In the twelfth century coins reappeared as a result of the revival of trade with China. By the fourteenth century Chinese copper coins were in wide use. The rise of a money economy made the control of copper, silver, and gold mines important, and they became the object of contention among the warring daimyō. In addition to coins, bills of exchange came to be employed by merchants engaged in long-distance commerce. They were also used to pay taxes. The earliest record of the use of bills of exchange comes from 1279.

The increased use and need of money resulted in the rise of moneylenders. Wealthy landowners, pawnbrokers, merchants—particularly sake merchants—and even monasteries and shrines engaged in moneylending. The borrowers, usually peasants, were charged high interest rates, starting at about 50 percent. The peasants, however, were not the only customers; the proprietors of the shōen also relied on the moneylenders. The Bakufu, too, borrowed money from the sake merchants and pawnbrokers. Many moneylenders later became government officials in charge of financial affairs and rose in the social hierarchy.

The expansion of commercial activities resulted as well in the emergence of wholesale merchants and in a growth of port cities. The ports around the Kinki region and the Inland Sea were the first to be built up, but cities were soon established on harbors in other parts of the country too. The city of Sakai near Osaka emerged as a flourishing port with considerable political power.

As an increasingly large volume of goods came to be transported on both land and sea, a large number of checkpoints and toll stations were established by local authorities to collect duty on goods in transit. It has been estimated that in 1462 there were 380 such toll stations between Kyoto and the mouth of the Yodo River in Osaka. Not only did the traveling merchants have to contend with these barriers to commerce, but they were frequently attacked by bandits and pirates.

A by-product of the increase in trade was the revival of the system of horse stations for official transportation and communication. This "pony express" system had been introduced as one of the Taika Reforms but was allowed to deteriorate. It was revived in many areas in the Kamakura period by the rising daimyō.

The merchants grew not only in number but also in importance in the market towns, ports, castle towns, and the towns that grew around monasteries and shrines. The dominant members among them were the wholesale merchants and the moneylenders. In some towns they collected taxes for the local lords and policed their communities. Sakai was an autonomous city run by thirty-six elders, primarily wealthy wholesale merchants. It had its own defense force and usually managed to defy the warlords in its vicinity. In 1568 it even refused to pay the levy demanded of it by Oda Nobunaga, although it was forced to submit the following year. Among other cities that retained a similar autonomy were Hakata in Kyushu and Ōminato and Uji Yamada, both in Ise. All this added up to a possibility that the towns of Japan would emerge as a significant political force, following the pattern of the medieval towns of Europe, but with the establishment in Japan of a strong central government in the late sixteenth century, the nascent urban forces were brought under control. In many instances the merchants cooperated with the daimyō who were working for the unification of the country, motivated no doubt by the desire to have peace and stability restored so that commerce could flourish.

A significant aspect of the expansion of commerce was the revival of trade with China. Following the decline of the T'ang dynasty the close relationship between China and Japan that had been maintained during the Nara and Heian periods abated, but with the unification of China under the Sung dynasty contact was reestablished. When the Sung court moved to the south (1127), Chinese commerce increased. Soon, however, as the Sung government became concerned with the excessive outflow of gold, silver, and copper, it began to restrict overseas trade. In 1245 it asked the Japanese authorities to limit the number of Japanese merchantmen sailing to China. Later, after the Mongol dynasty was established in China (1271), commercial contact between the two countries was again formally revived. Although the first official commercial exchange took place in 1325, informal trade had started earlier.

Around the fourteenth century Japanese pirates known as *wakō*, operating out of the islands of Iki and Tsushima off Kyushu, began to intensify their activities against the coastal cities of Korea. They also began to raid the coastal towns and villages of China. When the Ming government came into power in 1368 it sent an envoy asking the Japanese government to curb the pirates, but because the demand was presented in such a manner as to indicate that China considered Japan her subject state, it was rejected. The third Ashikaga shōgun, Yoshimitsu, was interested in expanding commercial relations with China, however, so he curtailed the wakō's activities to some extent. Nevertheless the pirates continued to make their attacks against Korea and China during the fourteenth and fifteenth centuries, frequently with the support of local lords in western Japan. The object of these raids was to steal food, such as rice and beans, and to kidnap villagers who could then be sold as slaves.

Legitimate trade between Ming China and Japan began to flourish under Yoshimitsu, who sought to ease the financial difficulties of his regime by such commerce. In 1404 a formal commercial treaty was concluded between the two governments, and the Bakufu periodically sent merchantmen to China. Formal commercial relations were ended under Yoshimitsu's successor but were revived by the fifth shōgun. In order to curb unauthorized trade with neighboring countries, the Ming government adopted a system of certification for those ships authorized to conduct commerce with China.

Trade with Korea was also reestablished around the same period and was conducted on an even larger scale than the commerce with China.

Commercial relations with China and Korea enriched the daimyō and merchants of western Japan. The city of Hakata in Kyushu was the center of commerce with Korea, while official trade with China was carried on through the port of Hyōgo. After the Ōnin War, the Ōuchi and Hosokawa families tended to dominate the trade with China. Commerce was also conducted with the Ryukyu Islands, and Ryukyu merchants frequently served as middlemen between Japan, Southeast Asia, and China.

Japan exported to China such things as swords, armor, copper, sulphur, lumber, fans, lacquerware, and pearls and, in return, imported raw silk, cotton thread, fine fabrics, dye, ironware, porcelain, paintings, books, medicine, and copper coins. From Korea Japan imported cotton goods, in exchange for copper, sulphur, and swords. Prior to this period Japanese garments had been made largely of silk and hemp. With the increased production of cotton in Korea in the fifteenth century, the Japanese began increasingly to utilize cotton fabrics for clothing. In the sixteenth century Japan began growing her own cotton.

The contacts between China and Japan during the Kamakura and Ashikaga periods not only had economic significance but also resulted in the re-exertion of Chinese influence in the cultural realm. A large number of Japanese monks visited China, Chinese books were imported to Japan, and the advanced Chinese printing technique was introduced. Chinese painting, calligraphy, and ceramics influenced Japanese art, and Chu Hsi philosophy (see page 159) came to be known to Japanese scholars. The latest Chinese medical knowledge and drugs, as well as new food and culinary practices, entered the country.

During the Ashikaga period, commercial intercourse with Southeast Asia was established for the first time. Emissaries from Southeast Asian countries appeared in Japan occasionally during the fourteenth and fifteenth centuries, but trade was conducted largely through Ryukyu middlemen.

THE INFLUENCE OF ZEN BUDDHISM
UPON CULTURE

The influence of Zen on art reached its apex in the Ashikaga period. It molded the aesthetic taste of the Japanese and established standards of excellence for later generations to emulate. It fostered an appreciation of the simple and the austere, and a preference for imbalance and asymmetry.

The upsurge of creativity in the arts was given a significant boost by the eighth shōgun, Yoshimasa, who concerned himself more with cultural activities than with the art of government. Even during the Ōnin War he paid more attention to culture than to the power struggle that was fragmenting his land. He constructed the Silver Pavilion in Higashiyama in the northeastern section of Kyoto, creating a cultural style referred to as Higashiyama Culture. He not only initiated the construction of a complex of buildings in his villa but also personally patronized the masters of landscape gardening, Nō, flower arrangement, the tea ceremony, and painting. Yoshimasa's taste in all these areas reflected the growing influence of Zen.

Even before Zen came to Japan, the Japanese had developed a refined sense of beauty and appreciation of nature. The stark, simple, and unadorned designs of the early Shinto shrines attest to a love of simple, uncluttered beauty. A Japanese writer remarks "I find it difficult to accept . . . [the] view that the aesthetic sensibility of the samurai civilization should be attributed entirely to Zen, since I believe this civilization had its roots still deeper, in the traditional Japanese sensibility as expressed in the classical civilization."[9] Zen, however, extended the aesthetic sensitivity of the Japanese into many new areas of life and art. It is manifested in such militaristic pastimes as swordsmanship and archery as well as in the artistic activities of the poet, the calligrapher, and the painter. It also molded the arts of gardening, flower arrangement, and the tea ceremony.

Regarding the relationship between the last-mentioned art and Zen, Suzuki Daisetsu observes, "What is common to Zen and the art of tea is the constant attempt both make at simplification. The elimination of the unnecessary is achieved by Zen in its intuitive grasp of final reality; by the art of tea, in the way of living typified by serving tea in the tearoom."[10] Tea was imported to Japan from China before the Kamakura period, but Eisai is credited with making it a popular beverage. The ritual of the tea ceremony was also introduced from China by Zen monks in the late thirteenth century, and the art was adapted to Japanese tastes. Formally the ceremony is conducted in a small, simple room in a thatched hut in the quietude of nature. Its object is to foster the spirit of harmony, reverence, purity, and tranquillity.

The aesthetic tastes fostered in the tea ceremony are *wabi* and *sabi*. Sabi is an objective quality manifested in things and the environment. It is associated with "age, desiccation, numbness, chilliness, obscurity—all of which are negative feelings opposed to warmth, the spring, expansiveness, transparency, etc."[11] It is a quality of mellowness and depth that is acquired through use and aging. Wabi is a subjective feeling fostered by simple, almost rustic, and serene surroundings. It embodies the sense of solitude and melancholy but also of tranquillity that one experiences as one's Buddha-nature comes to the surface in the simplicity and serenity of the teahouse and tea ceremony. An aesthetic taste related to these qualities is the preference for what is called *shibui*, that is, that which is austere, sober, and subdued. It is a quality that is in keeping with the Japanese taste for restraint and understatement.

The tea ceremony, then, is not merely a pleasant pastime. In its pristine form it has had profound aesthetic and spiritual significance, and the spirit fostered by it has deeply influenced Japanese art and life. In Suzuki's opinion such aesthetic and spiritual experiences take the place of spiritual constructs.

If Japan did not produce any philosophical system of her own, she was original enough to embody in her practical life all that could profitably be extracted from Confucianism, Taoism, and Buddhism and turn them into the material for her spiritual enhancement and artistic appreciation. . . .

The Japanese are great in changing philosophy into art, abstract reasoning into life, transcendentalism into empirical immanentism.[12]

The art of the tea ceremony also contributed to the development of ceramics, since the appreciation of the tea bowls used in the ceremony was an essential part of the art of tea. In the latter part of the Ashikaga era the influence of Korean pottery, which is characterized by crude simplicity in contrast to the highly finished style of Chinese pottery, came to be reflected in Japanese ceramics. The most significant developments in Japanese pottery, however, occurred in the latter half of the sixteenth century.

The tea ceremony also fostered the art of flower arrangement since the alcove in the tea room was decorated by a tray of flowers and twigs. Here, as in other areas of Japanese art, placement is crucial. A flower arrangement is, in effect, a three-dimensional design, with forms and colors arranged in an aesthetically satisfying manner.

The influence of Zen during this period can also be seen in the art of gardening. Gardens were laid out artistically earlier too, but during the Ashikaga period, under the influence of Zen, a new style developed. The master in this field was Musō Soseki (1275–1351), a Zen monk. Musō was not interested in imitating nature but sought rather to reduce things to the bare essentials. His work became highly symbolic. One of the most famous of his creations is the Moss Garden at Saihōji in Kyoto, a symbolic representation of the ideal "land of Zen." This style of landscape gardening culminated in the rock garden of Ryōanji, another temple in Kyoto. The rock garden was created at the end of the fifteenth century either by Sōami (?–1525), who was a master in all fields of artistic endeavor, or by his disciples. It consists of nothing but white sand and fifteen natural stones arranged in five groups surrounded by a meager growth of moss. The sand symbolizes the sea and the rocks signify islands. Here natural forms are presented in their simplest terms, not unlike an abstract painting.

In the residential buildings of this era, a style known as *shoin-zukuri* came into existence. The simplicity and austerity manifested in Zen teahouses were incorporated into the domestic architecture. The materials used were plain and simple. In the interiors straight lines created neat geometric patterns in the corridors, ceilings, floor mats, and sliding doors. The *shoin* was a room where Zen monks lived and studied, and its features were incorporated in private dwellings; for example, the recessed altar of the Zen monk's room became the alcove where artworks were displayed. These features have been retained to the present in Japanese houses.

Shōgun Yoshimitsu's Golden Pavilion, a three storied structure, was built in the shoin style. The building and its setting of trees, rocks, and a lake were carefully arranged to constitute a harmonious whole. Yoshimasa's Silver Pavilion was modeled after the Golden Pavilion but has only two stories. It, too, is surrounded by a beautiful garden, believed to have been designed by Sōami. Nearby is a building which contains a small tearoom that became the model for tearooms constructed subsequently.

Some authorities consider the influence of Zen to have been reflected most significantly in painting. About the middle of the thirteenth century

The rock garden of Ryōanji, a Buddhist temple in Kyoto. Sōami (?–1525) is thought to have designed the garden. Courtesy of the Consulate General of Japan, New York.

the paintings of a Chinese Zen monk, Mu-ch'i, were brought to Japan, where they made a lasting impact upon Japanese *sumie* (ink drawing). Zen injected into painting and calligraphy an air of virility. Bold, forceful strokes characterize the works of the master sumie painters and calligraphers of this period. In sumie painting once the brush touches the paper the brushstroke cannot be changed, so the mental control of a person disciplined in Zen becomes essential. The artist moves his brush delicately at first, then boldly across white paper, finally letting the imprint of the brush either fade out or end abruptly. The sumie painters of this period were not interested in a realistic imitation of nature but depicted the essence of things as they saw it. All unessential details are therefore left out of their paintings. The rhythm and movement of the brushwork, as well as its texture and overall design, are important in endowing these paintings with dynamism and vigor.

Josetsu (fl. 1400) is thought to have been the founder of the sumie school of painting in Japan, but only one of his works is extant. It depicts a man trying to catch a catfish with a gourd, a typical Zen proposition. It is generally agreed that the greatest artist to emerge out of this tradition was Sesshū (1420–1506). An authority on Japanese art commenting on the power of Sesshū's brush writes: "His strokes are sudden, strong, vehement, he seems careless of modulating them; and yet how magically all falls into place. It is this extraordinary mastery of forcible brush-stroke which gives Sesshū his supremacy with the Japanese: this, and the intensity and directness which he combines with unsurpassed greatness of spirit."[13] Ernest F. Fenollosa, a pioneer among Western students of Japanese art, asserts that Sesshū is the greatest master of the straight line and the angle in the history of world art. Sesshū used two styles: one utilizing sharp, angular, and relatively complex brushwork, and a soft, diffused, rather explosive yet highly simplified style. Although he was primarily a landscape painter, his paintings of the founder of Zen Buddhism, Bodhidharma, are known for their vigor and dramatic force. In the next era, another sumie artist, Miyamoto Musashi (1584–1645), who was also one of the greatest swordsmen of Japan, combined Zen aesthetics with the spirit of the samurai.

The influence of Zen can also be seen in the calligraphy of this period. In contrast to the gentle, cursive style that was popular during the Heian period, Ashikaga calligraphy was vigorous and masculine. As in sumie painting, the overall composition, the relationship between the brushmarks and the blank areas, and the movement and rhythm of the brushstrokes are important. But, in addition, the proper balancing of the component parts of each character, the relationship of adjacent characters, and the variations in the size and density of the brushstrokes are of equal importance.

It was also during this era that the Nō drama reached new heights of artistic refinement. The Nō play grew out of the popular folk dances and plays that were performed at Shinto festivals to pray to the gods for abundant harvest and to give thanks after the harvest. They also served as entertainment for the common people. These dances were refined through the ages and in the Ashikaga period emerged as a serious dramatic form. Nō was patronized increasingly by the upper classes and eventually came to be regarded as an aesthetic experience appreciated primarily by the culturally elite.

The Zen preference for simplicity and restraint is seen in the external aspects of the Nō plays. The stage, open on three sides, is simple and plain, having neither a curtain nor background scenery except for an old pine tree painted on the rear wall. The few stage properties that are used are symbolic and abstract. The movements and gestures of the all-male cast are highly stylized, formal, and carefully measured. Usually the principal actor wears a mask, but even without a mask the actor's face is frozen as if he were masked. Mime constitutes an important part of Nō dramas; feelings are expressed by symbolic gestures and movements. Weeping, for example, is signified by raising the hand to the eyes. The fan is manipulated to symbolize a variety of things, such as falling leaves, rippling waves, and an ascending moon. The Nō performance is accompanied by a chorus that chants the story in a sing-song. The actors are dressed in brilliant costumes, luxuriously embroidered and brocaded.

The art of Nō was perfected by two men: Kan'ami Kiyotsugu (1333–1384) and his son, Seami Motokiyo (1363–1443), who enjoyed the patronage of the third shōgun, Yoshimitsu. Seami's works are regarded as masterpieces and are still performed today. He was profoundly influenced by Zen and sought to convey in his works the sense of *yūgen*, or mystery, "what lies beneath the surface; the subtle as opposed to the statement."

OTHER CULTURAL DEVELOPMENTS

In the Ashikaga period learning began to spread downward into the society rather than being restricted to the elite, the court aristocrats and the priests. The warriors began to show an interest in education, and the local lords began to encourage learning among their followers. We have already caught a glimpse of this in the "house laws" of Hōjō Sōun. The process of cultural diffusion was facilitated during and after the Ōnin War when a large number of aristocrats and monks fled the turbulent capital, finding employment with the daimyō as educators and lecturers.

One manifestation of this growing interest in learning is the Kanazawa Library that was established in Kanazawa (near present-day Yokohama) in the middle of the Kamakura period. Even though it was allowed to deteriorate after the fall of the Kamakura Bakufu, twenty thousand volumes were recovered from this library. The Ashikaga Academy was also founded during the same period by the Ashikaga family in the Kantō region. Students from all over the country attended the academy. Although it was operated by Buddhist priests, Confucianism came to form the core of the curriculum, and students educated here returned to their home provinces to engage in educational work.

Another significant institution that emerged during this period was the temple school (*terakoya*). It became the practice of the samurai and wealthier peasants to send their children to Buddhist temples to learn how to read and write. Although this practice did not become widespread until the

Tokugawa period, the origin of the temple schools can be traced back to the Ashikaga era.

The art of woodblock printing, which had entered Japan from China during the Kamakura period, flourished in the Ashikaga years as many Chinese printers sought asylum in Japan during the period of turmoil at the end of the Mongol and the beginning of the Ming rule. The Zen temples of Kyoto and Kamakura (known as the Temples of the Five Mountains) sponsored the printing of Buddhist texts.

Several significant works of history were produced during this era. One such history was written by a loyal supporter of the southern court, Kitabatake Chikafusa (1293–1354). This is the *Jinnō Shōtōki* (*The Records of the Legitimate Succession of the Divine Sovereigns*), written in 1339. It records the history of Japan from its founding by the gods to the reign of Emperor Godaigo. Kitabatake emphasized that Japan was a unique land of the gods and that descendants of the Sun Goddess were destined to reign to eternity. Every subject of the emperor, he insisted, must serve him with utmost loyalty.

The *Jinnō Shōtōki* is significant as an important Shinto document. Shinto was keeping its flame alive even during this era when Buddhism was winning widespread support. The tradition of seeking to reconcile Buddhism and Shinto, which had emerged during the Heian period as Dual Shinto, prevailed during this age, too, but there was also a move to subordinate Buddhism to Shinto. The proponents of this movement contended that the Japanese gods constituted the original divine substance, and the Buddhas and Bodhisattvas were manifestations of this, a reversal of the position taken by the earlier Dual Shintoists, who regarded the Japanese gods as manifestations of the universal Buddha.

Another important historical work—actually a historical romance—of this era was the *Taiheiki* (*Chronicle of Grand Pacification*). It is believed to have been the work of several writers and was completed around 1370. It describes the events from 1318, the beginning of the reign of Emperor Godaigo, to 1367, focusing on the Kemmu Restoration and the conflict between the imperial and Ashikaga factions. It is sympathetic to the imperial cause and depicts the heroic exploits of such men as Kusunoki Masashige and Nitta Yoshisada. It has remained the chief source of information for the early Ashikaga period. The saga was also in its day a source of popular entertainment; storytellers went about retelling its tales of military exploits, heroism, and virtue.

The people were entertained by other romantic and melodramatic tales of heroic warriors as well. One of the most popular subjects of the storytellers was Yoshitsune, Yoritomo's younger brother, who was idealized as a young man of valor, courage, and military genius. Fairy tales were popular in this era, too.

Another form of recreation enjoyed by the people at large were the Buddhist Bon dances that came to be performed in the early years of the Ashikaga period. The people also found emotional release in the annual festivals of the Shinto shrines and were occasionally entertained by farcical plays known as *Kyōgen*, which often satirized the members of the upper classes. The Kyōgen was eventually incorporated into the Nō theater.

In the religious life of the people, the custom came into existence of paying homage to stone images of various Bodhisattvas who, it was believed, bestowed diverse benefits upon the worshippers. The practice of going on pilgrimages to a number of widely scattered Buddhist temples also became popular among devout believers.

As for the Buddhist sects that emerged in the Kamakura period, both Nichiren and True Pure Land Buddhism were endowed with dynamic leadership that effected a kind of renaissance in the sects. The beliefs of the Nichiren Sect were propagated vigorously by its leaders, among whom was Nisshin (1407–1488), who, it was said, disciplined himself by such means of self-torture as pulling out his fingernails and piercing the open sores with a needle. When he aroused the wrath of the sixth shōgun, the shōgun had a red-hot iron pot placed on his head. Undaunted, Nisshin continued his work to gain converts. The zealous efforts of such preachers won the Nichiren Sect a large number of converts, particularly among the townspeople. It became especially popular in Kyoto and became something of a political force in the sixteenth century in that strife-ridden city.

Because Shinran, the founder of the True Pure Land Sect, did not believe in institutionalizing his movement, it was loosely structured. This situation was changed by Rennyo (1415–1499), who welded the movement into a well-structured religious sect and a political power as well. The sect became especially popular among the peasantry in the north central and western regions of Honshu. In the age of political disorder, the converts organized themselves into military bands and fought against hostile military chieftains. The True Pure Land Sect came to be known as the *Ikkō* (One Direction) Sect, and the military campaigns they launched against the warlords were called Ikkō Uprisings. In the last quarter of the fifteenth century, the Ikkō adherents staged six uprisings and eventually gained control of the province of Kaga. By the sixteenth century the Ikkō forces had become a major power in the Kyoto-Osaka area as well as in the north central and central provinces, constituting a formidable obstacle to the ambitious daimyō.

NOTES

1. The Ashikaga era is also known as the Muromachi period, after the Muromachi section of Kyoto, where all but the first three Ashikaga shōgun resided.

2. In 1425 there were 342 sake brewers in Kyoto, many of whom also engaged in moneylending.

3. Quoted in Nagahara Keiji, *Gekokujō no Jidai* (*The Triumph of the Lowly Over the Mighty*) (Tokyo: Chūō Kōronsha, 1965), p. 2.

4. Sōun was not related to the Hōjō family of the Kamakura Bakufu. The Hōjō family name was adopted by Sōun's son. This family is also known as Go-Hōjō (Later Hōjō) to distinguish it from the earlier one.

5. Quoted in Tsuji Zennosuke, *Nihon Bunkashi* (*Japanese Cultural History*) 7 vols. (Tokyo: Shunjūsha, 1955), vol. 4, p. 176.

6. Firearms had been introduced from China in the fifteenth century and may have been used by some eastern daimyō before the Western muskets arrived. Since their use did not spread, the Chinese firearms were evidently not very effective.

7. Quoted in Tsuji Zennosuke, *op. cit.*, vol. 4, pp. 177–79.

8. Quoted in Satō Shinichi, *Nambokuchō no Dōran (Conflicts Between the Southern and Northern Courts)* (Tokyo: Chūō Kōronsha, 1965), pp. 390–91.

9. Nyozekan Hasegawa, *The Japanese Character: A Cultural Profile,* trans. John Bester (Tokyo and Palo Alto, Calif.: Kodansha International Ltd., 1965), p. 48.

10. Daisetsu T. Suzuki, *Zen and Japanese Culture* (New York: Pantheon, 1959), p. 271.

11. *Ibid.,* p. 285.

12. *Ibid.,* p. 307.

13. Lawrence Binyon, *Painting in the Far East* (New York: Dover, 1959), p. 180.

CHAPTER 6

THE RESTORATION
OF ORDER

During the Age of the Warring States, the Ashikaga shogunate not only lost its capacity to govern the outlying regions but found itself unable to maintain control over the provinces near Kyoto. Ultimately those provinces came under the control of new military leaders who emerged in that area. After the demise of the major constabulary houses, such as the Hosokawa family, the government fell under the domination of the Miyoshi family. It was then dominated by Matsunaga Hisahide, a vassal of the Miyoshi family, who rebelled against the Miyoshi clan and assassinated the thirteenth shōgun.

In the provinces a multitude of warring lords were contending for land and power. Their object was not to succeed merely as regional powers but to extend their authority over the entire country. The most critical power struggle occurred in the region between Kantō and Kyoto, where powerful warlords contended for supremacy. In the middle of the sixteenth century there were four major powers entrenched in this region: the Uesugis of Echigo, the Takedas of Kai, the Imagawas of Suruga, and the Hōjōs of Kantō. Among the lesser forces were the Oda family and the Matsudaira (Tokugawa) clan.

The clan that emerged triumphant was the Oda family, led by Nobunaga (1534–1582), who started the country on its path to reunification and order. The men who completed the task were Toyotomi Hideyoshi (1536–1598) and Tokugawa Ieyasu (1542–1616). These three men laid the foundation for the establishment of two-and-a-half centuries of stable military rule—the Tokugawa Bakufu. Their lives were closely interwoven. They were all born within one decade. Hideyoshi was Nobunaga's most able and trusted general. Ieyasu was at one time held captive by the Oda clan and later became Nobunaga's ally. Hideyoshi succeeded Nobunaga as the military chieftain of the entire land and in turn was succeeded by Ieyasu.

111

ODA NOBUNAGA

The Oda family had served as deputy constable of Owari and gained control of that province under the leadership of Nobunaga's father. Owari was located in a strategically critical spot, on the route from Kamakura to Kyoto. It was also a rich rice-producing and commercially active area with many market towns.

Nobunaga managed to extend his power by bold military tactics and politically beneficial alliances. For instance, he married his sister to a military leader of Ōmi, his adopted daughter to Takeda Shingen's son, and his daughter to Ieyasu's son. He was quick to take advantage of new tactics and weapons. He ended the traditional reliance on mounted knights by making effective use of foot soldiers armed with long pikes. When firearms became available he was among the first to arm his men with muskets. In a battle with the Takeda clan in 1575 he employed over three thousand musketeers, compared to the five hundred used by his foes, and won a decisive victory. He was also a daring tactician. In 1560 when the odds seemed to be overwhelmingly against him in his confrontation with the Imagawa clan, he launched a surprise attack against his rival's forces, which numbered ten times his army, and dealt them a crushing blow. This victory proved to be an important milestone in Nobunaga's rise to power. He proceeded to consolidate his position in central Japan and in 1568 moved into Kyoto where, after a struggle, Matsunaga Hisahide submitted to his superior force.

After he gained control of Kyoto, Nobunaga did not immediately claim suzerainty over the entire country but instead supported Ashikaga Yoshiaki as the shōgun of the land. He then turned to the conquest of the military chieftains controlling Ōmi and Echizen. In the process he encountered the opposition of the Ikkō (True Pure Land) forces and the monks of Mt. Hiei just outside of Kyoto. He turned his wrath against the latter, destroying the monasteries and seizing and executing not only the monks but the villagers, including women and children. About sixteen hundred people were killed in this bloodbath.

Shōgun Yoshiaki became uneasy about Nobunaga's growing power and began conspiring with his foes. This finally induced Nobunaga to put an end to the Ashikaga shogunate. In 1573 Yoshiaki fled to the west and sought the aid of the Mōri family, the dominant power in western Honshu. In the east, the major clans of Hōjō, Takeda, and Uesugi were engaged in a power struggle. Such rivalries among the daimyō played conveniently into Nobunaga's hands. By 1581 the Takeda forces were completely destroyed. The Uesugi clan remained a formidable power while it was led by Kenshin, who was an outstanding general and administrator, but its fortunes also began to decline after his death in 1578.

A situation that redounded to Nobunaga's benefit was the fact that, as it became evident that his power was ascendant, his foes' vassals began to defect to his side with increasing frequency.

The other political bloc that gave Nobunaga considerable trouble was the Ikkō forces, with their headquarters in Ishiyama Temple in Osaka.

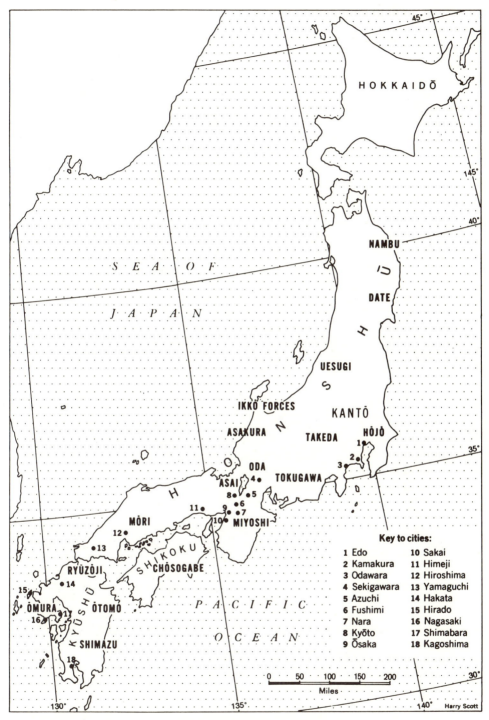

HOKKAIDŌ

SEA OF
JAPAN

NAMBU

DATE

UESUGI

IKKŌ FORCES

KANTŌ

ASAKURA   TAKEDA   HŌJŌ
                             1•
                          2•
ODA   3•
ASAI   4•   TOKUGAWA
8• •5
9• •6
MŌRI   11•   •7
        10• MIYOSHI
12•

13•
        SHIKOKU
RYŪZŌJI   CHŌSOGABE
15•   •14
ŌMURA   KYŪSHŪ   ŌTOMO   PACIFIC

16•
                              OCEAN
SHIMAZU

18•

Key to cities:

1 Edo   10 Sakai
2 Kamakura   11 Himeji
3 Odawara   12 Hiroshima
4 Sekigawara   13 Yamaguchi
5 Azuchi   14 Hakata
6 Fushimi   15 Hirado
7 Nara   16 Nagasaki
8 Kyōto   17 Shimabara
9 Ōsaka   18 Kagoshima

0   50   100   150   200
Miles

Harry Scott

MAJOR DAIMYŌ, AROUND 1570.

They were particularly powerful in the provinces of Kaga and Echizen. Kaga was under their complete control. In 1575 Nobunaga sent his men against the Ikkō forces in Echizen, capturing and massacring thirty thousand to forty thousand Ikkō adherents. In 1580 his men succeeded in driving the Ikkō forces out of Kaga. A peace settlement was finally effected between the Ikkō leaders and Nobunaga through the mediation of the imperial court.

Nobunaga then turned to the subjugation of the Mōri clan, which had been allied with the Ikkō forces. The general who was placed in charge of this campaign was Toyotomi Hideyoshi, who effectively used the siege, one of the favorite tactics of the contending warlords of this era, against his enemies. Hideyoshi turned two castles into veritable hells as he starved the defenders to death. He had placed still another Mōri fortress under siege when he received word of Akechi Mitsuhide's rebellion against Nobunaga.

Mitsuhide had joined Nobunaga's camp relatively late, after the latter captured Kyoto. Evidently he harbored a deep-seated resentment against the high-handed and sometimes abusive treatment accorded him by Nobunaga. In one battle Mitsuhide had sent his mother to the enemy as a hostage in order to persuade them to come out of their fortress to negotiate with Nobunaga. When the opponents did so Nobunaga, ignoring Mitsuhide's compact with them, apprehended and crucified them. Naturally the enemy forces executed Mitsuhide's mother.

When in June, 1582, Mitsuhide was ordered by Nobunaga to lead his men west to assist Hideyoshi against the Mōri forces, he decided to lead his army against Nobunaga instead. Caught wholly by surprise, Nobunaga was trapped in a Kyoto temple and committed suicide. Thus perished his dream of establishing his hegemony over the entire land. When he died he had possession of thirty-two of the sixty-six provinces.

Nobunaga was not only a masterful military leader, he was also an able administrator. He encouraged merchants to open markets in the areas under his control, offering them protection and immunity from taxation. He also curbed the monopoly of the guilds, opening the markets to all merchants. To facilitate the flow of goods he abolished toll stations and encouraged the building of ships and the construction of roads. He abolished corvée, sought to establish a uniform system of coinage, and initiated a cadastral survey. By Nobunaga's time contact with the West had already been established. He favored broadening ties with the outside world by encouraging foreign trade and welcoming the Christian missionaries.

Nobunaga was essentially a ruthless tyrant who was extremely self-willed. For example, he had a young serving maid executed because she had not cleaned the room thoroughly—she had left a stem of a fruit on the floor. He was also a vindictive man. A man once took a shot at him and was captured many years later. Nobunaga had the man buried in the ground with only his head exposed and had it sawed off. He was particularly merciless in his treatment of Buddhist monks. In addition to the massacre of the monks of Mt. Hiei, he at one time had one hundred and fifty monks who were attached to the Takeda clan's family temple burned to death merely because they had performed funeral services for the departed chief of the clan.

TOYOTOMI HIDEYOSHI

The man who succeeded Nobunaga as the foremost general of the land was born a son of a peasant in Owari. He left his stepfather's home when he was fifteen and became a servant of one of Imagawa's vassals. A few years later he entered Nobunaga's service as his sandal holder. He gained his master's recognition and eventually rose in rank, becoming one of Nobunaga's most successful generals. When he received word of Mitsuhide's mutiny, he quickly made peace with the Mōri forces, returned to Kyoto, and avenged his master's death. He then eliminated in battle those generals who were likely to challenge his claim to leadership as Nobunaga's successor, including the latter's son. He also managed to subdue the regional forces capable of threatening his aspirations for national leadership. He failed, however, to remove the man who was potentially his most dangerous foe, Tokugawa Ieyasu. With Ieyasu, Hideyoshi was compelled to conclude a negotiated peace. Otherwise he succeeded in gaining the allegiance or subduing all the major daimyō—the Hōjō clan in the Kantō region, the Date family in the north, the Shimazu forces in Kyushu, the Chōsogabe family in Shikoku, and the Mōri clan in western Honshu.

By 1590 Hideyoshi had accomplished what Nobunaga had failed to achieve: he had completed the task of national unification. All of his former rivals recognized his supreme authority as overlord and became his vassals, holding their domains as fiefs. They were no longer independent warlords beholden to no one. True, Ieyasu had not capitulated completely, but the two leaders had agreed to a truce. Hideyoshi sought to bind Ieyasu closely to him by adopting his son and by having Ieyasu marry his sister. Ieyasu supported Hideyoshi in the latter's campaign against the Hōjō clan and was given their Kantō holdings as a reward. In return, however, he was asked to relinquish his former holdings in the central region. This was no great sacrifice, since Ieyasu's new holdings—eight provinces—were immense. His domain constituted a little empire in itself, valued at 2.5 million koku.[1] Ieyasu built his castle in Edo (Tokyo) and consolidated his position in the Kantō region. His status was not that of a subservient vassal of Hideyoshi but virtually that of an ally.

Hideyoshi was made regent (kampaku) in 1585 and was appointed chancellor (dajō daijin) the following year. He also coveted the position of shōgun, but it had become customary to appoint only the descendants of the Minamoto family to that position. Hideyoshi contemplated having Ashikaga Yoshiaki adopt him as his son to qualify him for the post, but when he was appointed regent he pursued the shogunate no further.

Hideyoshi triumphed in the scramble for national supremacy by his superior generalship and his ability to make bold decisions and take resolute action. He could be ruthless but also magnanimous and is regarded as having been less cruel than Nobunaga had been. He was not as relentless in punishing his foes, permitting them to survive if they submitted. His vassals lived in fear of him nevertheless. A Jesuit missionary, Luis Frois, observed, "he is so feared and obeyed that with no less ease than a father of a family disposes of the persons of his household he rules the principal kings and lords of Japan."[2] Like all warlords of his era, he, too, had a vicious streak in him. He had adopted his nephew as his heir, but when his own son was born, he eliminated his adopted son by accusing him of disloyalty and forcing him to commit suicide. He then had the latter's wife, three young children, mistresses, and servants all put to the sword. Their bodies were thrown into a pit as if they were animals—hence their grave came to be known as "animal mound." When some unknown persons scribbled abusive remarks on his gate, Hideyoshi had eight townspeople of Kyoto arrested. On the first day he had their noses sliced off, the second day their ears, and on the third day they were strung upside down and impaled.

Hideyoshi was inordinately ambitious and, not satisfied with his conquests in Japan, harbored grandiose visions of building a great East Asian empire. After subduing all of Japan he turned his attention abroad to Korea and China and launched an invasion of the continent.

Evidently Hideyoshi had only a vague notion about Korea and China and undertook the invasion without weighing carefully the implications of this move. He seemed to have regarded Korea as an extension of Japan, a land that he could conquer in the same manner in which he had subdued the daimyō. Perhaps there was some economic motivation involved such as the desire to control the trade with Korea. The merchants of Sakai were known to have favored expanding commercial contacts with Korea and China. Hideyoshi may have also wished to acquire more land to distribute among his followers and at the same time to use the expedition as a means of channeling the energies of the samurai—many of whom were unemployed—now that there was no outlet in Japan. Apparently there was also a general imperialistic spirit rising in Japan. The desire to expand abroad is reflected in the fact that a number of people emigrated to Southeast Asia during this period. Thus around the same time that England was emerging as a major sea power and expanding abroad, Japan, too, seemed to be on the verge of rising as a major colonial power, propelled by the people's desire to seek new havens and embark on new adventures.

It may also be that Hideyoshi's desire for personal glory, a megalomaniacal urge to leave his mark on history, was behind the Korean venture. In May, 1586, before he had subdued all his foes in Japan, he expressed to a Jesuit priest his wish to conquer Korea and China. He remarked that "his sole ambition was to leave a great name behind him after his death, for which reason he had resolved . . . to cross the sea at the head of a vast expeditionary force with the object of conquering Korea and China."[3] He asked the Jesuits to charter for him two large Portuguese galleons for this purpose. In return he offered to build churches throughout China and to force the populace to embrace Christianity en masse.

In 1593 Hideyoshi boasted to the Franciscan ambassador from the Philippines, "When I was born, a sunbeam fell on my chest and when the diviners were asked about this, they told me that I was to be the ruler of all that lies between east and west." The ambassador related that "he said that the people of Luzon should obey him; if they did not, he would send his men against them because they had nothing to do as there were no wars at the time in Japan."[4] He did send several messages to the Spanish governor of the Philippines demanding his submission. Although his words regarding the Philippines remained idle threats, he did take action against Korea.

In the spring of 1592, Hideyoshi sent an expeditionary force of over 150,000 men into the peninsula. His armies—led by Konishi Yukinaga, a Christian general who came from a merchant family in Sakai, and by Katō Kiyomasa, who rose from the lower ranks with Hideyoshi—were able to move rapidly north and to capture Seoul in less than a month. Elated, Hideyoshi wrote his nephew, "I now intend to command the country of the Great Ming. And I shall appoint you Kwampaku [viceroy] of Han [China]." He also planned to send the Japanese emperor to Peking and even began thinking of the possibility of conquering India.

But as the Japanese forces moved further north, they began to encounter greater difficulties. Japanese naval forces were not powerful enough to control the seas, and Korean warships equipped with guns and incendiary missiles were able to prevent Hideyoshi from sending his troops sufficient supplies and reinforcements. Moreover, as the Japanese approached the Chinese border, the Ming government became alarmed and sent its troops into Korea to stop Hideyoshi's armies. After several major but indecisive battles, an armistice was agreed upon. Negotiations on the final settlement of the war were entered into but the talks dragged on for two years without any conclusive agreement. Hideyoshi failed even to obtain the terms that the Ming officials had originally accepted. The Ming emperor was misled by his officials into believing that Hideyoshi was prepared to become his vassal and sent an envoy to formalize the relationship. Hideyoshi, on the other hand, had been led to believe by his subordinates that the Chinese were ready to accept him as their emperor. When he realized that the Ming government was not about to submit to his wishes, he exploded in anger and launched another invasion of Korea in 1597. A force of about 140,000 men was sent overseas again. The invading armies were once more initially successful, but before a decisive victory was won, Hideyoshi died in August, 1598, and the expeditionary forces were withdrawn. The fact that Hideyoshi's death resulted in the immediate termination of the plan to conquer Korea and China would seem to indicate that the scheme was primarily Hideyoshi's own creation and did not represent any underlying factors that engendered an inexorable drive for expansion into the continent.

For Korea these military attacks wrought devastation and desolation of the land and starvation and death for the populace. When the Chinese commander recaptured Seoul during the first invasion, he found that

the country all about was lying fallow, and a great famine stared the Koreans in the face. . . . Famishing men fought and killed each other, the victors eating the vanquished, sucking the marrow from the bones, and then dying themselves of surfeit. . . . This state of things naturally brought on an epidemic of the native fever . . . and the dead bodies of its victims lay all along the road.[5]

Not all Japanese were elated with Hideyoshi's Korean campaign. Hearing of the impending invasion of Korea, a monk in Nara wrote in his diary, "As I think of the suffering and vicissitudes that will befall all segments of that society, I feel nothing but sorrow for their plight. . . . It is indeed difficult to understand the reason for this unprecedented undertaking."[6]

HIDEYOSHI'S DOMESTIC POLICIES

Once Hideyoshi had subdued all of his foes and consolidated his position at home, he proceeded to stabilize the social order. During the period of strife, the peasants, suffering from the predatory actions of the warring factions, often banded together to protect themselves. As we saw earlier, peasant uprisings against the moneylenders occurred frequently. Many peasants also left the soil to seek refuge in the provinces of the more powerful or more benevolent lords. Thus there was considerable mobility and disorder in the countryside.

In order to restore order and stability, and in effect freeze the social order, Hideyoshi issued a decree in 1586 forbidding the peasants to move from the land. This sort of ban had been imposed by many daimyō at the local level prior to this, but under Hideyoshi it became a national policy. In 1591 he reiterated the ban against movement from the soil and decreed severe penalties not only against the peasants who left the land but also against those who aided or abetted a peasant's flight. At the same time, he prohibited the lower-class samurai from becoming farmers, merchants, or artisans and forbade all vassals from leaving the service of a lord without his consent.

In 1588 Hideyoshi issued a decree ordering the peasants to turn in all their weapons—swords and firearms—to the ruling authorities. During the period of disorder, many peasants fought as warriors; Hideyoshi himself had risen from the ranks of the peasantry. Many samurai, on the other hand, had tilled their own farms. This decree, which started the so-called sword hunt, was designed to make the class distinctions between the samurai and the peasants rigid and at the same time prevent the peasants from causing any trouble in the countryside. Hideyoshi's object was to bind the peasants to the soil and turn them into a class of serfs. The decree stated:

The people of the various provinces are strictly forbidden to have in their possession any swords, short swords, bows, spears, firearms or other types of arms. The possession of unnecessary implements [of war] makes difficult the collection of taxes and dues and tends to foment uprisings.
. . . Therefore the heads of provinces, official agents, and deputies are ordered to collect all the weapons mentioned above and turn them over to the government.[7]

Another measure taken by Hideyoshi to extend his control over the countryside was the nationwide cadastral survey that was conducted during 1582–1598. This survey enabled him to assess the value of the lands and check the legality of landholdings. The findings determined the amount of tax the peasants had to pay on each piece of land. Taxation rates differed according to locality, but generally the peasants were expected to turn over to the lord 50 percent of the crop. (Because the practice was not uniform, some lords demanded as much as 70 percent while others asked for less than 30 percent.) In time of crop failure, however, instead of gaining relief, they were expected to pay up to two-thirds of the harvest.

Hideyoshi called for a ruthless implementation of the land survey. He instructed one of the daimyō in charge of the survey:

> If any manorial lord objects to it, drive him and his vassals into the castle and annihilate them. Adopt the same policy towards the peasants. If they complain, kill all the peasants in the village. Even if the entire area or province is turned into a wasteland it would not matter. Go deep into the mountains and far across the seas in order to conduct a thoroughgoing survey.[8]

His order was followed faithfully by his officials. In other respects, too, Hideyoshi employed harsh measures against the peasants. He decreed that any peasant asking for tax exemptions (and any official who indulged the peasants in this matter as well) be punished. Peasants who neglected to work the land were also chastised.

When the cadastral survey was conducted, it was decided to use the koku as the standard of measurement for rice rather than the *kan* (8.27 lbs.), which had been used prior to this. The daimyō and warriors' land allotments were calculated in terms of the amount of rice they were entitled to receive as stipends. If a samurai's stipend was to be 100 koku of rice, he was given a fief that supposedly produced that amount. For his actual income he then levied rice rents on the peasants in his fief. If he imposed a 50 percent levy, his income amounted to 50 koku.

In order to minimize the threat from the daimyō, Hideyoshi sought to prevent them from joining forces against him. Daimyō families were prohibited from establishing marital ties without his permission and were forbidden to make military alliances or political agreements. Hideyoshi could and did move the daimyō around to different provinces to prevent them from becoming entrenched in one region. He stationed those whom he trusted in strategic areas and placed mutually hostile lords next to each other so they might check one another. He held about 2 million koku as his own demesne. These holdings were scattered throughout the country. In order to strengthen his financial position he controlled the gold and silver mines and exploited them intensively. He also maintained close control over the merchants of Kyoto and Sakai in order to exploit their financial resources.

MOMOYAMA CULTURE

The era covering roughly the years in which Nobunaga, Hideyoshi, and Ieyasu dominated the land is referred to as the Momoyama period in art history. The term Momoyama comes from the site near Kyoto where Hideyoshi built his Fushimi Castle.

The art of this period conveys a sense of vigor and vitality. The symbolic representation of the temper of the age is found in the castles built by the military leaders. These were massive fortresses designed for defense against armies equipped with firearms. They were usually patterned after Western fortifications, surrounded by a series of walls and moats. The castle itself consisted of a central tower flanked by a number of smaller ones. The main tower was usually six or seven stories high and was used as a final holdout. At the base of the superstructure were huge stone blocks. The entire edifice, with its white plastered walls and handsome tile roofs, usually dominated the surrounding landscape. Himeji Castle west of Osaka is the best preserved of the fortresses of this period.

Nobunaga built a huge castle in Azuchi near Kyoto, but it was destroyed in the conflict that was touched off by Mitsuhide's rebellion. Its main tower was seven stories high and the rooms were elaborately decorated, containing paintings by the leading artist of this age, Kanō Eitoku. Hideyoshi constructed two massive fortresses, one in Osaka and the other in Fushimi. The former had forty-eight large towers; the main tower stood on a stone base 75 feet high, above which it rose 102 feet. Both of Hideyoshi's castles were destroyed in battle, but the Osaka castle was later rebuilt and is now equipped with an elevator. Many of the components of the Fushimi castle were removed to the Nishi-Honganji, headquarters of the True Pure Land Sect, and have been preserved to the present.

The construction of these castles and palaces fostered the other arts because the interiors of these edifices were elaborately decorated with painted walls, sliding doors, folding screens, and wood carvings. In tune with the military spirit of the age the predominant style of painting was vigorous and colorful. It was also grander in scale than that of the previous era, when elegance and gracefulness had been emphasized. Ink monochrome flourished in the preceding age but now opaque, bright color was used. The sliding doors and screens were painted in strong colors against backgrounds of gold leaf. The most renowned painter of this period was Kanō Eitoku (1543–1590), who painted for both Nobunaga and Hideyoshi. Unfortunately only a few of his innumerable works have survived, but those that remain are thought to typify his style: flat space, bold and simple designs, and bright colors. Some art historians consider Hasegawa Tōhaku (1539–1610) a greater artist than Eitoku. Tōhaku painted both in monochrome and color. He patterned his black-and-white paintings after the Chinese master, Mu-ch'i, using the soft-ink style in which everything is suggested rather than explicitly stated. In the use of color, also, he was a master, producing the finest works of this age. The paintings on sliding doors attributed to him display the brilliance of color and boldness of design

Himeji Castle in Hyōgo Prefecture took nine years to build; it was completed in 1609. Courtesy of the Consulate General of Japan, New York.

manifested by Eitoku but also show a delicacy of detail and a greater concern for perspective.

The warriors of this period displayed a great interest in the tea ceremony, resulting in the construction of a large number of teahouses and fostering of the craft of pottery. Hideyoshi was one of the most enthusiastic practitioners of the ceremony, sponsoring elaborate tea parties. He enlisted the master of the tea ceremony, Sen-no-Rikyū, who also served Nobunaga, as one of his advisers. Sen-no-Rikyū, a Zen Buddhist, perfected the art of tea ceremony and gave it the simplicity, restraint, and austerity traditionally associated with it. He not only prescribed the form of the ceremony but the kind of utensils to be used, the design of the tearoom, and the setting in which the teahouse should be located. Unfortunately for Sen-no-Rikyū he got embroiled in political intrigues, lost Hideyoshi's favor, and was compelled to commit hara-kiri.

Stimulated by the demand for tea bowls, pottery making flourished, resulting in what is regarded as the golden age of ceramics. Glazed wares reflecting Korean influence as well as plain unglazed pottery were produced. The *Shino* wares, with their heavy translucent white glaze applied thickly and unevenly and then embellished with simple abstract designs; the *Oribe* wares, which took a great variety of shapes and ornaments; the *Raku* wares, usually black, with strong, simple shapes; and the *Karatsu* wares, with a brownish gray crackled glaze and free-flowing abstract designs, were some of the noteworthy products of this era.

CONTACT WITH THE WEST

In 1543 some Portuguese seamen whose vessel was blown off course landed on the island of Tanegashima off the shore of southern Kyushu. They were followed by Portuguese traders who arrived to establish commercial relations with Japan. The Portuguese were in turn followed by the Spanish, who first arrived in 1584. The city of Nagasaki became the main port of entry for traders.

The Western merchants brought to Japan silk fabrics, gold, sugar, perfume, medicinal herbs, and apparel from China, India, and other Asian countries. With the introduction of firearms in Japan, the demand for imported lead and nitrate also increased. In return Japan exported silver, copper, lacquerware, and pottery. Silver was one of Japan's main attractions for the Western traders. Some historians estimate that Japan was probably producing at that time one-third of the silver in the world.

The Dutch and the British soon followed the Portuguese and Spanish to Japan. The first Dutch ship arrived in 1600; the British came in 1613. Eventually the Dutch replaced the Portuguese as the chief Western traders in Japan.

The advent of the Western merchants stimulated Japanese interest in overseas trade, and they, too, began to send merchantmen to the south. Around the middle of the sixteenth century Japanese vessels sailed to Taiwan, Luzon, Indochina, and Siam (Thailand). Both Hideyoshi and Ieyasu issued official certificates stamped with red seals to Japanese ships (thus known as *goshuinsen,* or red-seal ships) engaging in overseas commerce. Only those vessels possessing these certificates were permitted to participate in foreign trade. The Japanese merchantmen of this period averaged 200 to 300 tons in size.

As commercial contacts with Southeast Asia increased, a number of Japanese—mostly merchants, masterless samurai, and Christians—began emigrating to such places as the Philippines, Annam, Cambodia, Java, and Siam, establishing Japanese settlements. It is estimated that in 1621 there were three thousand Japanese living near Manila. The Japanese population in Siam was about fourteen or fifteen thousand. The leader of the Siamese settlement, Yamada Nagamasa, became a prominent general at the court of Siam. When the Tokugawa Bakufu adopted a policy of national seclusion in the 1630s, these emigrants were isolated from their homeland and were eventually assimilated into the societies where they had settled.

CHRISTIANITY IN JAPAN

In 1542 St. Francis Xavier, who had helped to found the Jesuit Order, arrived in Goa in India to spread Christianity in Asia. He went to Kagoshima in 1549 and received permission from the daimyō of Satsuma to spread his religion there. From Satsuma he traveled to Hirado near Nagasaki and then to Yamaguchi and eventually to Kyoto for a brief stay. At the end of 1551 he left Japan to return to Goa, leaving behind about a thousand Christian converts. Other dedicated missionaries such as Luis Frois and Alexander Valignano arrived to take St. Francis's place.

The missionaries were generally favorably received by the Kyushu daimyō, who were motivated in part by the desire to engage in trade with the Western countries. By 1569 there were fifteen thousand converts in the Nagasaki area. The missionaries' task was facilitated by the fact that several daimyō became Christians and then compelled their followers to accept the religion. As a result, the Jesuits won many converts among the samurai class. Among the early daimyō converts were Ōtomo Sōrin of Bungo and Ōmura Sumitada of Hizen. In 1582 they sent four youths to Rome to see the pope. Date Masamune, a daimyō of northern Japan, although not a Christian, sent an embassy of over sixty persons to Rome in 1613 primarily to facilitate trade with Spain. The embassy went to Rome by way of the Philippines, Mexico, and Spain, and returned in 1620 by the same route, after a two-year stopover in the Philippines.

The Christian missionaries were aided greatly by the fact that Nobunaga gave them his enthusiastic support. He did so in order to weaken and undermine his political foes, the Buddhists. A Jesuit missionary, Coelho, observed, "This man seems to have been chosen by God to open and prepare the way for our holy faith. . . . In proportion to the intensity of his enmity to the bonzes [Buddhist monks] and their sects, is his good will towards our Fathers who preach the law of God."[9]

In 1560 the Jesuits had received permission to preach their religion in Kyoto, but in 1565, because of the complaints of the Nichiren Sect, the emperor had prohibited the propagation of Christianity and compelled the missionaries to leave the capital. In 1568, when Nobunaga gained control of Kyoto, he lifted this ban. He also assisted in the construction of chapels in Kyoto and Azuchi. By 1576 there were over twenty thousand converts in the Kyoto-Osaka area alone. In 1582 it was estimated that there were about 150,000 Christians and 200 chapels throughout the country.

Although initially the missionaries were welcomed by the ruling class, who believed they could facilitate trade with the West and also inculcate such virtues as obedience and humility among the people, some men came to recognize the potential danger Christianity posed. A devout Christian might make an obedient vassal, but ultimately he was expected to serve and obey a higher authority, God. If ever a Christian's duty to his master and his duty to God came into conflict, he was expected to choose God. When some samurai abandoned their masters for God and some children left their parents for their new faith, a sense of uneasiness began to beset some members of the ruling class. Nonetheless the future of Christianity in Japan appeared to be bright even after Nobunaga was eliminated by Mitsuhide. Then in 1587 Hideyoshi suddenly moved against the Christian missionaries, ordering them to leave the country within twenty days. He did not require the Japanese converts to renounce their faith, but he forbade Christian daimyō and samurai from forcing their religion upon the inhabitants in their fiefs. Upper-class samurai were prohibited from adopting Christianity without official permission.

Hideyoshi's motives for this action have remained elusive. When he succeeded Nobunaga as the overlord of Japan, he did not change his predecessor's policy toward Christianity. In fact, he seemed to be sympathetic to the missionaries, and granted them the same favors that Nobunaga had accorded them. He was certainly not sympathetic to the Buddhists whose power he sought to undermine. In the battle with the Shimazu forces of southern Kyushu, he had the support of the Christian daimyō of northern Kyushu. Apparently, Hideyoshi's physician was anti-Christian and filled his ears with the dangers and evils of Christianity. When Hideyoshi ordered one of his Christian vassals to renounce his religion and was disobeyed he suddenly issued the anti-Christian decree.

Just prior to issuing the ban Hideyoshi asked Coelho these questions: (1) Why do the missionaries seek to persuade his vassals to become Christians? (2) Why do they persecute Buddhist monks and destroy their temples? (3) Why do they eat beef when cattle are useful to mankind? (4) Why do the Portuguese buy the people of Japan and export them as slaves? These may have been some of the issues brought to his attention by his doctor and other anti-Christian advisers. It was true that the Portuguese traders did purchase a number of Japanese, particularly young boys and girls, to be sold abroad as slaves. They were sold not only to other Asian countries but some ended up in places as distant as Mexico and Argentina. The Jesuits were, of course, opposed to this practice and had the Portuguese king issue a decree against the slave trade in 1571, but there was no way to enforce the ban. Hideyoshi was concerned about this problem. He was also critical of the Westerner's custom of eating meat. When he issued the edict restricting Christian missionary activities, he also issued decrees against slavery and meat-eating.

Differences in other customs and moral standards caused some friction between the missionaries and the Japanese. One issue the missionaries were critical of was the loose sexual standards of the Japanese men, who in effect practiced polygamy. The upper-class men, in particular, had many concubines. Hideyoshi remarked, perhaps in jest, that if it were not for the Christian insistence on monogamy, he, too, might become a convert. The Jesuits were also critical of the practice of pederasty, which was common among the upper classes.

Initially, Hideyoshi did not rigorously enforce his decree against the Christians. The missionaries were not made to leave the country, as called for by the edict. As a result they looked upon Hideyoshi's anti-Christian outburst as an act of caprice. Although there was some reason to believe that the spread of Christianity might disturb the political order, Hideyoshi seemed unconcerned about the presence of the Christian daimyō. If any problems arose he was in a position to deal with them decisively. For instance, when the lord of the Nagasaki, Ōmura, turned the city over to the Christian Church and forbade the residence there of non-Christians, Hideyoshi appointed a deputy to govern the city and removed it from the Church's control.

Even after the ban, then, missionary work was conducted by the Jesuits, who were, however, very circumspect in their behavior so that Hideyoshi's wrath would not be again aroused, but new difficulties arose when another group of missionaries, the Franciscans, arrived from the Philippines in 1593. They, too, were received cordially by Hideyoshi. Being unfamiliar with the situation that prevailed in Japan, they were less discreet and more zealous in their work. Soon a rivalry between the Jesuits and the Franciscans developed. The Jesuits had hoped to retain a monopoly in spreading Christianity in Japan and had sought to keep the Franciscans out. The way in which the two orders went about their work was different: the Jesuits concentrated on converting the upper classes, while the Franciscans won more converts among the poorer classes. The Jesuits did not think highly of the "poxy lepers" and seedy ragamuffins who frequented the Franciscan hospices. While the "blind, halt, burned, deaf, dumb, lame— nearly all lepers" went to the Franciscan centers, the stately samurai attended the tea ceremonies held at the Jesuit establishments. The rivalry was evidently stimulated in part by the antagonism between Portugal and Spain—the Jesuits came from the former, the Franciscans from the latter.

For about ten years after the anti-Christian edict was issued the missionaries were permitted to carry on their work, but in 1597 they began to encounter more serious difficulties. In the fall of 1596 a Spanish galleon was shipwrecked off the coast of Shikoku. This offered Hideyoshi a chance to confiscate its rich cargo, and while he was deciding what to do with the vessel, the Spanish pilot-major, perhaps hoping to intimidate the Japanese officials, boasted that it was usual procedure for Christian missionaries to be followed by Spanish conquerors. This seemed to confirm what Hideyoshi's anti-Christian advisers had been telling him, so he decided to apprehend and execute the Franciscan missionaries who were working in the Osaka-Kyoto area. In late 1596 six Franciscan missionaries, fifteen Japanese Franciscan neophytes, and three Japanese Jesuit lay brothers, who were included by mistake, were arrested, paraded through the streets of Kyoto, Osaka, and Sakai, and then marched on to Nagasaki. In February, 1597, the twenty-four victims, plus two more neophytes who were apprehended along the way, were crucified, becoming the first Christian martyrs in Japan. Before he could start any large-scale persecution, however, Hideyoshi died, and the Christians enjoyed a short breathing spell under Ieyasu, who succeeded him as the overlord of Japan.

Ieyasu was also interested in expanding foreign commerce and opened all the ports to trade without any restrictions. As part of this policy he tolerated the Christian missionaries, although he did not retract the ban imposed against them by Hideyoshi. Consequently the missionary work continued. Before long, however, Ieyasu also concluded that Christianity was a potential political menace. There is some reason to believe that fear of the Catholic powers was instilled in the minds of the Japanese authorities by the Catholics' Protestant rivals, the Dutch. For instance, in 1610 the stadtholder of the Netherlands sent a message to Ieyasu asserting that the object of the Catholics was to foment political dissension and civil strife. Moreover, unsavory behavior by some Japanese Christian officials undermined Ieyasu's complacency about the prevalence of Christian converts in Japan. With the way of distrust thus paved, the commissioner of Nagasaki had little trouble persuading Ieyasu to adopt an anti-Christian policy. Finally, on January 27, 1614, Ieyasu issued an edict banning the religion. Everyone was required to become a member of one of the major Buddhist sects, and records were kept on the people's religious affiliations. It is believed that there were about 300,000—some estimates run as high as 700,000—Christians in Japan when the edict was issued. Most of them were concentrated in northern Kyushu, with Nagasaki as the center, but some Christians could be found even in the northernmost areas of Honshu.

Persecution of Christians now began in earnest. The missionaries were ordered to leave the country. Many stayed behind, however, and went into hiding, but this time there were no powerful Christian daimyō to protect them and the converts. Daimyō who were suspected of harboring pro-Christian sentiments were compelled to prove their loyalty to the shogunate by purging their fiefs of Christians. Those who refused to renounce Christianity were burned to death. After Ieyasu's death in 1616, the attempt to root out Christians was carried out with even greater vigor. Hidetada, Ieyasu's successor, reiterated the decree ordering the missionaries to leave the country. Anyone helping them to hide was punished. To demonstrate its determination to root out Christianity, in September, 1622, the Bakufu publicly burned or decapitated fifty-five Christians in Nagasaki, including women and children.

The third Tokukawa shōgun, Iemitsu, who came to power in 1623, was an even more cold-blooded persecutor of the Christians than his father had been and often attended the torture sessions himself. A growing number of Christians were forced to become apostates through force and torture.

The most common methods of torture were by water, fire, mutilation, and hanging into a pit headfirst. Ironically enough, the samurai tended to apostatize more readily than the common people—"the lame and the halt"—who had been converted by the Franciscans. Those who refused to renounce their faith were executed. Before the execution some were thrown into prisons so overcrowded that there was barely enough room to move. They were forced to endure terrible hunger, thirst, filth, stench, and disease. Often they were left there to rot. Frequently when a prisoner died, the corpse was left there for days. During the period from 1614 to 1640 between five and six thousand Christians were executed.

The climax of the anti-Christian campaign came with the Shimabara Rebellion of 1637-1638, involving Christians from Shimabara Peninsula and the nearby island of Amakusa, where Christianity had been firmly implanted. There were about ten thousand Christians in Amakusa Island, and when, at the beginning of the seventeenth century, the daimyō sought to eradicate the religion he failed because of popular resistance. When persecution became more severe, most of the Christians renounced their religion outwardly but remained Christians at heart. In 1633 a new daimyō was enfeoffed who mercilessly taxed the impoverished peasants. The people of Shimabara, too, were suffering at the hands of a brutal and rapacious daimyō who tortured and abused those who were unable to pay their taxes. The peasants of Shimabara finally staged a general uprising against the daimyō in 1637.

Although the rebellion may have started out as a protest against the taxation policies of the lord, it soon took on a religious hue. The rebels openly proclaimed their adherence to Christianity and shouted the names of Jesus, Maria, and Santiago during their attacks. From Shimabara the rebellion spread to Amakusa, where the rebels chose a sixteen-year-old youth, Amakusa Shirō (1621–1638), as their leader. They also had the support of several resourceful masterless warriors who provided them with military leadership. After the Amakusa rebels were defeated on the island, they went to Shimabara and joined the insurgents there. About thirty-seven thousand people, including women and children, entrenched themselves in a strategically located castle and defied the Bakufu's forces that besieged them. They were finally reduced to near starvation and the stronghold was taken. Virtually all of the insurgents in the castle were massacred. The siege had lasted for three months, and the Bakufu had employed over 100,000 warriors against them, suffering a loss of 13,000 men.

The Shimabara Rebellion led to severe restrictions on contact with the outside world. Indeed, the process of curbing Japanese relations with the external world had started earlier. In 1616 all foreign merchantmen, except those from China, were prohibited from entering ports other than Nagasaki and Hirado. Foreigners were permitted to reside only in Edo, Kyoto, and Sakai. In 1624 the Spanish were denied the right to trade with Japan, and the British voluntarily abandoned their attempts to develop commerce there. In 1633 Japanese ships without official authorization were prohibited from leaving the country. In 1636 all Japanese ships without exception were forbidden to leave Japan. Not only could the Japanese no longer go abroad, but those who had gone abroad were prevented from returning. In 1639, after the Shimabara Rebellion, the final edict, calling for a strict policy of seclusion, was issued. No foreign ships were allowed to enter Japanese ports except for the Koreans, who were allowed to trade with Japan at Iki Island off Honshu, and the Dutch and the Chinese, who were allowed to trade at the small island of Deshima in Nagasaki Bay under restricted circumstances. The Dutch tradesmen were allowed to reside only on the island and could not travel elsewhere without special permission.

Initially there were no restrictions on trade with China. In 1685, however, the outflow of silver to China was limited to 6,000 kan (about 49,620 lbs.) and that to Holland to 3,000 kan. After 1715 only thirty Chinese ships were allowed to come to Japan each year, while Holland was permitted to send two vessels only. Export of copper was also restricted at this time. In 1813 the number of Chinese merchantmen allowed to call annually was reduced to ten.

All books from the West were banned in order to prevent Christian ideas from entering the country. From time to time Christians were uncovered and were either punished or executed. Between 1664 and 1667 two thousand Christians were arrested. The government remained vigilant, and it appeared as if Christianity had been successfully rooted out. But many hidden Christians survived, and when religious freedom was restored in the nineteenth century, a number of Christian families came out of hiding in the area around Nagasaki.

Japan was to remain closed to most of the world until Commodore Perry's arrival in 1853. This decision to restrict external contacts was a momentous one for it meant that Japan was to be virtually cut off from the great scientific, technological, and industrial developments that unfolded in the West in the following two-and-a-half centuries.

THE INTRODUCTION OF WESTERN THINGS

As we noted earlier, the Portuguese introduction of muskets to Japan changed the mode of warfare. The construction of castles was also affected by the Western mode of building fortresses. Western navigation and shipbuilding techniques as well as Western mining techniques were adopted. Movable type was introduced to Japan by Valignano, and initially the Japanese used it to print a number of books. Woodblock printing was found to be easier to produce, however, so movable type ceased to be used. Western-style oil painting was also introduced at this time, and for a period the naturalistic style of the West was employed by some Japanese artists. Aside from Christian texts, the only literary work that was brought to Japan by the missionaries was *Aesop's Fables*.

The kind of commodities introduced from the outside was indicated by the new words, derived from Portuguese or Spanish, that came into use. These included birōdo (*velludo*, velvet), rasha (*raxa*, woolen cloth), sarasa (*sarsa*, printed cotton), jiban (*gibao*, underwear), kappa (*capa*, waterproof coat), shabon (*jabon*, soap), karuta (*carta*, cards), and tabako (tobacco).

Among the new words for foods were jagaimo (*jacatra*, potatoes), kabocha (*camboja*, pumpkins), pan (*pan*, bread), and kasutera (*castella*, sponge cake). Even the popular Japanese dish tempura came from Portugal (*temporas*, meatless Friday). In addition, such articles as clocks, telescope lenses, and eyeglasses were introduced.

NOTES

1. The value of the fiefs was assessed in terms of the amount of rice they produced. In 1598 the official estimate of the rice yield of the entire land came to about 18.5 million koku. A koku equals 4.96 bushels.

2. Quoted in James Murdoch, *A History of Japan*, 3 vols. (New York, Ungar, 1964), vol. 2, p. 209.

3. Charles R. Boxer, *The Christian Century in Japan, 1549–1650* (Berkeley, Calif.: University of California Press, 1951), pp. 140–41.

4. Michael Cooper, S.J., ed., *They Came to Japan: An Anthology of European Reports on Japan, 1543–1640* (Berkeley, Calif.: University of California Press, 1965), p. 111.

5. Quoted in Murdoch, *op. cit.*, p. 346.

6. Hayashiya Tatsusaburō, *Tenka Tōitsu* (*Unification of the Land*) (Tokyo: Chūō Kōronsha, 1966), p. 476.

7. Ryusaku Tsunoda, W. T. de Bary, and Donald Keene, eds., *Sources of Japanese Tradition* (New York: Columbia University Press, 1958), p. 329. Reprinted by permission of Columbia University Press.

8. Okada Akio *et al.*, *Nihon no Rekishi* (*A History of Japan*), 12 vols. (Tokyo: Yomiuri Shimbunsha, 1959–1960), vol. 7, p. 114.

9. Quoted in Murdoch, *op. cit.*, p. 167.

CHAPTER 7

THE EARLY
TOKUGAWA PERIOD

With the death of Hideyoshi we enter a unique period in Japanese history: two-and-a-half centuries of military rule in which political peace and social stability were maintained. The Tokugawa rulers set about deliberately to freeze the political and social order and achieved their objectives remarkably well. Here, cut off from the rest of the world, was a small "world state." Arnold Toynbee characterizes the nature of this kind of world state in the following manner:

> The smallest human community constitutes the whole world for the people inside it if it is insulated from all other human communities on the face of the planet; and it will be insulated from them if its members feel that outsiders do not count. In this—and it is a very practical sense— even tiny Japan was a world state during her two centuries of insulation under the regime of the Tokugawa shoguns. . . . the world governments of the past have concentrated their energies on self-preservation; and they have tried to preserve themselves by a policy of freezing. They have tried to freeze not only their frontiers against the outer barbarians and not only the structure of public administration inside those frontiers; they have tried to freeze the private lives of their citizens as well. The most notorious recent instance of this policy is that of the Tokugawa regime in Japan.[1]

In this closed society the institutions, practices, values, attitudes, behavior, and mode of thinking of the Japanese were molded for two-and-a-half centuries. The present-day Japanese way of life and pattern of thinking cannot be clearly understood unless the nature of Tokugawa society is understood, for out of this setting the Japan and the Japanese of the nineteenth and twentieth centuries emerged.

THE TRIUMPH OF TOKUGAWA IEYASU

Of the three "unifiers" of sixteenth-century Japan, the man who finally triumphed and achieved the objective of establishing a new military dynasty was Ieyasu. He was the most patient, the shrewdest, and the luckiest of the three. Moreover, he had a broad vision—a historical perspective and political acumen—that the other two may have lacked. He was also willing to listen to criticisms about himself. "It is difficult," he said, "for anybody to recognize his own weaknesses. At the lower ranks friends and relatives can criticize each other. But those of higher standing do not have this advantage. They are approached by people who flatter them. . . . Thus, I appreciate all sorts of criticisms, even those dealing with minor faults."[2]

In order to survive in the ruthless world of the contending warlords, Ieyasu was willing to be just as pitiless as the next man. When Ieyasu and Nobunaga were allies, Nobunaga demanded that Ieyasu kill his wife and his son, who was married to Nobunaga's daughter, because he suspected them of intriguing against him. In order to avoid a conflict with the more powerful Nobunaga, Ieyasu complied by executing his wife and compelling his son to commit suicide. When Ieyasu set out to destroy the Toyotomi family he was merciless, sparing only two small children. Thousands of Toyotomi supporters were hunted down relentlessly, executed, and had their heads publicly exposed.

The experiences of his childhood taught Ieyasu to be patient and to endure hardships. His family, the Matsudaira clan, was a local power in Mikawa but was threatened by two powerful neighbors, the Oda and Imagawa clans. In order to avoid being crushed by them, Ieyasu's father allied himself with the more powerful Imagawa family and turned Ieyasu, who was then six, over to them as a hostage. Ieyasu was abducted by the Oda family, however, and remained their captive for two-and-a-half years. He was recaptured by the Imagawa forces and remained their hostage until the age of eighteen when, in 1560, Nobunaga defeated the Imagawa clan. After his liberation Ieyasu began building his family fortune in the Mikawa-Suruga region. As noted earlier, when Hideyoshi succeeded Nobunaga, Ieyasu had become such a formidable power that he could not be forcefully subjugated.

When Hideyoshi died his son and successor, Hideyori, was only five years old. Before his death Hideyoshi had established a council of five daimyō to assist Hideyori. The dominant figure in the group was Ieyasu, who soon made it clear that he had no intentions of being bound by the pledge to support Hideyori.

A development that played into Ieyasu's hand was the cleavage that occurred among Hideyoshi's generals between the "administrators" and the "combat officers." The former were led by Ishida Mitsunari (1560–1600); the latter included Katō Kiyomasa (1562–1611). The generals who made their reputation in the battlefields held in contempt those who had risen with the brush.

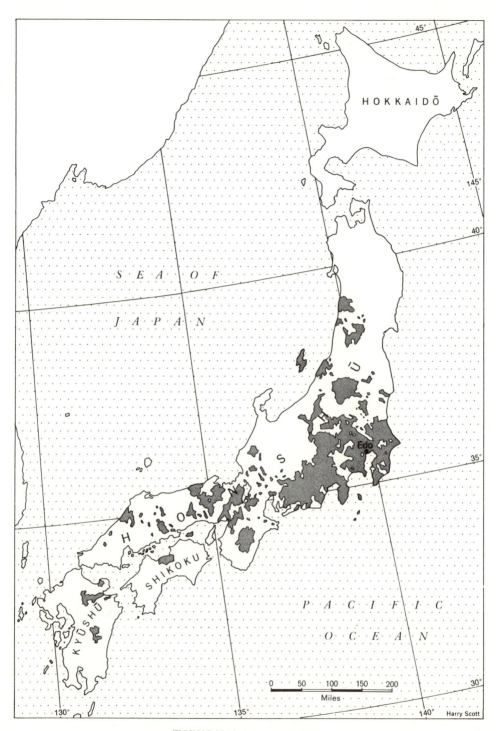

HOKKAIDŌ

SEA OF

JAPAN

Edo

35°

HONSHU

SHIKOKU

KYŪSHŪ

PACIFIC

OCEAN

0   50   100   150   200
Miles

45°

145°

40°

30°

130°   135°   140°

Harry Scott

TOKUGAWA DOMAINS. 1664.

When it began to appear that Ieyasu was seeking to gather power in his own hands, Mitsunari called upon the Toyotomi family's loyal supporters to join forces with him to oust Ieyasu. This led to a great confrontation at Sekigahara in central Honshu in October, 1600. The two factions could be divided roughly into geographical regions: the western clans supported Mitsunari, while the eastern clans sided with Ieyasu. Hideyoshi's "combat officers," disliking Mitsunari, all joined Ieyasu's camp. A pitched battle was fought on the 20th of October, but Ieyasu managed to persuade one of Mitsunari's generals, a member of the Mōri clan, to become a turncoat and thus won the day. Mitsunari's faction suffered a crushing defeat, and Mitsunari himself was captured, paraded around Kyoto, Osaka, and Sakai, and executed. Ieyasu finally emerged as the successor to Hideyoshi.

Ieyasu proceeded immediately to confiscate the holdings of the daimyō who had supported Mitsunari. Some lost all their holdings, others had their fiefs reduced drastically. Toyotomi Hideyori was allowed to retain three provinces with 650,000 koku. His presence still posed a threat to the Tokugawa family because strong pro-Toyotomi sentiments prevailed in the land. Many generals loyal to the Toyotomi family had supported Ieyasu at Sekigahara merely because of their distrust and hatred of Mitsunari. Consequently Ieyasu was forced to exercise caution in dealing with the Toyotomi family. He succeeded in dividing the pro-Toyotomi faction by sowing seeds of mutual distrust among them. He had also bound many of Hideyoshi's former generals to him by rewarding them generously. Thus when he decided to move against the Toyotomi family, few generals came to their defense. A large number of masterless samurai, perhaps as many as 100,000, who were on the losing side in the Battle of Sekigahara did, however, come to their support. In the winter of 1614 Ieyasu sent his forces against the citadel of Osaka, but it proved to be impregnable. Thereupon Ieyasu offered to conclude an armistice if the Toyotomi faction would allow him to destroy some of the fortifications of Osaka Castle. The Toyotomi faction was under the impression that the agreement called for the destruction of the outer ramparts and the outer moat alone and agreed to the armistice. When the fighting ceased Ieyasu had his men fill in not only the outer moat but the two inner moats as well. This caused the Toyotomi faction to recommence fighting. This time, though, the Tokugawa forces were able to overrun the fortress and eliminate the Toyotomi family.

In 1603 Ieyasu was named shōgun. Unlike Hideyoshi he managed, by making appropriate changes in his family tree, to trace his ancestry back to the Minamoto clan. He retained Edo as his headquarters, and it became the de facto capital. In 1605 he resigned the post of shōgun in favor of his son, Hidetada (1579–1632), but until his death was the real wielder of power. He concentrated on organizing the political and social systems in such a way as to ensure the continuity of Tokugawa rule even after his death. In order to appreciate this continuity, however, one must first have an idea of the political events of the first half of the Tokugawa era.

In 1623 Hidetada was succeeded by Iemitsu (1604–1651), the able but ruthless shōgun who uprooted Christianity and closed the country. Iemitsu also tightened the Bakufu's control over the daimyō and instituted the system of *sankinkōtai* (see page 138), requiring the daimyō to spend every other year in Edo. In fact, the political system of the Tokugawa government acquired its basic form during Iemitsu's regime. In 1651 he was succeeded by Ietsuna (1641–1680). There was a minor disturbance during the latter's reign when some unemployed samurai, led by Yui Shōsetsu, plotted to overthrow the Bakufu, but the conspiracy was quashed before an uprising was ever staged. Ietsuna failed to play an active role in running the government and left the management of the affairs of state initially largely in the hands of his uncle, who acted as regent, and later to the councilors, who ruled the land as a committee. Since the personal leadership of the shōgun ceased to be important during Ietsuna's shogunate, when he died some of his councilors favored following the practice of the Kamakura Bakufu and proposed installing a member of the imperial family as the shōgun. The suggestion was rejected, however, and Ietsuna's younger brother, Tsunayoshi (1646–1709), was installed as shōgun in 1680.

During the first part of his regime Tsunayoshi was assisted by an able councilor, and he exercised strong leadership. During the latter half, however, his personal attendants and chamberlains gained considerable power, which they somewhat abused. Tsunayoshi became a protector of dogs because he was born in the year of the dog and was advised by a charlatan that he would have a male heir if he treated dogs in a kindly manner. Ultimately he became fanatical about this and severely punished anyone who harmed a dog. Engelbert Kaempfer, a German doctor who visited Japan during this period, observed: "Many a poor man hath been severely punished in this country, under the present Emperor's reign, purely for the sake of dogs."[3] Finally the shōgun forbade the killing of any living thing. One samurai was executed for killing a swallow. In Edo no fish, clams, or fowls could be sold. No one was to swat even a mosquito. Although Tsunayoshi's desire to protect living creatures was based partly on his Buddhist beliefs, he did not extend the principle of non-killing to human beings.

On the positive side, Tsunayoshi became interested in learning. He encouraged the study of Confucianism and established a Confucian academy. He also sponsored the compilation of histories.

Initially the Bakufu's finances were in good condition. But in succeeding generations the expenses mounted, while the revenues failed to keep pace. Many expensive projects were undertaken, such as the construction of the Tōshōgū Shrine in Nikkō honoring Ieyasu. The city of Edo experienced many devastating fires, and the silver and gold mines began producing less. Tsunayoshi not only led an extravagant life but also initiated a program of renovating many temples and shrines. Consequently the Bakufu's deficits continued to increase. In order to deal with the growing financial crisis, Tsunayoshi debased the coinage in 1695 and created an inflationary situation. Although the government's revenues were increased substantially by this means, deficits had again increased by the end of his reign. In 1708, in the last year of Tsunayoshi's rule, the Bakufu's revenues came to about 760,000 to 770,000 ryō, as opposed to expenditures of 1.4 million ryō.[4]

It was during Tsunayoshi's rule, however, that the culture of the towns-people flourished. This was the era of the Genroku culture that will be discussed in the next chapter. A famous incident involving forty-seven samurai who avenged the death of their lord also took place during Tsunayoshi's shogunate. It came to be cited as a shining example of faithful warriors who fulfilled their obligations to their lord.

The sixth shōgun, Ienobu (1663–1713), employed one of the most able of the Tokugawa scholars, Arai Hakuseki (1657–1725), to correct the abuses of the previous regime. One of the first things the new shōgun did was to withdraw the edict protecting all living creatures and release those who had been imprisoned for violating the edict. Hakuseki sought to revitalize society by re-emphasizing the Confucian code of conduct that called for proper decorum and etiquette. In an attempt to cope with the economic problems, Hakuseki issued new coins to replace the debased ones and sought to curtail the outflow of gold and silver by further restricting foreign trade at Nagasaki. It is estimated that in the hundred years or so following the establishment of the Tokugawa Bakufu one-fourth of the gold and three-fourths of the silver mined in Japan had left the country.

Hakuseki was a scholar with broad interests. He informed himself about the outside world through an Italian Christian missionary, Giovanni B. Sidotti, who had smuggled himself into Japan in 1708. Sidotti was captured and imprisoned until his death five years later. Hakuseki wrote a book about the West on the basis of what he had learned from Sidotti. He came to the conclusion that Western science and technology should be allowed to enter the country, but Christianity should continue to be banned. Concerning his discussions with Sidotti, Hakuseki observed:

> When he came to speak about his religion, it appeared to be not in the slightest respect like the true way. Wisdom and folly became suddenly interchanged in him; at first I had thought him very intelligent, but when he began to explain his doctrine, he became like a fool. . . . At this point, though, I knew that although Roman learning is well accustomed to deal only with matter and mechanics, and is acquainted with things derived from matter, yet it is not acquainted with things above matter.[5]

After he left his official post Hakuseki turned to the study of history. He adopted a rational, positivistic approach in his examination of ancient Japan, thus removing the veil of mysticism that had traditionally surrounded the "age of the gods."

The seventh shōgun, Ietsugu, under whom Hakuseki also served, was in office only for a short period as an infant. Yoshimune (1684–1751), who became the eighth shōgun in 1716, was one of the ablest of the Tokugawa shōgun. He reasserted the authority of the office, which had been left largely in the hands of the high officials since Iemitsu's rule. Like his predecessors, however, he failed to get at the root of the economic problems confronting the Bakufu and sought to cope with the difficulties by forcing the people to be frugal through moral exhortations and sumptuary laws. The government's difficulties could be traced, he was convinced, to the easy living and sagging moral life of the people. He thus emphasized the military arts over literary efforts, and encouraged the samurai to engage in hawking and hunting.

Yoshimune also put into effect certain stop-gap measures, known as the Kyōhō Reforms (named for the Kyōhō period, 1716–1736), in order to increase government revenues. For example, he reduced the daimyō's stay in Edo (the sankinkōtai system; see page 138) to a half a year in return for rice contributions, a practice that was discontinued after a decade, however. In order to increase agricultural production he encouraged the reclamation of new land and the production of crops other than rice, such as sweet potatoes. To prevent the peasants from leaving the villages he attempted, with little success, to enforce the ban on the buying and selling of land. He also regularized tax collection by maintaining a fixed rate of collection over a number of years rather than relying on an annual assessment of the agricultural yield. He sought to disseminate practical knowledge. As part of this policy, in 1720 he eased the ban on the importation of foreign books, allowing them to enter the country as long as they did not contain Christian concepts.

The eighth shōgun also introduced legal reforms and in 1742 had the Code of One Hundred Articles—a compendium of the legal procedures and penal laws that were in effect up to his time—drawn up. He encouraged the populace to express their opinions through the use of suggestion boxes. In addition, he sought to utilize men of talent and was interested in aiding the sick and the poor.

Yoshimune was puritanical in his outlook and endeavored to uphold morality by censoring novels and other works of literature, insisting upon the expurgation of all lewd expressions. In order to discourage double suicides by lovers, he prohibited any mention of this practice. He also proscribed any discussion of the Tokugawa family in print. An effort was made to curb unlicensed prostitution and gambling.

Although Yoshimune succeeded in injecting a measure of energy into the Bakufu, the reforms that he instituted merely dealt with the external symptoms. The difficulties confronting the Bakufu arose from the basic nature of the society, and these attempts at reform were palliatives which merely delayed its deterioration.

THE POWER STRUCTURE

With the Battle of Sekigahara the supremacy of the Tokugawa family over the rest of the daimyō was established. Ieyasu did not seek to rule over the entire land directly, but the daimyō were no longer allowed to be the fully autonomous regional barons that they had been in the Age of the Warring States. They were in effect vassals of the shōgun and owed him loyalty and prescribed obligations. In the administration and control of the land, a division of power between the Bakufu and the daimyō, who retained authority in their han (domains), was effected. Thus the Tokugawa system of rule is referred to as the *baku-han* system.

The Tokugawa family retained a large portion of the country's land as its demesne. At the end of the Tokugawa rule the agricultural yield of the entire nation was estimated at about 30 million koku. The Tokugawa family retained about 7 million koku. Of this amount, between 2.6 million and 2.7 million koku were held as fiefs by the liege vassals or direct retainers of the Tokugawa family. The Bakufu's holdings were located not only in the Kantō region but in the central provinces and the Kinki area (the provinces around Kyoto) as well. The remaining 22 to 23 million koku were divided among the daimyō. The number of daimyō varied somewhat during the Tokugawa period but averaged about 270. Each daimyō held at least 10,000 koku, but the size of the daimyō's domain varied greatly. A large majority held less than 100,000 koku, and many held only the minimum 10,000 koku. Only sixteen han were officially valued as being worth more than 300,000 koku. The largest han was held by the Maeda family of Kaga, whose holdings were assessed at 1.02 million koku. Frequently the actual productive capacity was higher than the official estimate.

Initially the imperial court was granted an income of about 20,000 koku, but this was later increased to 30,000. The court aristocrats were restricted to meager stipends and led an existence of near privation.

There were three categories of daimyō: relatives of the Tokugawa family (*shimpan*), hereditary daimyō (fudai), and outside lords (tozama). There were only a few shimpan. The most important of these were the three main collateral houses established by Ieyasu's sons, the Owari, Kii, and Mito han. They, together with three houses established by the sons of the eighth and ninth shōgun, provided a successor to the shōgun if he did not have an heir. Other major shimpan included the Echizen and Aizu houses.

The fudai lords were by and large those daimyō who had been vassals of the Tokugawa family before the battle of Sekigahara. They not only functioned as rulers of their own han but served as high officials in the Bakufu. The tozama lords, of whom there were about a hundred, were those who had joined the Tokugawa faction later. Many had fought against it at Sekigahara, but some had remained neutral, and others had even fought on its side. The last group were regarded as friendly tozama lords and were rewarded after Ieyasu gained mastery over the land. Those who had fought against him at Sekigahara, with a few exceptions, found their holdings reduced substantially. The tozama holdings, however, tended to be larger than the fudai holdings. Of the sixteen largest han, eleven were held by tozama lords, four belonged to the shimpan, and only one was held by a fudai daimyō.

For a few decades the Bakufu pursued a policy of eliminating those lords it considered untrustworthy, even those who had supported it at Sekigahara. It also confiscated the holdings of those daimyō houses that experienced internal conflict over succession. In addition it exercised the right of escheat when a daimyō died without leaving an heir. Deathbed designations were not recognized. During the first half of the seventeenth century, 120 daimyō families lost their fiefs for diverse reasons, but the Bakufu discontinued exercising its right of escheat at about the middle of the seventeenth century.

The Bakufu kept strategic areas under its direct control or else allotted them to the shimpan or fudai daimyō. Those tozama lords who were not fully trusted by the Bakufu were generally located in the outlying regions or were placed in between two reliable houses.

The Bakufu took great care to prevent the daimyō, particularly the tozama daimyō, from endangering its supremacy. Daimyō families were prohibited from concluding marital ties without the Bakufu's approval. Castles could not be repaired without permission from the shogunate. An elaborate system of spies was developed to ferret out any budding conspiracies.

In order to maintain a close check on the daimyō, the Bakufu instituted the sankinkōtai (alternate attendance) system, requiring the daimyō to spend every other year in Edo. This compelled them to spend huge sums of money moving their households back and forth to the capital and maintaining expensive residences there. The resulting drain on their resources prevented them from accumulating funds that could be used against the Bakufu. In addition, the daimyō were required to leave their wives and children in Edo as hostages. Barriers or checkpoints were established at strategic points to control their movements.

The daimyō were also required to sign an oath of allegiance to the shōgun. As each new shōgun came to office, the daimyō had to renew their pledges and also to acknowledge the *Buke Shohatto* (Laws Governing the Military Households), which prescribed the mode of conduct for the samurai and daimyō.

The major obligation of the daimyō to the shōgun was to come to his aid in time of trouble with a fixed number of warriors, horses, and weapons. The number of warriors each daimyō was obliged to provide was determined by the amount of land he held and came to about two men per 100 koku. The daimyō was also required to provide material assistance and men for corvée when the Bakufu required them for special projects.

The daimyō was allowed a fairly free hand in the administration of his own han, but certain matters were placed outside his jurisdiction. The Bakufu retained the right to manage the country's foreign relations, and it also controlled such internal matters as coinage, weights and measures, and inter-han transportation.

The liege vassals of the shōgun were classified into two groups: the bannermen (*hatamoto*) and housemen (*gokenin*). They were in a way members of the "palace guard." The bannermen had the privilege of approaching the shōgun directly whereas the housemen did not. The latter also held smaller fiefs or stipends. These immediate servitors of the shōgun were at first given either fiefs or stipends, but the Bakufu eventually adopted the policy of removing the liege vassals from the land and having them reside in Edo, and thus by 1722 most of them were receiving stipends rather than holding fiefs. In the early eighteenth century there were over five thousand bannermen and seventeen thousand housemen. The daimyō also adopted the practice of paying their retainers stipends rather than alloting them fiefs. By 1690, 83 percent of the daimyō had their vassals on stipends.

ADMINISTRATIVE STRUCTURE

The administrative structure of the shogunate took its more or less final form during the third Tokugawa shōgun's regime. The shōgun, as the chief administrator, was assisted by several councilors. The highest ranking post was that of the *tairō* (great councilor). This position, however, was filled only under such special circumstances as the minority of a shōgun or in such extraordinary situations as the crisis caused by the arrival of Commodore Perry. During the early years of the Tokugawa Bakufu three tairō were appointed to function as a group, but eventually the number was reduced to one. They were chosen from among those fudai daimyō who were especially close to the Tokugawa family. The standing conciliar positions were those of the *rōjū* (senior councilors). Usually there were four or five rōjū who took turns each month managing the administrative affairs of the Bakufu. They were chosen from among the fudai daimyō with holdings of over 25,000 koku. Under their supervision were a number of important officials, such as the *ō-metsuke* (inspector general), whose function was to oversee the shogunate's relationship with the daimyō and keep a check on them. Various commissioners (*bugyō*) in charge of the major cities, financial affairs, and monasteries and shrines were under the direction of the rōjū. The city commissioners managed the administrative and judicial affairs of Edo and the other major cities under the Bakufu's jurisdiction.

There was also a group of three to five junior officials, the *wakadoshi-yori* (junior councilors), who were also chosen from among the fudai daimyō. Their task was to supervise the bannermen and housemen and to oversee the affairs within Edo Castle. Under their authority were the *metsuke* (inspectors), who also kept an eye on the bannermen and housemen. To manage its demesne the Bakufu appointed intendants. There were four intendants known as *gundai* and forty to fifty referred to as *daikan*. The former were in charge of Tokugawa domains with incomes of over 10,000 koku and the latter controlled areas with incomes between 5,000 and 10,000 koku. In order to maintain a close check on the imperial court, the Bakufu assigned a deputy in Kyoto. All of the court's activities were closely supervised, even its nominal ceremonial functions. The administrative machineries of the daimyō resembled those of the Bakufu, although there were local variations.

The manner in which the administrative system was established indicates that one of the chief concerns of the Bakufu was to maintain stringent controls over all elements in the society in order to ensure that its position would not be threatened from any direction. The other major preoccupation of the Bakufu was financial. It had to manage its affairs with income derived largely from its own demesne. It could not tax its vassals or the daimyō, although it could ask for contributions. Its primary source of income was the taxes levied on the peasants in its own demesne. It usually collected 40 percent of the harvest. In addition it imposed special levies to pay for public works, the horse stations, and extraordinary projects.

The Bakufu also derived some income from the mines, having kept the major ones under its direct control. It obtained loans, which were in effect forced donations, from the merchants. It retained the right to mint coins for the entire land, and it debased the currency from time to time when its financial situation became acute. The daimyō were permitted to mint their own coins and issue paper currency for use in their own han. These, however, had little value in other parts of the country.

THE ADMINISTRATION OF JUSTICE

The legal system that prevailed in Tokugawa Japan was not based upon the concept of rule-of-law as it evolved in the West. Rule-of-law upholds the supremacy of regular law as opposed to the exercise of arbitrary power; it means equality before the law with no immunities for the ruling or official class. In contrast, justice in Tokugawa Japan was administered according to "rule-by-status," in which discretionary powers were held by superiors within a multistatus social structure. The entire society was ruled by a concept of hierarchic relationship; distinctions between superior and inferior persons were constantly made. Not only could governing officials exercise arbitrary power over the common people, but the samurai class as a whole could exercise such power over them. There was little recourse for the commoner against the samurai, because bringing suits against superiors was proscribed and punishable.

Law to the common man meant submission to the will of those above. The ruling class justified its authority in terms of a moral order that stemmed from natural law, the basic principle of which was that men were unequal. Hence the decrees issued by the shōgun and the daimyō took the coloring of moral precepts and admonitions.[6] Laws, primarily sumptuary and proscriptive in nature, were issued in various forms from the beginning of the Tokugawa period, but little effort was made to systematize them. Some laws were applicable throughout the land, while others applied only to the Bakufu's demesne. Some laws were intended for the common people, some for the samurai, and some for the monasteries and shrines. Penalties for violating the laws were not clearly spelled out, although a common practice of a sort eventually emerged as magistrates followed precedents.

Under Shōgun Yoshimune an attempt was made to regularize the administration of justice with the compilation in 1742 of the Code of One Hundred Articles. Further additions and amendments were made, but by 1754 it had more or less assumed the form that was to prevail during the rest of the Tokugawa era. Altogether there were one hundred and three sections in the code.

A large number of crimes were punishable by death. Among such crimes was the failure to try to save one's parents trapped in a burning house. The code liberalized somewhat the penal practices that had prevailed prior to this, however. For instance, formerly a wide range of crimes resulted in the punishment not only of the culprit but also of his parents, brothers, wife, children, and in some cases even nephews and nieces. In 1691, for example, in the Bakufu's demesne in the north, a servant fell in love with his master's daughter, and they committed double suicide. Since he had evidently killed her first and then killed himself he was judged guilty of having murdered his master's daughter. Not only did the authorities crucify the corpse of the servant as an example, they also executed the servant's father and his older brother. The Code of One Hundred Articles limited the imposition of capital punishment for crimes committed by family members to the children of persons guilty of murdering their masters and parents. Capital punishment in such instances, however, was not inflicted upon samurai children. Instead they were banished to outlying regions.

Because of this practice of holding family members jointly responsible, the custom of legally disowning members of one's family came into existence. Family members would then be protected from the misconduct of, say, a profligate son.

The hierarchical social structure and the concept of rule-by-status allowed a samurai to take the law into his own hands against the common people. The code permitted even the lowest of the samurai to execute on the spot petty townsmen or peasants if they addressed him in "coarse and improper language" or behaved insolently toward him. The code stipulated that "when one slays a rude fellow, it is to be deemed a [justifiable] cutting down, owing to the difference of high and low."[7]

As for the modes of execution, depending on the nature of the crime, a condemned man was crucified, beheaded with a sword, burned at the stake, or decapitated with a bamboo saw. In the last instance, the victim was pilloried for two days, and any passerby was permitted to saw away at his head with a bamboo saw that was placed beside him. Condemned men were frequently led through the streets, decapitated, and gibbeted. Other modes of punishment included banishment, house arrest, flogging, tattooing, handcuffing, and imposition of fines.

Under Tokugawa criminal procedures no one could be punished unless he confessed, so torture was used against those who, despite strong evidence of guilt, refused to confess to crimes involving murder, arson, robbery, breach of government barriers, or treasonable conspiracy. The modes of torture used included flogging, weighing down with stones, trussing up by binding the arms, legs, and body into a tight little bundle, and suspension on a beam with the arms pinioned and hands tied behind the back.

All the Bakufu officials, including the senior councilors, junior councilors, commissioners, and inspectors general, performed judicial duties by hearing disputes brought to the Bakufu by the daimyō, bannermen, housemen, townspeople, and peasants. Cases involving daimyō were heard by the higher officials. In special cases the high officials deliberated as a group and acted as the Bakufu's supreme judicial body. The peasants were denied the right to make direct appeals to the Bakufu so they remained at the mercy of their lords and the local officials. Those who made direct appeals did so with the full awareness that they would be executed regardless of the merit of their case.

The villagers had their own system of justice. There was a village code that dealt with such basic concerns of the village as taxation, agriculture, and community activities. Those who violated the code of conduct, written or unwritten, that regulated village affairs and the relationship between villagers were punished by the community. The punishments included, in ascending order of severity, apologies, fines, ostracism, and banishment. Ordinary disputes between villagers were mediated by the village headman or elders, and differences were usually resolved through compromises.

SOCIAL STRUCTURE

Prior to the Age of the Warring States it was common for the samurai to farm in time of peace and go off to the battlefield in time of war, but during the era of the Warring States, the samurai began to congregate in the castle towns. Thus a division of labor between the samurai and the farmers began to develop. Hideyoshi's sword hunt and freezing of occupation resulted in a four-class division of samurai, peasants, artisans, and merchants. The Tokugawa Bakufu adopted a policy of perpetuating this situation and maintained a rigid division of these four main classes. Birth determined every individual's social status. A samurai's son belonged to the samurai class, and the peasant's son remained a peasant. The establishment of the hierarchic social structure fixed the character of Tokugawa society and, to a large extent, of modern Japan. Class status and group relationship governed all social relations, and individualism was thoroughly repressed.

The ruling class justified this class structure in terms of Confucian concepts. Knowing one's proper place in society was one of the points emphasized by the Confucian scholars, particularly the Chu Hsi school, which eventually became the official philosophy of the regime. An early Tokugawa Chu Hsi philosopher, Hayashi Razan (1583–1657), wrote,

> Heaven is august, Earth is ignoble. Heaven is high, Earth is low. Just as there is a distinction of high and low between Heaven and Earth, in the society of men, a prince is noble while the subject is common. Proper decorum calls for a hierarchy between the noble and the common, the elder and the younger persons. . . . Unless the distinction between the prince who is noble and the subject who is common is maintained, the land cannot be governed. . . . If the Way that distinguishes the prince and the subject, and the father and the son is followed, and the principle of distinguishing the high and the low, the exalted and the vulgar is upheld, the Way of Heaven will prevail above, and human relationships will be clear below.[8]

The Bakufu's laws governing the military household stated that lord and vassal should observe what was proper to their stations in life. A person was expected to be totally submissive and obedient to his superiors and would never dare, of course, to criticize them.

The object of the Bakufu was to fix the social order and preserve the status quo. All innovations were rejected. An official decree stated, "Generally speaking in all things the ancient laws must be followed. New practices must be prohibited." An eighteenth-century Confucian scholar wrote, "It seems that in state affairs, if the laws and practices of those who founded the state are followed exactly and are not changed, the state will endure forever. If the descendants turn against the laws of their ancestors and devise new ones the state will fall into chaos and will surely perish."[9]

THE SAMURAI

In the hierarchic Tokugawa society the privileged class was the samurai, the governing class. It constituted about one-fifteenth to one-tenth of the total population. At the end of the Tokugawa era, there were fewer than two million members of the samurai class and about twenty-seven million commoners. Although the samurai was basically a military man, Ieyasu sought to identify him with the Confucian scholar-officials of China. Thus, he insisted that the samurai must not only be skilled in the military arts but must be well educated, particularly in the Confucian classics.

Within the samurai class itself there was a hierarchy of rank and status. In general there was a broad division between the upper- and lower-class samurai. A nineteenth-century intellectual leader, Fukuzawa Yukichi, who came from a small han in northern Kyushu, reported that there were more than one hundred different degrees of rank in his han where there were only fifteen hundred samurai. Proper distinctions of status were maintained at all levels.

At the end of the Tokugawa regime there were 1,282,000 upper-class and 492,000 lower-class samurai and their family members. Between these two groups rigid social barriers existed. Ordinarily the lower-class samurai could not rise into the upper class regardless of how well they performed their duties or how faithfully they served their lords. There were considerable differences in the privileges enjoyed by the two classes. Upper-class samurai could ride horses and go hunting and fishing, but the lower-class samurai were denied these pleasures. Foot soldiers had to kneel on the ground when they encountered upper-class samurai. Intermarriage between the two classes was prohibited. There were, of course, great differences in the stipends they received. Toward the end of the Tokugawa era many lower-class samurai were unable to live on their stipends and were forced to engage in handicraft work at home to supplement their income—a truly humiliating thing for a samurai to have to do. There were complex rules and regulations to abide by in one's relations with other members of the samurai society, including intricate rules concerning the use of the proper style of language befitting the conversing parties' social status. There were also differences in apparel and the kind of fabrics that could be used.

At the beginning of the Tokugawa period, there was a considerable number of unattached samurai because a fairly large number of daimyō lost their domains in the early years of Tokugawa rule. The masterless warriors (known as *rōnin*) usually retained their samurai status and became teachers of swordsmanship or Confucianism. Some, however, were assimilated into the townspeople, while others became warrior-farmers known as *gōshi*. Among the gōshi were peasants who were given the privileges of samurai as a reward for some meritorious conduct or special service performed.

It was during the Tokugawa period that the code of the samurai came to be discussed in idealistic terms, largely by Confucian scholars such as Yamaga Sokō (see page 164). In time of strife the principle that guided the conduct of most of the samurai was self-interest, and the means to success was brute force and guile. The Tokugawa era, however, was a peaceful age. Hence the samurai was expected to be more than just a skilled swordsman; he was expected to be well-versed in the Confucian classics and to conduct himself in a manner befitting a gentleman-scholar. Whereas formerly his loyalty to his master was dependent upon the benefits his master could bestow upon him, now he was expected to remain loyal to his lord regardless of the latter's behavior. It was said, "Even if the prince does not behave like a prince, the subject must behave like a subject."

In the early eighteenth century a Saga Han warrior's thoughts concerning the ideal mode of samurai behavior were recorded by his disciple. The collection of his remarks, *Hagakure* (*Hidden Among Leaves*), came to be regarded as an embodiment of the essence of the samurai spirit. In emphasizing the importance of selfless service to one's master, the Saga warrior asserted, "As long as a person values his master, his parents will be happy and the Buddha and the gods will respond to his prayers. I have no other thought but to serve my master." Another point he emphasized was the need to come to terms with death. "I have discovered," he said, "that *bushidō* means to die."[10] By thinking continuously of death, he contended, a person will become free and be able to perform his duties more perfectly.

But the era of peace compelled the Bakufu to discourage the samurai from dying needlessly. In the early years of the Tokugawa period the practice of devoted vassals committing hara-kiri upon the death of their lords became widespread. When Shōgun Iemitsu died, thirteen men, including three high officials, committed hara-kiri. In order to put an end to the needless deaths, the fourth shōgun proscribed this practice in 1663. The Bakufu also sought to discourage vendettas, although it did not ban them. Those samurai who planned to avenge the death of their parents or masters were required, however, to obtain the permission of the Bakufu. From 1615 to the end of the century there were over a hundred instances in which vendettas were carried out. The most celebrated case was that of the forty-seven warriors who in 1702 avenged the wrong done to their daimyō. Although their action was regarded as a noble deed, they were ordered to commit hara-kiri by the Bakufu for having disturbed the public peace.

THE PEASANTS

The peasantry, constituting more than 80 percent of the population, theoretically ranked next to the samurai in the social hierarchy but in reality their status was lower than that of the townspeople. Like the townspeople, the peasants could not wear swords or use family names. They were bound to the soil and could not change their occupation.

In order to prevent the peasant landholdings from being reduced in size and to avert a rise in tenancy, in 1643 the Bakufu prohibited land from being bought and sold. In 1673 it proscribed the division of land among family members if it resulted in reducing the family holdings to below 10 koku or 1 *chō* (2.45 acres). This was designed to prevent family holdings from becoming so small as to make the payment of taxes difficult. This meant that younger sons could no longer become independent farmers. They had to remain in their parents' households as dependent members or become hired workers or indentured servants. The daimyō usually followed the Bakufu's policies in managing peasant affairs, but some did not adopt these proscriptive measures.

The peasant's life was regulated in minute detail by the ruling class. In the samurai's way of thinking, the peasant's raison d'être was to serve the ruling class's economic needs. Everything was therefore directed to this end. The peasant was told to limit his crops to the five cereals (rice, wheat, beans, German millet, and millet) and to produce only rice in the wet fields. No arable land was to be left idle. In some han the officials determined when the peasants should get up and when they should start and stop their day's work. They were told not to waste their evening hours but to make straw ropes and sandals. Women were instructed to spin and weave.

In addition to advocating the virtue of industry, the ruling class sought to instill the concept of frugality among the peasants. They were instructed to consume as little food as possible. Millet rather than rice was to be their staple. Smoking, tea-drinking, and, above all, consumption of sake— for rice was used to produce it—were discouraged. They were also told to utilize barnyard grass and vegetable leaves as food. They were instructed to use only cotton for clothing and to bind their hair with straw instead of ribbons. Their dwellings were to be simple hovels. All forms of recreation and games were forbidden except on special occasions. Any peasant found amusing himself any other time was punished. Wives who idled their time away by such pastimes as flower-viewing and tea-drinking were to be divorced. Many of these admonitions were embodied in the Bakufu's edict issued in 1642. As the influence of the towns began to be felt in the villages, the officials began to concern themselves about ways to prevent the peasants from being contaminated by the extravagant ways of the townspeople.

The taxes usually amounted to about 40 to 50 percent of the crop, but the percentage tended to increase as the ruling class began to experience increasing financial difficulties. The general policy, it would appear, was to squeeze as much as possible out of the peasants, leaving them just enough to stay alive. "Sesame seed and peasants are much alike," an eighteenth-century senior councilor said. "The more you squeeze them, the more you can extract from them."[11] In a political guidebook written by Honda Masanobu, an influential adviser to Ieyasu, it is stated that all the rice except the amount needed by the peasants to stay alive during the year should be collected. In practice, however, not all daimyō and officials followed these maxims.

The amount of rice and other products each village was expected to pay was determined by land surveys. If the officials estimated that a particular village was capable of producing 500 koku of rice and rice equivalents in other crops, the village was classified as a 500-koku village. If the tax rate was 50 percent, under normal circumstances the officials counted on reaping 250 koku in rice and rice equivalents. The village as a whole was held responsible for the payment of the assessed tax. Each household's share of the tax burden was determined by the villagers themselves.

Because the actual yield in a given village differed from year to year, each year the officials came to examine the quality of the harvest and fix the exact amount to be paid. As noted earlier, in the Kyōhō era (1716–1736), Shōgun Yoshimune abandoned the annual crop survey and allowed a fixed rate to prevail for three to five years. The last previous nationwide cadastral survey had been made during the Kambun and Empō eras (1661–1681). This meant that in many instances newly reclaimed plots were not included in the tax assessment, although some han did make surveys of just the newly reclaimed areas.

In addition to the land tax, as the years passed, a large number of miscellaneous taxes came to be levied on the peasantry. By the late eighteenth century there were, according to a high Bakufu official, "a tax on the field, a tax on doors, a tax on windows, a tax on female children according to age, a tax on cloth, a tax on sake, a tax on hazel trees, a tax on beans, a tax on hemp . . . if the peasant added a room to his hut a tax was levied on it. . . ."[12]

Furthermore the peasants were called upon to provide labor to maintain roads and other public facilities. Villages along the main highways, such as those connecting Edo and other major cities, were required to provide men and horses to maintain the horse stations that were located at fixed intervals. For example, on the Tōkaidō connecting Edo and Kyoto, there were fifty-three such stations. Each station had a hundred men and a hundred horses ready for the use of travelers, especially the daimyō, on their way to and from Edo. Hamlets located within 10 to 20 miles of the main road had to provide three or four men and five or six horses for every 100 koku of rice produced.

In some han the officials were directed to confiscate the peasants' possessions, even their wives and children, if they failed to pay their taxes. Slavery was prohibited but temporary bondage was permitted. Thus, in order to pay their taxes and debts, the peasants frequently sold their family members into temporary servitude. In reality this resulted in permanent enslavement, because the contract could not be dissolved until the debt was repaid, and this the impoverished peasants could seldom do. The brothels of the big cities were filled with daughters of indigent peasants. In the villages themselves there were a considerable number of hereditary and indentured servants who were employed by the wealthier farmers. That the peasants' lot was a hard one was remarked upon frequently by contemporary observers. An eighteenth-century Bakufu official claimed that peasants were treated like beasts of burden.

Broadly speaking there were two classes of peasantry: those who possessed their own land and those who were tenants. The former came to be called *hombyakushō* (full-fledged farmers). They were recorded in the land registries and had to pay taxes. On the other hand, they had a voice in village affairs, belonged to the five-man group (see page 148), and had priority in the use of the woods, meadows, and irrigation water. The size of the landholding of the full-fledged farmers differed from place to place, but 1 chō (2.45 acres) was probably the average size, since they were forbidden to reduce their holdings below this figure.

Although records of peasant incomes and expenditures are rare, the few that do exist show that the average peasant led a hand-to-mouth existence. A handbook written around the 1680s for officials of an unidentified region estimated that a peasant with a half a chō of rice field and a half a chō of upland could, by double cropping, produce 22.5 koku of rice and rice equivalents. His farming, living, and household costs came to 18 koku, leaving him 4.5 koku to pay his land taxes.

The farmlands were usually graded into three categories: superior, medium, and inferior. Although the expected yield differed somewhat depending on the location, 1 chō of superior rice field was expected to yield about 15 koku, medium grade field 13 koku, and poor field 11 koku. The expected yields for uplands were lower.

In the case of the above peasant, the handbook states that if his fields were rated medium, his taxable yield would be 12 koku. If they were rated superior, it would be 14 koku. The normal tax rate being 40 percent, he would have to pay 4.8 koku in the former instance and 5.6 koku in the latter. Thus he would have to go into debt to pay his tax. This tendency prevailed throughout the country, and the situation grew worse with the passing years.

Normally the peasants had their own plots of land to farm on a more or less permanent basis, but in some areas land was held in common by the entire village and periodic land distribution took place. This practice prevailed to some extent in twenty of the sixty-six provinces, and in some villages it survived until the end of the Tokugawa era.

In most villages there were a few fairly wealthy farmers who owned considerably more land than the average villager. They also retained a number of servants to work on the land. Some of these workers were hereditary servants who were in effect slaves. Others were indentured servants whose terms of service might run from ten years to a lifetime, depending upon the amount of money they or their families had borrowed. It is estimated that these servants accounted for as much as 10 percent of the population in the seventeenth century. In the latter years of the Tokugawa era their number decreased as their masters found it more beneficial to allow them to work the land as tenants instead of indentured workers.

At the beginning of the Tokugawa rule, there was in certain regions a segment of the rural population who were in effect serfs of rural landlords. These workers were called *nago* (children of the landowners) and were attached hereditarily to their masters' households. Holding none of the rights and privileges of the independent peasants, the nago were completely dependent on their masters for the means of farming and were usually among the most impoverished members of the village. By the end of the Tokugawa era, the nago also were practically nonexistent; they, too, had become independent or tenant farmers.

The basic administrative unit in the Tokugawa era was the village (*mura*), which emerged after the shōen system collapsed. The shōgun and the daimyō's agents supervised village affairs and the collection of taxes, but each village enjoyed a degree of autonomy in the management of its affairs and in effect constituted a corporate body. It owned, bought, and sold property, borrowed and loaned money, and entered into agreements with other villages. Although all independent farmers had a voice in village affairs, an elite group of wealthy and prominent villagers dominated the community. Members of the elite families functioned as headmen and elders, serving as agents of the lord of the domain.

The headman was held responsible for keeping records, allocating each family's share of the land tax, collecting the taxes, adjudicating local disputes, maintaining public works, reporting infractions of the law, and so on. He was assisted in his work by the elders and other leading members of the village. When an important matter arose, a meeting of the hombyakushō was held to deal with it.

There was also a five-man group or neighborhood association consisting of five to ten householders. Members of this group were held jointly responsible for the payment of taxes and criminal acts committed by any of its members. In other words, the authorities used it as a self-policing body to maintain a close check on peasant life and enforce its many rules and regulations. The association also served as a mutual aid society, with members helping each other in time of need and sickness. This system first came into existence under Hideyoshi and was probably patterned after a similar institution that existed in China.

It was the Bakufu's policy to keep the peasants intimidated. When Ieyasu heard that the peasants were disturbed at the high-handed behavior of the falconers he is said to have remarked, "Let the falconers be as high handed as they please. This will make the peasants think 'if mere falconers act in such a manner how much more overbearing would high officials be?' and they will be afraid to harbor any disloyal thoughts. Willful farmers are the cause of peasant disturbances."[13]

The peasants' mental horizon was limited because each village tended to be isolated from the surrounding areas. Moreover, the ruling authorities deliberately kept the villages insulated from the towns. Their object was to keep the villagers ignorant. "A good peasant is one who does not know the price of grain," was a common saying among the ruling class. It was said that peasants and townspeople should be forbidden from studying. They were to be indoctrinated with the ideals and values convenient to the ruling class, that is, with such virtues as humility, obedience, and loyalty. By and large, the peasants endured their hardships with great patience, but toward the end of the Tokugawa era, as economic difficulties increased, peasant uprisings began to break out with growing frequency.

THE TOWNSPEOPLE

The third and fourth classes in the social hierarchy were the artisans and the merchants. They were placed at a lower level than the peasantry because the economy was supported by the tillers of the land and, in theory, the samurai class respected and valued the peasants. In the official social hierarchy the merchants found themselves at the bottom of the order because the orthodox philosophy, Confucianism, held money-making in disdain. Confucius stated, "The superior man thinks of virtue; the inferior man thinks of possessions. . . . The superior man understands righteousness, the inferior man understands profit."[14]

A Confucian moralist of Tokugawa Japan, Kaibara Ekken (1630–1714), wrote that "the enlightened kings of the ancient period valued agriculture and curtailed industry and commerce. They respected the five grains and held money in disdain." Another Confucian remarked, "Merchants gain wealth without laboring, encourage luxurious living and undermine the people's minds. Farmers not only must be aided but they must also be respected while merchants must be suppressed and held in contempt."[15]

It was considered to be in bad taste for the samurai to concern himself with money, and ignorance about financial matters was seen as a sign of good breeding. This attitude prevailed to the end of the era and even into the Meiji era. Fukuzawa Yukichi reports that his father was outraged to hear that his children were being taught how to work with numbers. But the merchant class accepted its lot and function as dealers in money and made it its philosophy to accumulate as much money as possible. Chikamatsu Monzaemon (1653–1725), a Tokugawa playwright, had a merchant remark in one of his plays,

A samurai's child is reared by samurai parents and becomes a samurai himself because they teach him the warrior's code. A merchant's child is reared by merchant parents and becomes a merchant because they teach him the ways of commerce. A samurai seeks a fair name in disregard of profit, but a merchant, with no thought to his reputation, gathers profit and amasses a fortune. This is the way of life proper for each.[16]

A writer who depicted the life of the townspeople, Ihara Saikaku (1642–1693), wrote, "Money is the townsman's pedigree, whatever his birth and lineage. No matter how splendid a man's ancestors, if he lacks money he is worse off than a monkey-showman."[17]

An early member of the famous business house of Mitsui, Mitsui Takafusa (1684–1748), compiled in the 1720s a history of merchant houses, focusing in particular upon houses that fell because of extravagance, neglect of business, and the practice of loaning money to the daimyō. The purpose of the work being didactic, Takafusa warned repeatedly against falling into these pitfalls. Merchants were admonished to never forget that their primary object was to make money. "For the townspeople," he wrote, "though there are many businesses, there is nothing that they can rely upon but the profits that accrue from gold and silver." A merchant must be frugal, prudent, and stick to his business. "Never waste your attention on matters which have nothing to do with your work," he advised. "Merchants who ape samurai or think that Shinto, Confucianism or Buddhism will preserve their inner heart will find that they will only ruin their houses if they become too deeply engrossed in them. How much more true is this of other arts and entertainments! Remember that it is the family business that must not be neglected for a moment."[18]

A significant spokesman for the merchant's point of view was Ishida Baigan (1685–1744), a philosopher who is regarded as the founder of the school of thought referred to as *Shingaku* (Teachings of the Heart). Baigan was born a farmer's son and found employment in a Kyoto merchant's shop at the age of twenty-three. He read everything he could get his hands on and later asserted that learning consists of reading books. He remarked, however, that "if one reads the books and does not know the heart of the books, it is not called learning. The books of the sages contain their own heart. Knowing their heart is called learning."[19] Hence the name for his school of thought.

Baigan upheld the opinion that the business of a merchant was to make money, and he sought to make the pursuit of profits a part of the Principle of Heaven. The merchant performed a useful function in society and in return received his "stipend" in the form of profits, just as the samurai received his stipend. He wrote, "If one calls receiving a stipend from one's lord 'greedy' and 'immoral,' then from Confucius and Mencius on down there is not a man who is moral. What sort of thing is it to say, leaving samurai, farmers and artisans aside, the merchants' receiving a stipend is 'greed' and that they cannot know the Way?"[20]

Baigan also emphasized the point that the common people, just as much as the samurai, were doing their duty as the shōgun's subjects. He rejected the distinction that the samurai made between themselves as subjects and the rest of the populace as common people. Peasants, merchants, and artisans were also subjects of the ruler; the only difference was in the work they performed. As proof of this common quality of the four classes, he cited a common principle that governed all classes. This was the principle of frugality. It was essential, he argued, not only for the merchants but also for the peasants and artisans as a principle that would cause them to "fear those above and realize their lowly status." It was also the basis of government. "The principle of loving the people," he asserted, "can be put into effect if in managing financial affairs frugality is practiced. Even if one wishes to love the people, it would not be possible if financial resources are lacking. Thus, it is clear that frugality is the basis for governing the land."[21] Frugality, then, was made the basis of the Confucian concept of benevolence (*jen*). It fitted in well with the ruling class's continuous interest in fostering frugality as a means to solve its economic difficulties.

Baigan and his followers gave public lectures to the townspeople to propagate their views. Their ideas even filtered into the countryside, as rural leaders invited them to speak in their villages. It would appear, then, that the virtues of frugality, diligence, and devotion to moneymaking were firmly embraced by a substantial segment of Tokugawa society. This fact no doubt contributed in part to the rapid rise of Japan as a commercial and industrial power after the Meiji Restoration.

Although the samurai held the merchants in contempt, in reality the townspeople's lot in general was much better than that of the peasants. It continued to improve as the merchants accumulated more and more wealth and eventually gained financial power over the ruling class. And, as we shall see below, they dominated the cultural world of the Tokugawa era.

As we noted earlier, commerce and a money economy were on the ascendancy during the Ashikaga period. Even during the period of the Warring States commerce was encouraged by the contending daimyō. Nobunaga sought to foster commerce as did Hideyoshi. With the advent of peace and stability under the Tokugawa Bakufu, conditions became even more favorable for commercial expansion, even though this growth was limited to the internal market.

The area under cultivation increased considerably between 1600 and 1730, and it is estimated that the population grew from about eighteen million in the latter part of the sixteenth century to about twenty-six million by the early eighteenth century. These developments stimulated commercial expansion and, therefore, increased the number and size of cities, particularly castle towns. About one hundred and thirty cities emerged and flourished primarily as castle towns. Between thirty and forty of these had populations of over ten thousand.

As the Bakufu's seat of government and the secondary home of the daimyō, Edo grew into a major city almost overnight. Estimates of the size of its population in the early eighteenth century run from 800,000 to one million. As the chief port and commercial center of western Japan, Osaka had a population of about 400,000, and Kyoto, the traditional capital, remained the center of commerce and culture, with a population of about 350,000.

For purposes of transportation and travel the Bakufu improved old roads and built new ones extending out of Edo to key areas. Because the daimyō had to travel back and forth under the sankinkōtai system, there was a great deal of activity along the main roads. The most heavily traveled route was the Tōkaidō connecting Edo and Kyoto. Towns along the route flourished, with inns and shops serving the daimyō and their retinues.

The major cities had to be supplied with rice and other consumer and luxury goods by the wholesale and retail merchants. To transport rice and other commodities to these cities, coastal shipping was extensively used because of the difficulties involved in overland transportation. The most important sea route was that connecting Osaka and Edo, but the entire island of Honshu was ringed with sea routes linking the main cities.

Those among the merchant class who prospered most as purveyors of consumer goods to the major cities were the wholesale merchants and brokers. The daimyō of western Japan maintained warehouses in Osaka and those in eastern Japan kept similar ones in Edo. Rice was shipped from the home provinces to these cities and stored in warehouses for future dispersal. The daimyō employed merchants to manage these warehouses and brokers to convert their rice into money. These merchants enjoyed some of the privileges of the samurai and were paid retainers' stipends. Some merchants served as financial agents for several daimyō and received huge remunerations.

Osaka was the commercial center for sake, soy sauce, rape-seeds, dried sardines, cotton cloth, paper, and iron, in addition to rice. Kyoto was the center of textile and other handicraft trades. Later in the Tokugawa era, as regional specialties were developed, a large number of wholesale merchants and shippers dealing in inter-han trade grew in importance and wealth.

Among the townspeople there were two classes: those who owned their own houses and those who were tenants. The former were treated as citizens and were recorded in the official registries. In addition, of course, there was a great distinction between the wealthier merchants and the ordinary townspeople. The moneychangers and wholesale dealers grew enormously wealthy, particularly those dealing in rice, lumber, and textiles.

Some merchant houses lost their fortunes by incurring the wrath of the ruling authorities, but many wealthy merchant houses flourished and survived throughout the Tokugawa era. A few emerged in the Meiji period as major business and financial firms. Among them were the house of Mitsui, which started out in the moneylending and drapery businesses and flourished as brokers; the Kōnoike family, which got its start in sake brewing, moved on to shipping, and eventually became financial agents for many major han; and the Sumitomo family, which made its fortune mining copper.

The Bakufu appointed commissioners to administer the major cities. Edo, Kyoto, and Osaka each had two commissioners. The cities were generally allowed considerable autonomy, and mundane local affairs were managed by officials chosen from the townspeople. In Edo there were town elders and district headmen. The elders, who were chosen from three prominent families, acted as liaison officers between the townspeople and the city commissioners. The headmen coordinated the affairs of the local districts in the city. Like the villagers, the townsmen were also organized into five-man groups. Townspeople who owned real estate were required to pay taxes to defray the cost of maintaining public facilities. The taxes were paid in lieu of the corvée that they were originally required to perform.

The residents of Edo and the castle towns consisted primarily of the retainers of the Bakufu and the daimyō, and merchants, artisans, and workers. At the end of the Tokugawa era, 60 percent of the area of Edo was occupied by the samurai class, and 20 percent by temples and shrines. The townspeople, constituting about 50 percent of the populace, were crowded into the remaining 20 percent. They were usually located in fixed sections of the city on the basis of their trade. That is, the carpenters were located in one section, the masons in another, the smiths in still another, and so on. Likewise, the dealers in rice, fish, paper, dry goods, etc., were apt to be located in fixed sections of the town.

Merchant and craft guilds were organized by the townspeople to limit the number of merchants or artisans in a given trade. Among the artisans and craftsmen, a master-follower relationship developed, and personal ties similar to those that bound the samurai and his master came into existence. A similar relationship existed between the merchant and his helper, who was expected to serve the employer loyally in accordance with feudalistic ideals. In return the employer was expected to treat him as a member of his family and eventually provide him with his own shop.

One of the chief fears of the city dwellers was fire. In Edo alone there were eighty major fires during the Tokugawa period, adding seriously to the Bakufu's financial burden. The conflagration of 1657 destroyed 60 percent of the city and killed 102,000 people. In the early decades of the eighteenth century the Bakufu sought to compel the homeowners to use tile roofs in key sections of the city. The maintenance of effective fire-fighting units became a major concern of the officials and townspeople.

OTHER CLASSES

In addition to the four main classes, a fairly large segment of the society was treated as outcastes. The ruling class classified the common people into ryōmin (good people) and semmin (lowly people). The majority of the commoners belonged to the former category, but at the end of the Edo period there were about 380,000 people who fell into the latter group. Of this category there were two major classifications, *hinin* (non-people) and *eta*.[22] Before the Tokugawa era the two were not clearly differentiated, but in the Edo period the eta were classed as people who were outcastes by birth, while the hinin were outcastes by occupation and social status, and could in rare instances rejoin the ranks of the ryōmin.

The origin of the eta class is not known, but it is believed that engaging in occupations considered to be defiling (such as slaughtering animals, butchering, and tanning hides), racial distinctions made in antiquity, descent from slavery, physical abnormalities, and diseases may have accounted for the beginnings of discriminatory treatment.

In the Tokugawa period the eta engaged in a variety of trades aside from tanning and butchering, such as the manufacturing of leather goods, baskets, straw sandals and mats, and tea whisks. Although they tended to be located in urban or semi-urban settings, there were also eta communities in rural areas, where they engaged in farming.

The hinin were itinerant entertainers, beggars, scavengers, prostitutes, and cast-off commoners. As an example of how this category of people came into existence we find Shōgun Yoshimune punishing those who attempted double suicide by dropping them into the ranks of the hinin. The Bakufu used the hinin to take care of prisoners and to execute and bury criminals.

Usually the outcasts were ignored in official surveys, and in some maps their settlements were left out. Roads passing through these communities were not included in the calculation of distance. Although the hinin were not considered defiling, the eta were regarded as such and were severely discriminated against. They were required to live in fixed areas and were not allowed to marry outside of their caste. They were not permitted to socialize with or enter the houses of the "good people." They could not wear *geta* (wooden clogs) or anything but cotton clothing. In the late Tokugawa era, an Edo magistrate handed down a decision that held that the life of an eta was worth only one-seventh the life of a non-eta.

FAMILY HIERARCHY AND WOMEN

In addition to the social class structure, there was a hierarchical order within the family. The father was at the top of the family hierarchy and held absolute authority. Filial piety was a virtue prized equally with loyalty to the lord. It was a moral ideal upheld by all thinkers and embraced by all segments of the society. There was, in addition, a hierarchy of age and sex. The younger brother had to defer to the elder brother and women to men.

The treatment of women, in particular, illustrates the authoritarian nature of the family system, especially in the samurai family. A samurai's wife was to be absolutely obedient to her husband and serve without any complaints, enduring all forms of hardship and abuse. Kaibara Ekken, who wrote a tract on the ideal conduct expected of women, said, "A woman has no prince to serve. She must consider her husband her master, and serve him with respect and deference."[23]

While a samurai's wife was expected to remain faithful to her husband and was punished by death for adultery, he was not restricted by similar moral strictures. She was taught that although a lower-class woman might display jealousy, it was unbecoming to a samurai's wife. While a man was permitted to have many wives, a woman was allowed only one husband in her lifetime. It was said that "even if the marriage had been arranged when the parties concerned were three or five years of age, if her mate dies, the girl must remain loyal to him all her life. This is the proper behavior for a member of a samurai family."[24]

A girl's marriage was arranged by her parents; she was given no voice in the matter. On the other hand, she could readily be divorced by her husband if he or his parents so desired. The ties between husband and wife were not to be sealed by love and affection. Their relationship was to be that of a superior and an inferior person. Thus proper decorum and etiquette had to be observed in their relationship. The son was required to place his parents' interests above those of his wife and children. It was said that "it is the normal way of the filial son to neglect his wife and children to serve his parents' interests."[25]

In one of Chikamatsu's plays a mother tells her daughter that "the most important test of a woman's training comes after she's married. You must treat your parents-in-law with the same devotion you have shown to your own parents, and your husband's brothers and sisters as if they were your own. When you are alone together with any other man you are not so much as to lift your head and look at him."[26]

This kind of total subservience to the husband was not demanded of the women of the lower classes, though the samurai's ideals did filter down somewhat. Writers representing the townspeople's ethos defended the natural expression of love between husband and wife, unlike the stoic samurai ideal that required the warrior to keep under complete control all his inner emotions. One writer, expressing the attitude of the townsmen, observed, "For the husband to love his wife, and the wife to be affectionate towards the husband and maintain a gentle and friendly relationship is the proper Way. If the affection of the husband and wife appears syrupy sweet to outsiders, an authentic relationship between husband and wife prevails."[27]

The notion that a woman should serve only one man was not adhered to rigidly by the townspeople. Ihara Saikaku wrote, "We cannot label as immoral the longing of a married woman for another man, or her desire to have another man after her husband's death." Another writer observed, "Among the townspeople, for a woman to remarry after parting from her husband is not an unsavory matter. She is free to do so, and her relatives will help arrange the affair for her."

The ideal of filial piety, which superseded all other considerations—except, of course, loyalty to the lord—in the samurai family was not insisted upon quite so rigorously in the townsman's family. Love of one's wife and children was considered to be more powerful than love of one's parents by some men. "On being parted by death," one writer asserted, "it is sadder in the case of one's wife than one's parents and it is much more grievous in the case of one's child than one's wife." Some townsmen even made the relationship between husband and wife the basis of all ethical conduct. "The way of men originated with husband and wife. First there was man and woman, and then husband and wife. After that came the gods, Buddha and the sages. Thus, husband and wife constitute the source of all things." The complete subservience that was demanded of the samurai's wife to her mother-in-law was rejected by some townspeople who advised the mothers-in-law not to harass their sons' wives. These attitudes, however, ran counter to the mainstream of Tokugawa thought, which was primarily Confucian in nature.

NOTES

1. Arnold Toynbee, "How to Change the World without War," *Saturday Review*, May 12, 1962, p. 17.

2. Watsuji Tetsurō, *Nihon Rinri Shisōshi* (*A History of Japanese Ethical Thought*), 2 vols. (Tokyo: Iwanami, 1952), vol. 2, pp. 372–73.

3. Engelbert Kaempfer, *History of Japan*, 3 vols., trans. J. G. S. Schenchzer (Glasgow: MacLehose, 1906), vol. 3, p. 205.

4. Although the value of both gold and rice fluctuated, one ryō is estimated to have been worth about 1.5 koku of rice around 1700 and about 1 koku around 1800.

5. "The Capture and Captivity of Pere Giovan Batista Sidotti in Japan from 1709 to 1715," a translation by W. B. Wright of Arai Hakuseki's *Seiyō Kibun*, in *Transactions of the Asiatic Society of Japan*, vol. 9, p. 166.

6. Perhaps this tradition of moralistic decrees being issued by the wielders of power accounts in part for the fact that even in the modern era a tendency to equate morality with power prevailed. "We find a tendency . . . to estimate morality, not by the value of its content, but in terms of its power, that is, according to whether or not it had a power background." Masao Maruyama, *Thought and Behaviour in Modern Japanese Politics* (London: Oxford University Press, 1963), p. 10.

7. J. C. Hall, "The Tokugawa Legislation," in *Transactions of the Asiatic Society of Japan*, vol. 41, p. 776.

8. Ienaga Saburō, *Nihon Dōtokushisōshi* (*A History of Japanese Moral Thought*) (Tokyo: Iwanami, 1951), p. 106.

9. Both quotations are from *ibid.*, p. 110.

10. Yamamoto Tsunetomo, *Hagakure*, 2 vols., ed. Shiroshima Masayoshi (Tokyo: Jimbutsu Ōraisha, 1968), vol. 1, pp. 27, 41.

11. Furushima Toshio, *Nihon Hōken Nōgyōshi* (*Japanese Agricultural History*) (Tokyo: Shikai Shobō, 1931), p. 83.

12. Quoted in E. H. Norman, *Japan's Emergence as a Modern State* (New York: Institute of Pacific Relations, 1940), p. 23.

13. Rekishi Chiri Gakkai, ed., *Nihon Nōminshi* (*A History of Japanese Peasants*) (Tokyo: Rekishi Chiri Gakkai, 1924), p. 110.

14. These Confucian statements are quoted from Wing-Tsit Chan, *Source Book in Chinese Philosophy* (Princeton, N.J.: Princeton University Press, 1963), pp. 27, 28.

15. Both quotations are from Ienaga Saburō, *op. cit.*, p. 120.

16. Chikamatsu Monzaemon, *The Major Plays of Chikamatsu*, trans. Donald Keene (New York: Columbia University Press, 1961), p. 332.

17. Howard Hibbett, *The Floating World in Japanese Fiction* (New York: Grove, 1960), p. 37.

18. Mitsui Takafusa, "Some Observations on Merchants," E. S. Crawcour, trans., in *Transactions of the Asiatic Society of Japan*, vol. 8, pp. 103, 115.

19. Robert N. Bellah, *Tokugawa Religion: The Values of Pre-Industrial Japan* (Glencoe, Ill.: Free Press, 1957), p. 149.

20. *Ibid.*, p. 158.

21. Watsuji Tetsurō, *op. cit.*, vol. 2, p. 612.

22. Today they are referred to as *burakumin* (people of the hamlet).

23. Ienaga Saburō, *op. cit.*, p. 112.

24. *Ibid.*, p. 113.

25. *Ibid.*, p. 115.

26. Chikamatsu, *op. cit.*, p. 76.

27. This and the rest of the quotations in this chapter are from Ienaga Saburō, *op. cit.*, pp. 143–46.

CHAPTER 8

INTELLECTUAL AND CULTURAL DEVELOPMENTS IN TOKUGAWA JAPAN

CONFUCIANISM

In the Tokugawa period, Confucianism, which had entered Japan with the introduction of Chinese civilization, finally emerged as the dominant mode of thought. Specifically it was the Chu Hsi school of Confucianism that was adopted as the official philosophy of the Bakufu. At the core of the doctrine were the teachings of Confucius and Mencius along with interpretations made by later Confucian scholars, including Chu Hsi.

Confucianism was a practical moral philosophy concerned primarily with government and society. The restoration of order and stability during the troubled days of the late Chou period was Confucius' goal; thus he addressed himself mainly to the rulers—the princes and the officials. He looked back to the golden age of the Three Dynasties, that is, Hsia, Shang, and Chou. Confucius believed this was a time when wise, benevolent, and moral leaders governed over an orderly society. The rulers of this period had to follow the examples set by the ancient sage-kings, who governed in accordance with the Will of Heaven. Confucius said, "The superior man stands in awe of three things. He stands in awe of the Mandate of Heaven; he stands in awe of great men; and he stands in awe of the words of the sages."[1] The ruler, having this reverent attitude toward Heaven and the sages, was expected to acquire the virtues of benevolence (*jen*), righteousness (*i*), propriety (*li*), faithfulness (*hsin*), and wisdom (*chih*). Benevolence and righteousness were given special emphasis by Confucius and Mencius. Benevolence can be equated with love, humanity, or human-heartedness. Righteousness is justice, a categorical imperative demanding "what ought to be." Propriety, also translated as rituals, etiquette, or rites, has to do

with human relationships and a scrupulous respect for distinctions of
status. In other words, proper conduct meant conforming to what was
regarded as the natural order of things. An individual must know the
proper meaning of what he claims to be in order to behave properly. A
prince cannot behave as a prince unless he knows the true meaning of
the word "prince." The same is true of the subject, the father, and the
son. Therefore, wisdom and the rectification of names are important.
Confucius said: "Let the ruler *be* a ruler, the minister *be* a minister, the
father *be* a father, and the son *be* a son."

The concept of loyalty was also stressed by Confucius and Mencius.
The Analects of Confucius states, "Confucius taught four things: culture,
conduct, loyalty, and faithfulness." Mencius said, "Humanity, righteousness,
loyalty, faithfulness, and the love of the good . . . constitute the nobility
of Heaven."

The ruler was to govern by moral example through the acquisition of
these virtues. Mencius said, "Let the ruler be humane, and all his people
will be humane. Let the ruler be righteous, and all his people will be
righteous. Let the ruler be correct, and all his people will be correct. Once
the ruler is rectified, the whole kingdom will be at peace." Accordingly,
the role assigned to the ruler in the Confucian political system was highly
paternalistic. The ruler was "the parent of the people" and he was "to
dispense a benevolent government." If the ruler should fail to be virtuous,
Heaven would reveal its displeasure and revoke the mandate to rule by
bringing about natural calamities and social disorder. The people would
then be justified in overthrowing the ruler. This aspect of Confucianism,
however, was not stressed by the Tokugawa rulers and their Confucian
supporters.

Confucius posited five cardinal relationships for man in social intercourse:
lord–subject, father–son, husband–wife, elder brother–younger brother,
friend–friend. In all of these relationships, an individual was to comport
himself in accordance with the moral ideals propounded by the ancient
sages. The most important of these relationships for the Confucians was
that of father and son, or parent and child. Mencius rejected the ideal of
universal brotherhood because he contended it was natural for a man to
love his parents more than strangers.

Confucius also emphasized the importance of understanding and adhering
to the rites (*li*) and music-dance (*yüeh*) compositions of antiquity. These
were the manifestations of the wisdom and virtue of the ancient sages.
Rites were to regulate and refine human desires so that they would remain
within proper bounds; music-dance compositions were to regulate human
emotions so that they would be expressed in accordance with right principles.

In theory, Confucianism would seem to have the ingredients for creating
an open society: the prince was admonished to employ men of talent and
the distinction between the superior and inferior man was based upon
moral character, not birth or wealth. Basically, however, it was an elitist
philosophy. Confucius said, "The common people may be made to follow
it [the Way] but may not be made to understand it." Confucianism held
the laboring man in low esteem while emphasizing the superiority of the

learned class. Mencius wrote, "It is said 'some labor with their minds and some labor with their strength. Those who labor with their minds govern others; those who labor with their strength are governed by others.' Those who are governed by others support them; those who govern them are supported by them. This is a universal principle."

Confucianism was not a philosophy that encouraged independent or original thinking, since one was to follow the example of the ancient sages. Complete reliance on the words of the sages—not just the ancient sage-kings, but all the Confucian thinkers since Confucius—characterized the intellectual behavior of the later Confucians, including most of the Japanese Confucian scholars. In Tokugawa Japan, it was the Chu Hsi version of this philosophy, or Neo-Confucianism, that became the dominant Confucian school. After the mid-seventeenth century it virtually became the official philosophy. Traditionally the founding Tokugawa shogun, Ieyasu, has been credited with giving his official blessing to this school, but Ieyasu was not committed exclusively to Chu Hsi Confucianism but was also influenced by Buddhist and Shinto thought.

THE CHU HSI SCHOOL IN JAPAN

The ascendancy of Confucianism in the Tokugawa period can be explained in part by objective circumstances. For one thing, the social and political features of Tokugawa society were comparable to those of imperial China at the time of the emergence of Confucianism. Secondly, when the Tokugawa Bakufu was founded, Confucianism in Japan had changed in character compared to the earlier period.

Regarding the first point, the Tokugawa social structure resembled the feudal class structure of Chou China with its hierarchy of emperor, feudal lords, ministers, high officials, officials, and common people. Thus Confucianism, which was used to justify the social structure of Chou China, could also be used to justify the Tokugawa class structure.

Prior to the Tokugawa era, Confucianism was studied primarily at the imperial court as a philological discipline. It was also pursued by Buddhist monks for their personal intellectual interest and enjoyment. By the time the Tokugawa government was established, it had been transformed into a moral philosophy of broad interest and significance. This transformation was induced by the importation of Sung or Chu Hsi Confucianism. Sung philosophy was introduced into Japan during the Kamakura period by the Zen monks and was treated as an integral part of Buddhist learning. The scholars who liberated Sung Confucianism from this dependence on Buddhism were Fujiwara Seika (1561–1619) and his disciple, Hayashi Razan (1583–1657).

Ieyasu and his successors sought to equate the samurai with the Confucian scholar-officials of China. They were not to be merely skilled in the martial arts but were to be steeped in Confucian learning as well.

Although various schools of Neo-Confucianism based on Chinese and Korean interpretations were present in the early Tokugawa years, Razan and his descendants perpetated the myth that a monolithic school of Chu

Hsi Confucianism was adopted by the Bakufu with Ieyasu's patronage. Razan was depicted as the Bakufu's house scholar and upholder of orthodoxy. But it was not until the latter half of the seventeenth century that Chu Hsi philosophy gained the Bakufu's imprimatur.[2]

It can be argued that the reason why Chu Hsi philosophy appealed to the Tokugawa authorities was simply that it was the school of Confucianism that was gaining currency at that time among Confucian scholars. No doubt other Confucian schools could have been utilized just as effectively to uphold the authority of the ruling family. In Chu Hsi thought, however, certain characteristics can be discerned that might have had special appeal to the Tokugawa rulers.

Scholars of the Chu Hsi school held that all things in nature are governed by a universal principle, *li* (Principle), derived from the Supreme Ultimate, which may be equated with Heaven. The physical nature of all things is determined by *ch'i* (Ether). All men are endowed with the same Principle, but differences in their Ether are responsible for physical and moral variations. Some men have purer Ether than others, but everyone can strive to allow the Principle to emerge by clarifying the turbid Ether that obscures it. This can be achieved by "the extension of knowledge through the investigation of things."[3] As a person begins to understand the Principle he will be able to live in accordance with it and the Way of Heaven. The Japanese Chu Hsi scholars emphasized this linkage between Principle and Heaven: since all things are governed by Principle, which is related to Heaven, the ruler, in performing his task, acts in accordance with the Way of Heaven. He is in effect an agent of Heaven who acts to enforce the principle of things. Accordingly, it becomes imperative for the people to obey the ruler.

The Japanese Chu Hsi scholars placed special emphasis on *taigi meibun* (doing one's duty to the lord in accordance with one's place in society). *Taigi* means supreme righteousness or supreme duty; *meibun* has to do with one's name and place, that is, knowing one's proper place. This concept was particularly convenient for the ruling authorities since the Principle required each man to observe what was proper to him. The ruler, thus, has certain duties to perform according to his "name" and "place" and in a similar manner, subjects have their duties to perform.

The Chu Hsi school, like earlier Confucians, emphasized the need to maintain proper human relationships in terms of the five basic relationships. This aspect of Confucianism was useful to the Tokugawa rulers who wished to establish a hierarchic society based upon the relationship between the lord and subject, between superior and inferior persons.

The Chu Hsi school of Japan adopted the Chinese Confucian scholars' point of view that the teachings of the ancient sages were unquestionable truths to be followed with absolute fidelity. One Confucian scholar remarked, "If I were to err because I had studied Chu Hsi, I would be erring in accordance with Chu Hsi's teachings so I would have nothing to regret."[4] As a result of this kind of thinking, there was a tendency on the part of the Tokugawa Chu Hsi scholars merely to repeat what their Chinese counterparts had written. A significant exception to this was Fujiwara

Seika, the scholar who introduced Ieyasu to Chu Hsi philosophy. He was not as narrow in his outlook as later Chu Hsi scholars, and he did not reject outright the rival Wang Yang-ming school. He sought to interpret Shinto and Buddhist ideas with an eye toward reconciling them with Confucianism.

Seika's disciple, Hayashi Razan, was considerably more rigid, as evidenced by his highly critical attitude toward Buddhism and Christianity. On the other hand, he was interested in trying to reconcile Confucianism with Shinto. "Some people," he wrote, "ask what the difference between Shinto and Confucianism is. I would reply, the principles are the same. They only differ in needs. . . . The Way of the Kings transforms into the Way of the Gods, and Shinto transforms into the Way. The Way is the Confucian Way."[5]

Razan also emphasized the importance of studying history because he believed it would reveal moral principles that were just. History could also be used to provide the ruling family with a legitimate claim to power. It is not surprising then that the Bakufu asked Razan to start compiling its family genealogy.

In his Confucian teachings Razan did little more than repeat the Chu Hsi doctrines. He emphasized the importance of combating human desires or selfishness and permitting one's "illustrious virtue" (the li endowed upon man by Heaven) to manifest itself. He also stressed the five human relationships and the five virtues. Particular emphasis was given to benevolence because he believed it encompassed the other four virtues. Righteousness, he said, was the basis of *giri*, man's moral duty and obligation. The principle of propriety was used by Razan to justify the hierarchical relationship between the noble and the base, the high and the low. Wisdom, he explained, consisted in understanding the principles of benevolence, righteousness, and propriety. Finally, faithfulness was equated with *makoto*, or sincerity.

The scholar who was influential in making Chu Hsi philosophy the orthodoxy of Tokugawa Japan was Yamazaki Ansai (1618–1682). He accepted Chu Hsi's words as unquestionable truth and did not permit his students to read any book that did not contribute to what he considered to be the essence of Chu Hsi philosophy: the principle of "devotion within, righteousness without." Like Seika and Razan, he sought to reconcile Confucianism with Shinto. This led him to what is known as *Suika Shinto*, a combination of the ethical ideals of Confucianism and the religious doctrines of Shinto. This was in tune with the growing tendency on the part of the Confucian scholars to syncretize Confucianism and Shinto. This trend persisted throughout the Tokugawa period.

Another Chu Hsi scholar worthy of attention is Kaibara Ekken (1630–1714), who played a significant role in molding the ethical ideals of Tokugawa society. He wrote moral tracts in a plain and straightforward style that were designed to disseminate Confucian ethical values among the common people. His work was easily understood and widely read. His didactic tract for women is an interesting example of his work and an illuminating statement of the concept of masculine superiority and feminine inferiority.

In his *Great Learning for Women* he operates from the premise that the sole purpose of existence for a girl is to get married and serve her husband and his family faithfully, subserviently, and selflessly. A woman can accomplish this only by completely suppressing her individuality and natural emotions.

In the later years of his life Ekken began to disagree with the theoretical aspects of Chu Hsi philosophy, but he did not go so far as to reject them. He turned his attention, instead, to scientific research. He was trained as a physician, and his interest in natural science led him to do some significant work in botany.

Muro Kyūsō (1658–1734) was a scholar who remained an ardent defender of Chu Hsi philosophy, even as it came under increasing criticisms by the adherents of the Wang Yang-ming school and the school of Ancient Learning. "The Way of Heaven and Earth," he wrote, "is the Way of Yao and Shun. The Way of Yao and Shun is the Way of Confucius and Mencius. The Way of Confucius and Mencius is the Way of Ch'eng-Chu [Sung philosophers Ch'eng Hao, Ch'eng Yi, and Chu Hsi]."[6] He even went so far as to suggest that "useless" books of all other schools should be burned.

Kyūsō emphasized the Confucian notion that the ruler must govern for the good of the people, and he apparently favored the concept of equality among men. He wrote,

> The ruler is not inherently superior. He is superior in relationship to the people. . . . The people and the prince were in the beginning alike in being mere mortals. The people then came to the prince asking him to serve them. He agreed to do so. For this reason the people pay their respects to him and treat him as their prince. The fact that he has become prince and works for the people is merely the fulfillment of the agreement.

Here Kyūsō's political concepts resemble the theory of the social contract. The ruler, Kyūsō contended, derives his authority from the people. "The [feudal] domain is not given [to the feudal lord] by Heaven, nor is it given to him by the Prince. Needless to say he cannot seize it by force. It is given to him by the people." Thus it is the duty of the ruler to "work for the interest of the people." This theory, though unorthodox, was not intended to arouse the people. It was essentially an exhortation to the ruling class to live up to the Confucian ideal of benevolent rule.

THE WANG YANG-MING SCHOOL

One of the leading rivals of the Chu Hsi school in Japan was the philosophy of Wang Yang-ming of Ming China. Wang Yang-ming (1472–1528) began his philosophical career as a follower of Chu Hsi philosophy, but he departed from it and adopted the position that li (Principle) is a subjective or intuitive thing. "Mind is li. How can there be affairs and li outside the mind?" he asked. "The substance of the mind is the nature and the nature is li. Therefore, since there is the mind of filial love, hence there is the li of filial piety. . . . And since there is the mind of loyalty to the sovereign, hence there is the li of loyalty."[7]

Wang Yang-ming emphasized the importance of a person acting upon the truth as he individually perceives it. He spoke of the unity of knowledge and action: "There have never been people who know but do not act. Those who are supposed to know but do not act simply do not yet know."[8] This thesis that the truth can be apprehended subjectively and that the individual must act upon it held special appeal for the samurai. The Wang Yang-ming school thus had a particularly strong following at the end of the Edo period in those han, such as Satsuma and Chōshū, where militant activists emerged who participated in the political movements leading to the downfall of the Bakufu.

The founder of the Wang Yang-ming school in Japan was Nakae Tōju (1608–1648). He was attracted to the philosophy by the thesis that truth is to be grasped intuitively, and that one had to act upon the truth so apprehended. In accordance with this tenet, Tōju believed that the way to clarify "the illustrious virtue" was to have "the mind read the mind." He focused upon the Confucian virtue of filial piety as an ideal of tremendous importance because of his belief that it constituted the very essence of man. This was the principle that distinguished man from the birds and the beasts. Tōju gave special emphasis to this quality because he was searching for a principle that would be common to all men and could thus serve as the basis for a moral outlook that would encompass all elements of the society.

Tōju's disciple, Kumazawa Banzan (1619–1691) denied that he belonged to any particular school of Confucianism and asserted that his source of ideas was the ancient sages. He claimed that he was willing to adopt the best aspects of both the Chu Hsi and Wang Yang-ming schools. He departed radically, however, from the Chu Hsi philosophy by embracing the concept that the principle of all things was located in the human mind. "Everyone knows," he contended, "That myriad principles and the mind are one. Myriad things in heaven and earth do not exist outside of the mind."[9]

Banzan may have made a greater impact on the society than did his master, but his influence was similarly limited primarily to the samurai class. As a good Confucian he believed that the samurai had to follow the Way in order to qualify as the ruling class. It was for this reason that he focused upon ethical conduct and maintained that the samurai should strive to become like the scholar-officials of ancient China.

Banzan was a staunch supporter of the welfare of the peasants for he insisted that "the foundation of the nation is the people, and the foundation of the people is food."[10] His concern over the peasantry's economic difficulties led him to favor a return to the era of the warrior-farmers, that is, to the time before the class system was devised to separate the samurai and peasants into distinct classes. According to Banzan, taxes were low before the class division occurred. Afterwards, the tax burden on the peasants was increased in order to support the samurai and enable the warrior class to live in the castle towns. As an adviser to the lord of Bizen, he managed to have his plan tested but found that it was received unfavorably by both the samurai and the peasants.

Another reason for the difficulties of the peasantry, according to Banzan, was the rise of the merchant class and a money economy. To eliminate the consequent hardships imposed on the peasantry, he advocated a return to a rice economy. In this sense he may be labeled a reactionary. In order to relieve the lot of the people to some extent, he also urged a less stringent enforcement of "laws and etiquette." He believed that the rules of proper conduct and the laws of his day failed to reform bad men but caused hardships to honest men.

ANCIENT LEARNING

The other Confucian circle that challenged the orthodox scholars was the school of Ancient Learning. Actually, it is an oversimplification to classify these Confucians into a single school because they held divergent views and concerned themselves with different problems. The only justification for grouping them together is the fact that they all shared the belief that the essence of Confucianism was to be comprehended, not by studying what later scholars such as the Sung philosophers said, but by going directly to the texts of the ancient philosophers. The first of these philosophers of the school of Ancient Learning was Yamaga Sokō (1622–1685). He contended that the scholars of the Han, T'ang, Sung, and Ming dynasties had misled and confused the world by their interpretations of the ancient classics. Sokō claimed that since what the sages taught as recorded in the classics was self-evident, there was no need for lengthy commentaries. His criticism of the official philosophy led him into serious difficulty with the authorities, and he was banished from Edo for a time.

Sokō felt that it was necessary to justify the existence of the samurai class, which in many ways had lost its function since peace prevailed under Tokugawa rule. Consequently, he set about defining the function of the samurai and the ideal way of life for them in his *Shidō* (*The Way of the Warrior*). In essence, he argued that the samurai were the custodians of the moral principles of the land, a role the warrior could claim only if he maintained his moral superiority. Sokō agreed with the Bakufu's contention that the samurai had to be well educated in the Confucian classics and history as well as skilled in the military arts. Above all, however, the samurai had to lead lives grounded upon just principles. It was essential that they comport themselves properly in all familial and social relationships. As guardians of the Way, the samurai had the responsibility of summarily punishing any member of the common classes who transgressed against the Way.

Unlike many Confucians, particularly the Neo-Confucians who insisted upon suppressing human desires, Sokō believed that the natural expression of human desires was good as long as it was done in conformity with the rules of proper conduct. If excesses were avoided, as they definitely must be, humanity and justice were sure to prevail.

Sokō was popular among the samurai as a teacher of military science. In his later years he became a royalist and a nationalist who looked upon the imperial family as the ultimate ruling authority. The shōgun was merely overseeing state affairs on behalf of the emperor, as a good Confucian subject should. Sokō did not, however, seek to base the imperial authority on Shintoist notions of divine origin. He interpreted early Japanese history primarily in terms of Confucian concepts and explained that the emperor was to be served in the manner that a loyal Confucian subject served his king. Sokō thus set the stage for the later Confucian scholars who became supporters of the imperial court.

Sokō was also an early nationalist who sought to assert the superiority of Japan over China. He referred to Japan as the Middle Kingdom, the center of the world. He thought she was superior to China, because, as he argued, only in Japan had proper relationships between lord and subject, father and son been truly observed and the moral ideals of the sages fully manifested.

Itō Jinsai (1627–1705) is another scholar who is identified with the school of Ancient Learning although there is no direct link between him and Sokō except for their common rejection of the Chu Hsi school and insistence upon going directly to the works of the early Confucians. Jinsai gave special emphasis to the Confucian *Analects* because he held that it alone could serve as "the standard and guide for the teaching of the Way in all times." Next to the *Analects* he stressed the importance of the *Book of Mencius*, which was the key to the understanding of Confucianism. Unlike Sokō, Jinsai did not link Confucianism primarily with the samurai class. He refused to accept any of the positions offered him by a number of daimyō and remained an independent scholar, living in poverty. Jinsai's influence, nevertheless, extended to a large number of people, for during his forty years of teaching, three thousand students attended his academy. After his death, his sons and disciples carried on his work.

Jinsai rejected the Neo-Confucian distinction between li and ch'i as well as the theory that li governs all things including human nature and moral principles. He restricted li to physical things and separated the Way of Man, which was his primary concern, from this. The Way of Man and the moral principles that constitute it are not, according to Jinsai, principles grounded upon the natural world, or human nature, which is part of the natural world. They are *ideas* and as such they exist independently.

Jinsai was not greatly interested in metaphysical theories; he was concerned primarily with practical morality. He placed special emphasis on benevolence, which he described as "a compassionate and loving heart reaching everywhere," and he considered this to be the ultimate goal of learning in Confucianism.[11]

Another Confucian scholar who defied the orthodox school and charted an independent course was Ogyū Sorai (1666–1728). He too emphasized the importance of studying the ancient Chinese texts and was known as a great Sinologist. He believed that in order to understand the Way of the sages, one had to understand ancient terms. Philological studies were extremely important, according to Sorai, because the meaning of words change in time and thus the true meaning of ancient terms could not be understood by applying later meanings of words to them. He also emphasized the six classics,[12] that is, works believed to have been produced during the era of the Three Dynasties. The fundamental principles of Confucianism were, he contended, to be found in these classics rather than in later interpretations.

Sorai was employed by Shōgun Tsunayoshi's personal adviser, and his opinion was often solicited by Shōgun Yoshimune's high officials. He did thus exert some influence on the Bakufu. A number of brilliant scholars emerged from his academy, and his school of thought dominated the intellectual scene during the mid-eighteenth century.

In many ways Sorai was one of the most radical Confucian thinkers of the Tokugawa era. Like Jinsai, he disagreed with the Neo-Confucian theory that li governs the nature of all things, including human nature and moral principles. He believed that the Way was not based on any principle of the universe, nature, or Heaven. It was in fact created by human personalities, the ancient sage kings of the Three Dynasties. All rules, regulations, and institutions were man-made, and so there could be no such things as a "natural" order of things or an order ordained by Heaven. The Way, according to Sorai, had absolute validity even though it was created by human beings, who became sages because of this rather than because they were morally perfect. The fact that he held the order of things to be man-made opened the way for later thinkers to entertain the idea that the existing feudal order, which had been created by man, was subject to change. The emergence of this line of thinking coincided with the entrance, in the nineteenth century, of Western political thought, which also held institutions to be man-made.

In discussing the Way, Sorai rejected the concept that the cultivation of personal morality necessarily leads to good government. He separated private morality and public affairs, and concluded that the Way, as formulated by the ancient sage kings, was primarily political in character. It was concerned with "how to govern the state and preserve peace in the land."[13] To achieve these ends, the ruler may, Sorai argued, use any means he deems necessary. This somewhat Machiavellian conclusion was tempered by his belief that benevolence and wisdom were virtues required of a ruler. Sorai said that benevolence meant "giving peace and security to the people," and that wisdom had to do with "recognizing good men and raising them to positions of responsibility."

Sorai claimed that the ruler had to emphasize "rites and music, and law enforcement and political administration" in order to govern effectively. He did not consider it worthwhile to argue, as the other Confucian scholars did, about the metaphysical basis and abstract meaning of morality. It is pointless, he held, to debate the question of whether human nature is basically good, as Mencius believed, or basically evil, as Hsün Tzu (ca. 300–237 B.C.) maintained. Man's nature is what it is and cannot be changed. Man can, however, pattern his behavior after certain moral standards and in this way learn to behave virtuously. Sorai opposed the constant moralizing of the other Confucian scholars and insisted that he was primarily interested in facts and substance, not idealistic concepts about morality. In this, he was unique among the Confucians. His emphasis on philological studies and his belief that Confucian concepts were man-made rather than based upon universal or natural principles influenced the thinking of the scholars in the school of National Learning.

NATIONAL LEARNING

The truly unorthodox school of thought of the Tokugawa period did not grow directly out of Confucianism but emerged as an independent intellectual movement. This school, referred to as National Learning, was influenced by Confucianism, Shinto, and even Buddhism. Essentially, however, it was an attempt to free Japanese learning from its excessive dependence on Chinese philosophy and literature. It failed to diminish significantly the influence of Confucianism during the Tokugawa period, but it did succeed in slowly extending its influence over the intellectual world until finally, in the Meiji era, it emerged as the central force of the nationalistic intellectual movement.

There was, as we observed, a movement to establish Japanese literature as an independent entity as early as the Heian period, but this attempt was not wholly successful. When the Tokugawa government made Neo-Confucianism the orthodox philosophy, Chinese learning enjoyed increasing domination over the Japanese intellectual scene. Partly as a reaction against this, and partly as a response to the Confucian emphasis on the past and historical studies, cultural nationalism emerged as an important force. Another contributing factor in the formation of National Learning was the interest in philological studies, which was stimulated by the scholars of Ancient Learning. Actually there were two schools of nationalistic learning: one developed in Mito Han and the other formed around Motoori Norinaga. It is the latter that is generally referred to as National Learning (*kokugaku*).

The Mito school grew out of the desire of Tokugawa Mitsukuni (1628–1700), the lord of Mito and grandson of Ieyasu, to compile a definitive national history. The project, *Dainihonshi* (*The Great History of Japan*), was started in 1657 but work on it was conducted sporadically, and it was not completed until early in the twentieth century. At the outset, Mitsukuni brought together more than one hundred scholars, including many Chu Hsi scholars, to work on the history. In compiling their work these men were guided by the concept of taigi meibun, the very principle that was stressed by Chu Hsi himself when he wrote his outline history of China. In Chou China the subjects owed supreme loyalty to the king; in a corresponding notion, Mito scholars concluded that in Japan supreme loyalty was due the emperor. The shōgun, according to the scholars, was merely acting as the emperor's loyal minister. By defining the relationship in this way, they saw no conflict between the two authorities. During the last stages of the Tokugawa era, the Mito scholars became more volatile in their expression of royalist sentiments, and eventually they came to favor direct imperial rule. Mito became one of the centers of opposition to the shogunate.

The origin of the National Learning school can be traced back to Keichū (1640–1701), a Buddhist monk who was interested in examining the *Man'yōshū* from a literary viewpoint. He did not go beyond that to attempt to uncover the Way as it was embodied in ancient Japanese literature. A tenuous move was made in this direction by Kada-no-Azumamaro (1669–1736), who was interested primarily in conducting philological studies of ancient Japanese works such as the *Man'yōshū, Kojiki,* and *Nihongi.* Kada-no-Azumamaro was also interested in establishing an academy where "imperial learning" would be pursued, but it was actually his disciple, Kamo-no-Mabuchi (1697–1769), who developed the concept of National Learning. Mabuchi wanted to study ancient Japanese literature with the hope of uncovering the Way of the sages by examining ancient words and making critical analyses of their meanings. In addition to studying ancient poetry and literature, Mabuchi included Shinto prayers among his objects of study.

His interest in ancient Japan and the imperial Way made him critical of Confucianism and the Chinese influence. He rejected the Neo-Confucian concept of li (Principle) and claimed that although the theories based upon this concept sounded reasonable, the fact that li was merely an abstract principle and not a practically applicable guide to experience was proven by the chaos and disorder that had characterized Chinese history. He advocated a rejection of this abstract philosophy and a return to the simple and pure ways of ancient Japan. He observed that the Way of the sages laid down all sorts of complex rules and regulations about proper conduct, which served to create a highly artificial society that prevented man from behaving naturally.

Mabuchi blamed all of Japan's evils on the introduction of Confucianism and artificial ways of China. He went so far as to claim that before Japan fell under Chinese influence, the nation was governed in accordance with the natural ways of the universe. "Confucianism made men crafty," he explained, "and led them to worship the ruler to such an excessive degree that the whole country acquired a servant's mentality. . . . the Confucian teachings had not only repeatedly thrown China into disorder, but they now had the same effect in Japan." He went on to declare the necessity of returning to the natural and simple ways of old Japan. "In ancient times," he wrote, "words and things were few. When things are few, the heart is sincere, and there is no need for difficult teachings. All will go satisfactorily even without teachings because men are honest."[14]

This condemnation of the influence of Confucianism and the emphasis on the simple, natural ways of ancient Japan were echoed and developed further by the most prominent figure among the scholars of National Learning, Motoori Norinaga (1730–1801). Norinaga, though born into a merchant family, was trained to become a doctor and studied medicine and Confucianism in Kyoto. His interest in Japanese literature and philology brought him under Mabuchi's influence. When the two men first met, Norinaga expressed his desire to study the *Kojiki* and Mabuchi advised him to begin instead with the *Man'yōshū* because he felt it offered the best foundation for the understanding of ancient words. He claimed that without this knowledge the "true intentions of the ancients" could not be understood, and it would be impossible "to make a complete break with the Chinese mind."[15] Under the guidance of Mabuchi, Norinaga commenced work on the *Man'yōshū* and then the *Kojiki*, which he ultimately devoted thirty years to studying.

Norinaga believed that the *Kojiki* embodied the Way of the gods, which was a political philosophy, not a religion. It was the "way in which the emperor governs the land." Norinaga rejected the attempts to synthesize Confucianism and Shinto as well as the efforts to reconcile Shinto with Buddhism. These syncretic endeavors were intended to endow Shinto with theoretical doctrines, and he maintained that this was invalid because pristine Shinto did not really possess any abstract concepts at all. True Shinto, Norinaga claimed, was the Way of the gods that prevailed before the contaminating influence from the continent was felt. Consequently, he adopted a rigidly anti-Chinese, highly ethnocentric position, refusing to recognize the wisdom or superiority of the Chinese sages. He condemned them as imposters and asserted, "Sages surpass other people only in their cleverness."

In rejecting Chinese thought and all interpretations of the past by later scholars, Norinaga was even inclined, by virtue of his absolute faith in the Way of the gods, to reject rationalistic thought. "The acts of the gods," he said, "cannot be fathomed by ordinary human reasoning." He believed that man's intellect was limited and thus incapable of comprehending all things. This left open the possibility for "mysterious things," but, as he lamented, "disbelief in mysterious things has been brought about by the misguidance of the Chinese mode of thinking."

His belief in the mysteries of the universe and life enabled Norinaga to accept the *Kojiki* as factual history. The Way of the gods was created by the ancestral gods of Japan, who were not abstract concepts like the Confucian "Heaven." They were divine beings that actually existed and were in fact the ancestors of the emperors. Norinaga believed the Sun Goddess, who casts her light over the entire universe and is the founding Goddess of Japan, to be none other than the sun itself. Japan thus occupies a unique place in the world as the land favored by the gods.

An essential feature of the unique quality of Japan, according to Norinaga, was the imperial dynasty, which had survived unimpaired since it was established by the Sun Goddess. Consequently, the imperial family acquired special significance in his political thinking. The people did not belong to the shōgun or the daimyō but were subjects of the emperor. This belief did not, however, lead him to reject the Bakufu because an integral part of his philosophy was to let nature take its course. As a result, he was willing to accept the status quo. "Things of this world," he held, "are beyond the scope of the human mind and designs. . . . Thus new laws must not be put into effect casually. If one were to rule in accordance with the trend of the times, and by following earlier precedents in all things, there may be slight defects but there will be no serious mistakes." He justified the rule of the shogunate by claiming, "Great shōgun have ruled the land ever since Azumaterunokami [Ieyasu] founded the government in accordance with the designs of the Sun Goddess Amaterasu, and by the authority vested in him by the imperial court. . . . The rules and laws of the founder and succeeding shōgun are all rules and laws of the Sun Goddess Amaterasu." Consequently, he could conclude that, "to obey the laws of the day is to follow the true Way of the gods."

Like Mabuchi, Norinaga believed in following the natural path, and he rejected the artificial rules and regulations about decorum and propriety that were stressed by the Confucians. "Man's feelings," he observed, "do not always follow the dictates of his mind. They arise in man in spite of himself and are difficult to control."[16] These spontaneous feelings, he insisted, should not be curbed unnaturally. As an example of this he noted that while alien philosophies teach man to transcend the sorrow and fear of death, these teachings are essentially invalid because they are contrary to the ways of human nature. To weep at the death of someone dear is an expression of true human nature and feelings.

Norinaga believed in the superiority of Japanese over Chinese poetry and ascribed its excellence to the fact that the former expressed human sentiments in an unrestrained fashion, whereas the latter sought to keep human emotions under control. In this sense we might say that Norinaga was a romantic. He observed that before the Chinese influence acquired roots in Japan there were many poems dealing with love. The reason for this was that the ancient poets gave free expression to natural human sentiments. Poetry, Norinaga insisted, should not be used for moral, didactic purposes. That is, the poet should not choose the good and reject the bad, instead, he should express in a natural and unadorned fashion both the good and the bad. In this Norinaga clearly ran against the dominant current of didacticism so prevalent in Tokugawa society.

AGRARIAN EGALITARIANISM

A thinker who stands virtually alone in that he cannot be included in any particular school of thought was Andō Shōeki (active during the first half of the eighteenth century), who rejected all the existing philosophies and religions. Shōeki was a physician who came from northern Japan, where the impoverishment of the peasantry was most severe. He was a forgotten figure until the twentieth century when his multivolume work was discovered.

Angered by the unjust system that exploited the peasantry, and motivated by his compassion for them, Shōeki became one of the harshest critics of the existing institutions and ideologies. He was not, however, an active revolutionary, and his views were known only to a small circle of friends. He traveled extensively and lived in Edo, Kyoto, Osaka, and Nagasaki, but he does not appear to have exerted a significant influence over the thinking of his age. He does, nevertheless, stand out as an example of one of the few independent-minded Tokugawa thinkers, and as a formulator of a uniquely utilitarian, egalitarian philosophy.

Shōeki regarded the existing order as an unjust system established by the usurpers of the people's land. "Rulers and sages," he charged, "have taken the country which was given by Heaven to the multitudes as their property, and turned it into their own domain from one end of the land to the other."[17] He believed that the agrarian class constituted the backbone of the society, and he was highly critical of the other classes. The samurai were corrupt and flattered their superiors while oppressing their inferiors; the artisans concerned themselves only with profits; the merchants relied on their clever tongues to make money and lead lives of comfort and ease. Only the peasants were engaged in "honest living by direct cultivation." Shōeki believed the country had fallen into a desperate plight, and the root of the problem, he said, could be found in the existing class system. Simply stated, the consumers of rice had increased while the producers had not, and this plunged the country into terrible difficulties. "All this arises from the errors of the ancient sages," he wrote, "who created the four classes and discriminated between them, whereas originally all men were equal, one with the other."

Shōeki was severe in his criticism of the teachings of the sages, and like the Taoists and Rousseau, he believed that before "learning and civilization" arose man was free, happy, equal, and moral. The invention of writing and the emergence of many religions and philosophies gave rise to illusions and superstitions that served to replace the simplicity and purity of the "original world of Nature." He berated those who did nothing but talk while remaining idle and gluttonous, not producing "a single grain of rice." What the so-called saints and sages had said, he asserted, was less useful than "horse-dung."

Shōeki's touchstone was utility, not abstract moral concepts or theories. Ideologically his point of departure was the necessity of satisfying man's basic material needs. "Does the theory contribute to the economic well-being of man?" is the question he asked of all schools of thought. "Direct cultivation and happy eating, direct weaving and happy clothing—there is no Way but this. Talking of thousands of ways is false." Shōeki considered that the ideal society was one in which everybody performed economically productive work, following the course of nature and living in harmony. "In Nature there is neither order nor disorder. The people, all alike, cultivate as one man." In such a society there would be no need for anyone to rule over others. Man's natural activity, according to Shōeki, was to till the soil. Thus, if everyone engaged in "direct cultivation" complete freedom and equality would prevail because no one would have to take anything from or oppress his fellow man.

THE CULTURE OF THE TOWNSPEOPLE

In theory the townspeople were at the bottom of the social structure, but in fact they had acquired a great deal of economic power and had emerged as the most energetic and creative element in Tokugawa society. Tokugawa culture was, in reality, largely the creation of the townsmen. A high point in the economic well-being and cultural activities of the townspeople was reached in the Genroku period (this era name technically refers only to the years 1688–1703, but in practice this period actually encompasses a decade or more on both ends, thus covering at least the thirty years of Shōgun Tsunayoshi's rule, 1680–1709). This is not meant to suggest that the creative work of the townspeople promptly ceased with the end of the Genroku era. It was sustained to some extent throughout the remaining years of the Tokugawa period. The townsmen made lasting impressions on Japanese culture through their contributions to woodblock prints, haiku, novels, and drama—in both Kabuki and puppet plays.

This outburst of creative energy can be explained in part by the fact that the townspeople lacked outlets for their considerable wealth and energy in the political realm. Consequently, they applied themselves to the pursuit of physical and material pleasures that in turn stimulated the rise of town culture. The Kabuki and puppet plays emerged as popular forms of entertainment for the townsmen. The brothels where the wealthy merchants went to seek their pleasures provided material for the storytellers, the dramatists, and the woodblock artists. The various arts and crafts were able to flourish to the considerable extent that they did because the townspeople had the money to spend on expensive clothing, lacquerware, screens, tea bowls, books, prints, etc.

The Genroku era is known for the townsmen's exuberant, colorful, extravagant, and often ostentatious way of life. The mores, values, attitudes, and behavior of the rich merchants of Osaka, Kyoto, and Edo had a unique aura that fixed the tone of Genroku culture. It was Osaka that originally set the pace, for here the wealthy merchants dominated society. Kyoto was still under the cultural dominance of the court aristocracy, and Edo was under the control of the ruling samurai class. Engelbert Kaempfer, a German doctor who visited Japan in the late seventeenth century, said of Osaka,

> Even what tends to promote luxury, and to gratify all sensual pleasures, may be had at as easy a rate here as anywhere. For this reason the Japanese call Osacca the universal theatre of pleasures and diversions. . . . Hence it is no wonder, that numbers of strangers and travellers daily resort thither, chiefly rich people, as to a place, where they can spend their time and money with much greater satisfaction, than perhaps any where else in the Empire.[18]

In their pursuit of material happiness the wealthy townspeople were relatively free from the rigid code of ethics that regulated the conduct of the samurai. The literature of this era yields a vivid picture of their way of life, and it would be quite accurate to describe it as a blatantly hedonistic mode of existence. They lived in what was referred to as the *Ukiyo*, the floating world where the pleasures and joys of life were pursued without a thought for the future. This entailed "living for the moment, gazing at the moon, snow, blossoms, and autumn leaves, enjoying wine, women, and song, and, in general, drifting with the current of life 'like a gourd floating downstream.'"[19]

The wives of rich merchants vied with one another to gain recognition as the most elegantly attired lady of the land. Young men went about dressed as dandies, and homosexuality became widespread. Wealthy merchants replaced the samurai as patrons of the brothels, where the hedonism of the pleasure-seeking townsmen was paid for by the heartbreak and degradation of the girls that had been sold into slavery.

PROSE FICTION

The hedonistic, erotic life enjoyed by the townspeople was reflected in their literature, that is, in the works described as *ukiyo-zōshi* (notes of the floating world). The originator and master of this form of prose fiction was Ihara Saikaku (1642–1693) of Osaka. Saikaku, a former merchant, began his literary career as a haiku poet and wrote primarily about the love lives of the men and women of his world. At one time he composed 23,500 haiku in twenty-four hours, a feat that attests to his prolific imagination and zestful energy. He wrote his first humorous, erotic novel, *The Man Who Spent His Life in Love*, in 1682 and produced more than two dozen volumes of this kind during the next decade. In his first book he described the love life of a rake whose amorous exploits began at the precocious age of eight and continued into lecherous old age. The hero has 3,742 women before he turns philosophical at the age of sixty. "I've been around every one of the pleasure quarters in this wide world, till I find," he says, "I'm quite emaciated by love; and now at last the floating world has lost all attraction for me."[20] His "emaciated" condition, however, does not stop him from sailing off in search of the fabulous Island of Women.

Saikaku did not moralize in his love stories; instead, he displayed an optimistic and sympathetic attitude toward man's foibles by depicting the exploits of his characters in a realistic but good-humored fashion. His novels demonstrate his keen awareness of the serious conflict between love and duty that confronted the lovers of the floating world. This was a theme that was also of particular interest to the playwright Chikamatsu (see page 175).

In his later works Saikaku dealt with the economic life of the townspeople. He was an enthusiastic supporter of the system that enabled clever, resourceful, and diligent men to amass great wealth. This did not blind him, however, to the economic hardships besetting the townsmen of the lower class who were constantly involved in a desperate struggle to make ends meet. Despite his awareness of the negative aspects of his society, he retained a fundamentally optimistic and positive outlook. The qualities needed for success in business, he held, were frugality, persistence, a pleasant manner, honesty, and imagination.

The popularity of the works of humorous and satirical writers like Saikaku attest to two significant facts: first, the printing of books had become common by the Genroku period and second, many Genroku townsmen, though not erudite, were at least literate. In numerous cities there existed something that was comparable to a lending library where books could be borrowed inexpensively.

Many didactic tales reflecting the moralism of the ruling class were written by Tokugawa writers. The master of this kind of prose fiction was

Takizawa Bakin (1767–1848). He was born into the warrior class but married into a footwear merchant's family in order to be able to pursue his writing career. Bakin devoted twenty-eight years of his life to the completion of his major work, *Nansō Satomi Hakkenden*, which consists of ninety-eight parts. The novel is set in the period of the Warring States and has eight heroes, each having a noble dog for his ancestor. The dogs represent the Confucian virtues of benevolence, righteousness, propriety, wisdom, loyalty, sincerity, filial piety, and obedience. Bakin made clear distinctions between good and evil, for his primary goal was "to encourage the good and chastise the bad." This was a theme that had the approval of the ruling authorities.

Stories designed to entertain or morally uplift the townspeople continued to be written, and they were widely read during the remainder of the Edo period. The quality of the literature declined considerably as many writers sought merely to imitate the earlier masters.

THEATER

Another area that reflected the culture of the townspeople was the theater. The puppet theater (*Jōruri* or *Bunraku*) that originated in the Muromachi period as a ballad-drama and saw the addition of marionettes in the early seventeenth century was perfected during the Genroku era. The Kabuki also gained a solid footing in this period.

Osaka was the center of the puppet plays. In these shows puppets perform actions that are described by a singer-narrator who is accompanied by *samisen* (a three-stringed instrument) players. The puppets are about one-third life-size, and each one requires three men to operate it. Official restrictions that were placed on Kabuki for moral reasons led to the domination of the theatrical world by the Jōruri by the middle of the eighteenth century. In order to compete with this form of theater, Kabuki borrowed heavily from it both in the style and in the actual plays performed. By the end of the eighteenth century Kabuki regained its popularity and has remained the leading dramatic form in Japan to the present.

The nature of Kabuki is described by a leading authority as follows:

Kabuki fuses into a single form the arts of music, dance, acting, literature, as well as graphic and plastic arts. . . . Each of the arts within the combined art of Kabuki is responsible for certain effects. Music gives Kabuki its dynamics, its rhythm, and its continuous pace. Dance makes the actors concentrate on grace and determines a large part of Kabuki's special kind of movement and gesticulation. Acting adds the qualities of pantomime, speech, and declamation, and of course provides the important dramatic factor. . . . Graphic arts are utilized in the wide variety of scenery, properties, and costumes. . . . Plastic arts are rivalled in the frequent poses and studied groupings of the actors.[21]

Spectacle, providing the framework for all this, is specifically designed to please the eye, which is the primary objective of Kabuki. Color and motion are thus the two most important elements in this kind of drama, and they serve to make Kabuki a much more spectacular dramatic form than the Nō plays. Ingenious mechanical devices such as the revolving stage, trapdoors, and the passageway that runs directly through the audience enabled the Kabuki producers to solve many technical problems and thereby heighten the dramatic effects of the plays.

The Kabuki theater comprised one of the key elements of the Genroku world of pleasure. The colorful day-long performances attracted people from all ranks of society, "from shop-boys to samurai." Kabuki actors became the focus of popular attention, gaining as much fame as today's movie stars. Theatrical giants like Ichikawa Danjurō I and Onoe Kikugorō I founded acting dynasties that have survived to the present day and have sustained the essence of the Kabuki theater.

The playwright who made the greatest contribution toward increasing the repertory of the puppet and Kabuki plays was Chikamatsu Monzaemon (1653–1725), who wrote about one hundred and sixty plays. He was born into a minor samurai family but joined the ranks of the townspeople as an unemployed samurai. Chikamatsu wrote his first play when he was thirty and devoted the rest of his life to writing historical dramas and domestic plays about the ordinary people of his time. When he wrote about love affairs, the plot usually involved a hero who was either a samurai or a townsman, and a heroine who was a courtesan from the brothels. The play generally focused upon the conflict between love and duty or *ninjō* (human feelings) and *giri* (social and moral obligations). Frequently, the only way out of this conflict for the lovers was suicide.

The harsh demands of giri often necessitated heartless treatment of loved ones. Fortunately, however, ninjō tempered such actions. In one of his plays, a woman is almost forced to disown her son because of the dictates of giri, but ninjō leads her instead to steal money in order to help him. Ninjō, then, humanizes giri, which "denies the individual's right to be happy at the expense of society. In so doing it preserves society, as ninjō unchecked by giri must eventually destroy it."[22]

WOODBLOCK PRINTING AND PAINTING

Another art form that emerged from the world of the townspeople was woodblock printing, known as *ukiyo-e* (paintings of the floating world). The prints were made not only to be appreciated in themselves but also to illustrate the stories written by Saikaku and other novelists. Saikaku had done the illustrations for some of his works himself, but the artist who is usually given credit for making the woodblock print an important art form, Hishikawa Moronobu (1618–1694), also did some illustrations for him. Moronobu was followed by a galaxy of prominent woodblock artists: Harunobu, Utamaro, Sharaku, Hokusai, Hiroshige, to name a few. These artists created a sense of movement, form, and atmosphere by relying solely on line and color. They made no use at all of chiaroscuro or linear perspective because they did not want to give the prints a sense of the three dimensions; they were not to be realistic paintings. These artists did, nevertheless, succeed in conveying a feeling of gracefulness, sensuality, and warmth in their depiction of lovers, courtesans, and actors. In landscape paintings, artists such as Hokusai were able to capture the atmospheric tone of the scene and convey a sense of dynamic force and energy.

Among the more prominent of the woodblock artists was Suzuki Harunobu (1725–1770), who, it is believed, was the first artist to produce a full polychrome print. He did not restrict himself to conventional colors to brighten his prints but experimented with rosy pink skies, kelly green earth, jet black skies, etc. As was the style with other woodblock artists, his subjects lacked individuality and consequently looked rather similar. His primary interest was not in depicting individual personalities but in portraying the essence of femininity through the creation of doll-like creatures. Harunobu's trademark is his delicate and coquettish feminine figures. Feminine frailty is conveyed through the depiction of abnormally small hands and feet on his subjects. In order to accentuate their sensuous, erotic characteristics, Harunobu never has the ladies stand erect but has their heads and bodies curved gracefully. The lines emphasize the richness of the fabrics adorning the figures and this adds considerably to their sensuousness.

Kitagawa Utamaro (1753–1806) is also known for his sensuous feminine figures. His subjects, more voluptuous than Harunobu's, are generally tall and willowy with elongated faces. Many of them are seminudes, and the lines are ingeniously used to convey a sense of the smoothness and softness of the flesh. Utamaro was inclined to concentrate on the head and the upper part of the body, usually dispensing with the setting.

In contrast to Harunobu and Utamaro, who focused upon delicate or sensuous women, Tōshūsai Sharaku (d. 1801) concentrated upon Kabuki actors. Departing from his activities as an obscure Nō actor, he produced about one hundred and forty-five prints in ten months during 1794/1795. He realistically depicted the intense facial expressions and exaggerated poses employed by Kabuki actors at climactic moments in the plays. His prints lack the gentleness and charm of the other artists' works, but because the lines are stronger, they convey a powerful sense of vigor, vitality, and movement. His unconventional realism did not endear him to this contemporaries, who were accustomed to stylized portraits of handsome actors, and he disappeared from the public scene after his very brief career as a woodblock artist.

Katsushika Hokusai (1760–1849) and Andō Hiroshige (1797–1858), known for their scenic color prints, are perhaps better known in the West than the other woodblock artists. Hokusai, who led a flamboyant and turbulent life, is regarded as a giant among the Tokugawa printmakers. He first called attention to himself by painting an enormous portrait of the Bodhidharma, which was 60 feet high. He then drew two sparrows that were so tiny they could be seen only with a magnifying glass. He perfected his art late in life and produced his masterpieces after he was sixty. Among the better known of his prints are the series on *The Thirty-Six Views of Fuji, Waterfalls, Bridges,* and *Imagery of the Poets.* The last series shows great poets placed

This and the following two illustrations are color woodblock prints by Tokugawa masters of *ukiyo-e* ("pictures of the floating world"). This page, "Lovers Sharing an Umbrella" by Harunobu (1725–1770).

"The Great Wave," a print from the series "Thirty-Six Views of Mt. Fuji" by Hokusai (1760–1849).

in a variety of natural settings, such as Li Po admiring a tremendous waterfall. He also produced thousands of sketches of human beings in every conceivable posture and situation.

His prints project an aura of majesty, as manifested in some of his views of Mt. Fuji, and a tremendous sense of force and energy, as seen in his prints of waterfalls and towering waves. Hokusai was also a master of dramatic composition who was able to use color in such a way as to capture the unique atmosphere of a particular moment. A striking example of this is the *Red Fuji*, one of his masterpieces. "Light effects as a device in art reached a high watermark in this picture, and it is no wonder that it served as a source of strong inspiration to painters of the impressionist school in France."[23] Like the other woodblock artists, Hokusai produced erotic prints. His "spring pictures" are considered to be the most profound, constituting "one of the major accomplishments of ukiyo-e."

Hokusai was a dedicated craftsman who devoted his entire life to this art. At the age of seventy-five he wrote,

Since the age of six I have had the habit of drawing forms of objects. Although from about fifty I have often published my pictorial works, before the seventieth year none is of much value. At the age of seventy-three I was able to fathom slightly the structure of birds, animals, insects, and fish, the growth of grasses and trees. Thus perhaps at eighty my art may improve greatly; at ninety it may reach real depth, and at one hundred it may become divinely inspired. At one hundred and ten every dot and every stroke may be as if living.[24]

He signed this essay, "The old man crazy about drawing."

Hiroshige's series, *Fifty-Three Stations of the Tōkaidō*, is probably the best known work of the Tokugawa woodblock artists. Hiroshige was interested in the relationship between light and natural phenomena and sought to capture the moods of nature and the atmospheric conditions—the mist, the moonlight, the raindrops, and the falling snow—of the different seasons. He was particularly successful with his snow scenes, as he made effective use of blank space while taking full advantage of the beauty of Japanese paper. His rain scenes were rendered in a unique and refreshing fashion by his use of bold parallel lines to indicate rain. "No one," writes an art historian, "had revealed to us so freshly the beauty of the rain; rain showering like light javelins that shine in the returning sun, or mingling with the mist and with the wind that bends and tosses a long ridge of blotted pines, or descending in straight rods that hiss on ground or water, or trailing delicate threads that caress the trembling willows."[25]

Japanese woodblock artists profoundly influenced the French impressionists of the nineteenth century. In particular it was the manner in which light and atmosphere were treated in the scenic color prints by Hokusai and Hiroshige that impressed the French artists.

Traditional decorative art—screen paintings and paintings on lacquer and pottery—also flourished during this era. One of the most prominent of the decorative style painters, and certainly the greatest lacquer artist of the age, Ogata Kōrin (1658–1716), emerged from among the townspeople. His works are known for their simplicity and elegance of form and color as well as the forcefulness of the brushstrokes. His most famous work is a pair of screens representing a row of irises with their dark-and-light blue blossoms and soft-green leaves arranged in an overall design that is set against a gold background.

An artist who painted in a more naturalistic style than the men who preceded him was Maruyama Ōkyo (1733–1795). A folding screen depicting pine trees in the snow reveals his preoccupation with modeling as a technique for evincing the roundness of forms. His paintings also possess more realistic details than the works of other decorative style painters.

A school of painting that evidently emerged as a reaction against the naturalistic school of Ōkyo was the *Nanga* (Southern painting), which sought to follow the Southern School of China. Nanga painters relied upon inspiration rather than a studied technique, and they regarded painting as an activity that educated men pursued for enjoyment. The best artist to emerge from this school, Ike-no-Taiga (1723–1776), showed an impressive mastery of calligraphic lines and subtle tone variations. His paintings are characterized by a brush-dotted texture and a rolling rhythm. A master haiku poet, Buson (1716–1783), was also a Nanga painter.

In pottery, porcelainware came to be produced in the Edo period. Such products as *Imari* wares with their elaborate decorations and rich colors, and *Kakiemon* wares with their elegant decorations on a pure white body

"Rain Shower on Ōhashi Bridge" by Hiroshige (1797–1858). Courtesy of The Cleveland Museum of Art, gift of J. H. Wade.

gained renown even in the West. The Kakiemon wares in particular were imitated by the porcelain makers of Holland, Germany, and England.

HAIKU

Another significant cultural development of the Tokugawa era was the emergence of haiku—a seventeen syllable poetry—as a major literary form. It is usually identified with the culture of the townspeople even though the greatest haiku poet, Matsuo Bashō (1644–1694), was born into a samurai family and traveled around the countryside as a Buddhist priest in order to avoid the bustling towns. Haiku was popular among the townspeople—for that matter, it was greatly favored by men of every walk of life.

Haiku is linked intimately with Zen Buddhism. Suzuki Daisetsu points out that haiku "ought to be an expression of one's inner feeling altogether devoid of the sense of ego. The haiku poet in this sense must also be a Zen-man." In explaining the brevity of the haiku poem, he remarks, "At the supreme moment of life and death we just utter a cry or take to action, we never argue, we never give ourselves up to a lengthy talk. Feelings refuse to be conceptually dealt with, and a haiku is not the product of intellection. Hence its brevity and significance." Therefore, "a haiku does not express ideas but . . . it puts forward images reflecting intuition."[26]

Its extreme brevity occasionally makes haiku sound flat, pointless, and even nonsensical when it is translated into another language. Donald Keene explains that the effectiveness of haiku depends upon the realization of the basic principle that the poem have these two elements: a general condition and the momentary perception. "The nature of the two elements varies but there should be the two electric poles between which the spark will leap for the haiku to be effective; otherwise it is no more than a brief statement."[27] As an example, here is one of the most frequently cited haiku by Bashō:

The ancient pond
A frog leaps in
The sound of the water.

In this haiku Bashō was seeking to express two principles, change and permanence. The first line evokes the eternal component: the timeless, motionless water of the pond. The second line gives the momentary element in the form of the frog's movement. The point where the momentary intersects the eternal is the splash of the water.[28]

In his book *Narrow Road of Oku*, Bashō discusses the circumstances that induced him to compose some of his poems. He mentions the time, for example, when he came upon Minamoto-no-Yoshitsune's last battle scene and, as he sat there weeping, he recalled this poem by the T'ang poet, Tu Fu:

Countries may fall,
But their rivers and mountains remain.
When spring comes to the ruined castle,
The grass is green again.

The result of this experience was his writing of the following haiku:

The summer grasses—
Of brave soldiers' dreams
The aftermath.[29]

The keen sense of finesse possessed by a great haiku poet distinguishes him from an ordinary poet, as this story about Bashō will illustrate. When he was just starting out as a haiku teacher, he was out walking one day with a student who, upon seeing the darting dragonflies in the field, composed this haiku:

Red dragonflies!
Take off their wings,
And they are pepper pods!

Bashō is said to have exclaimed, "No! That is not haiku. If you wish to make a haiku on the subject, you must say:

Red pepper pods!
Add wings to them
and they are dragonflies![30]

Haiku has come to be composed by people from all segments of the society since Bashō's days, and in this sense it can be said to have contributed to the growth of cultural democracy in Japan. In the Tokugawa era even the peasantry produced a great haiku poet, Issa (1763–1827). He wrote of insects, birds, and animals, manifesting a strong compassion for all living things. For instance, seeing a fly about to be swatted, Issa felt that it was praying for mercy and cried out:

Oh, don't swat
the fly! He wrings his hands!
He wrings his feet![31]

EDUCATION

One further noteworthy aspect of Tokugawa culture is the fairly widespread diffusion of learning that took place. Education of the common people was carried on in the terakoya (temple schools) by Buddhist and Shinto priests in the rural areas and frequently by masterless warriors in the towns. Children were taught the rudiments of reading and writing and the use of the abacus. Girls also attended these schools and learned the skills and modes of behavior deemed at the time to be suitable to their sex.

A considerable number of children successfully learned how to read and write in the towns. In the villages, however, education was largely restricted to the children of prominent farmers. The number of terakoya increased greatly toward the latter part of the Tokugawa period, and, although no accurate figures are available, it is estimated that perhaps there were from ten to fifteen thousand temple schools in existence. Twenty or thirty pupils attended an average-sized terakoya.

The children of the samurai were especially well educated. They attended private schools or han academies where they were taught calligraphy, the Chinese classics, some arithmetic, etiquette, and the military arts. In the later years of the Edo period, the han academies began to admit some students from the common classes. It is believed that literacy among the samurai men was almost 100 percent. This is a rather astonishing achievement. Overall, slightly more than 40 percent of all boys and about 10 percent of all girls were receiving some kind of formal education outside of their homes by the end of the Tokugawa era. In 1870 the literacy rate in Japan was considerably higher than that which exists in most underdeveloped nations today. It is likely that Japan compared favorably in this respect with some of the European countries of the nineteenth century. In light of this, it is not at all surprising that Japan was able to launch so successful a program of modernization and industrialization after she opened her doors to the outside world again.

THE STATE OF BUDDHISM

In addition to performing funeral services, Buddhist priests did contribute to the education of the common people, but little creative work was actually done by them in the way of furthering the spiritual well-being of the masses. They had captive clienteles because everyone was required to affiliate with a Buddhist temple, and their work with the laymen tended, as a result, to fall into a regular routine.

Buddhism as a religious and philosophical movement remained relatively stagnant during the Tokugawa period. The main intellectual activities of the various sects consisted in the formulation of doctrinal systems and orthodox dogmas. None of the sects challenged the orthodox philosophy, Neo-Confucianism, and they all seemed content to cooperate willingly with the ruling authorities. The Bakufu had some difficulty with a small segment of the Nichiren Sect who refused to participate in officially sponsored ecumenical religious functions. This was the only group that caused any trouble and eventually those who did not cooperate were suppressed. Some of the dissenters managed to survive by going underground, much like the Christians did.

A renaissance of a sort took place in the Zen Rinzai Sect under the leadership of Hakuin (1685–1768). He systematized the existing kōan and created a number of new ones, formulated a method of achieving satori, and trained a large number of disciples. The kōan system and method of training that Hakuin established have remained in effect to the present. He insisted upon continuous zazen practices and kōan study. The discipline of a Zen disciple, Hakuin taught, did not cease with the attainment of satori, because the training that followed was of equal or greater importance. He emphasized the importance of moral behavior, without which satori was not possible, and the value of good health, which was necessary for the rigorous training. Hakuin was also a talented painter and calligrapher.

The age of creativity that characterized the Genroku period and the few decades that followed it also coincided with the period in which the Bakufu began to feel, with increasing intensity, the pressures of the growing economic crisis. We shall now turn to an investigation of this and other related problems that plagued the Bakufu for the last remaining century of its rule.

NOTES

1. The quotations from Confucius and Mencius that appear in this chapter were selected primarily from Wing-Tsit Chan, *Source Book in Chinese Philosophy* (Princeton, N.J.: Princeton University Press, 1963), pp. 18 ff.

2. Herman Ooms, *Tokugawa Ideology, Early Constructs, 1570–1680* (Princeton, N.J.: Princeton University Press, 1985), pp. 72 ff.

3. On Chu Hsi's views see Wing-Tsit Chan, *op. cit.*, pp. 588 ff., and Fung Yu-lan, *A History of Chinese Philosophy*, trans. Dirk Bodde, 2 vols. (Princeton, N.J.: Princeton University Press, 1953), vol. 2, pp. 533 ff.

4. Watsuji Tetsurō, *Nihon Rinri Shisōshi* (*A History of Japanese Ethical Thought*), 2 vols. (Tokyo: Iwanami, 1952), vol. 2, p. 416.

5. Maruyama Masao, *Nihon Seijishisōshi Kenkyū* (*Studies in the History of Japanese Political Thought*) (Tokyo: Tōkyō Daigaku Shuppankai, 1954), p. 155.

6. The quotations from Muro Kyūsō are from Nagata Hiroshi, *Nihon Tetsugaku-shisō-shi* (*A History of Japanese Philosophical Thought*) (Tokyo: Mikasa Shobō, 1938), pp. 112–16.

7. Fung Yu-lan, *A Short History of Chinese Philosophy* (New York: Macmillan, 1953), p. 309.

8. W. T. de Bary *et al.*, eds., *Sources of Chinese Tradition* (New York: Columbia University Press, 1960), p. 579.

9. Nagata, *op. cit.*, p. 81.

10. Naramoto Tatsuya, ed., *Nihon no Shisōka* (*The Thinkers of Japan*) (Tokyo: Mainichi Shimbunsha, 1954), p. 117.

11. Ryusaku Tsunoda, W. T. de Bary, and Donald Keene, eds., *Sources of Japanese Tradition* (New York: Columbia University Press, 1958), p. 421.

12. The books of *Odes, History, Music, Changes,* the *Rites of Chou*, and the *Spring and Autumn Annals*.

13. The quotations from Sorai and analyses of his thinking are based on Maruyama Masao, *op. cit.*

14. Tsunoda *et al.*, *Sources of Japanese Tradition*, pp. 517, 519.

15. This and the following quotations from Norinaga are from *Motoori Norinaga Zenshū* (*The Complete Works of Motoori Norinaga*), 6 vols. (Tokyo: Yoshikawa Hanshichi, 1900–1903), vol. 4, pp. 49, 607, 393, 387, 853, 565, 556, and vol. 6, p. 219.

16. This and the following quotations from Norinaga are from Tsunoda *et al.*, *Sources of Japanese Tradition*, p. 534.

17. The quotations from Andō Shōeki are from E. H. Norman, "Andō Shōeki and the Anatomy of Japanese Feudalism," in *Transactions of the Asiatic Society of Japan*, series 3, vol. 2, *passim*.

18. Engelbert Kaempfer, *History of Japan*, 3 vols., trans. J. G. S. Schenchzer (Glasgow: MacLehose, 1906), vol. 3, pp. 6–7.

19. Howard Hibbett, *The Floating World in Japanese Fiction* (New York: Grove, 1960), p. 11.

20. *Ibid.*, pp. 42–43.

21. Faubion Bowers, *Japanese Theatre* (New York: Hill & Wang, 1959), pp. 177–78.

22. Monzaemon Chikamatsu, *The Major Plays of Chikamatsu*, trans. Donald Keene (New York: Columbia University Press, 1961), p. 35.

23. Tokuzo Sagara, *Japanese Fine Arts* (Tokyo: Japan Travel Bureau, 1955), p. 198.

24. Robert T. Paine and Alexander C. Soper, *The Art and Architecture of Japan* (Baltimore, Md.: Penguin, 1955), p. 153.

25. Lawrence Binyon, *Painting in the Far East* (New York: Dover, 1959), pp. 266–67.

26. Daisetsu T. Suzuki, *Zen and Japanese Culture* (New York: Pantheon, 1959), pp. 225–27, 240.

27. Donald Keene, *Japanese Literature: An Introduction for Western Readers* (New York: Grove, 1955), pp. 40–41.

28. *Ibid.*, p. 39. Reprinted by permission of Donald Keene.

29. Donald Keene, ed., *Anthology of Japanese Literature from the Earliest Era to the Mid-Nineteenth Century* (New York: Grove, 1955), p. 369.

30. Harold G. Henderson, *An Introduction to Haiku* (Garden City, N.Y.: Doubleday, 1958), pp. 17–18. Reprinted by permission of Doubleday.

31. *Ibid.*, p. 133. (The author has substituted "swat" for "mistreat" in Henderson's translation.) Reprinted by permission of Doubleday.

CHAPTER 9

THE LATE
TOKUGAWA PERIOD

POLITICAL DEVELOPMENTS

In 1745 Shōgun Yoshimune turned over the shogunate to his son, Ieshige, but he remained the de facto ruler until his death in 1751. It is not surprising that Ieshige proved to be a rather ineffective shōgun— he was an invalid with a rather serious speech defect. During the reign of the next shōgun, Ieharu, chamberlain Tanuma Okitsugu and his son became influential figures wielding great power. In fact, during the last fourteen years of Ieharu's reign, Okitsugu, acting as senior councilor, held near dictatorial power. As a result, Ieharu's regime (1760–1786) is referred to as the Tanuma era.

Unlike Yoshimune, who sought to solve the Bakufu's economic difficulties by reducing expenses, encouraging frugality, and increasing agricultural production, Okitsugu hoped to resolve the difficulties by debasing coinage, granting monopolistic rights to wholesale dealers in return for payment of fees, and taxing the merchant guilds. In order to reverse the unfavorable balance of trade and curb the outflow of bullion, he sought to increase exports. He also initiated various reclamation projects. There is little question that Okitsugu sought to serve the public good; but there is also no doubt about the fact that he was more than casually interested in advancing his own private interests in the hopes of accumulating a vast fortune. Consequently, standards of rectitude began to decline throughout the official hierarchy, while graft and bribery, though surely engaged in to some extent under previous administrations, became widespread practices. One observer noted, "Villagers rush about in agitation crying out that officials are coming to assess the tribute; for days on end shrines and temples are piled high with all kinds of rare presents for them."[1]

In spite of Okitsugu's efforts to solve the Bakufu's financial difficulties, natural calamities aggravated the situation, and conditions failed to improve.

A great famine broke out between 1783 and 1787, the prices of goods soared, and rice riots occurred frequently. Okitsugu was blamed for most of the difficulties and, with the death of Ieharu, he was summarily removed from office.

Under Shōgun Ienari (1773–1841), Yoshimune's grandson, Matsudaira Sadanobu (1758–1829), emerged as the chief Bakufu official. Sadanobu had gained a reputation as an able and enlightened administrator while he was the head of a small han in northern Honshu. During the great famine of 1783, while hundreds of thousands of people starved in the neighboring han, he took measures to ensure that not a single person in his han would perish from lack of food.

The treasury was nearly depleted when Sadanobu became the Bakufu's chief councilor in 1787, a year of great floods, inflation, food shortages, and rioting. In order to cope with the crisis, Sadanobu started what has been called the Kansei Reforms (the Kansei period, for which the reforms are named, was 1789 to 1801). The policies that he adopted were conservative in nature and patterned after those of his grandfather, Yoshimune. He concentrated, for instance, on reducing expenditures and encouraging frugality. He also imposed price controls, but they proved to be ineffective. In order to be prepared to cope with future famines, he increased the Bakufu's rice reserves and required the daimyō to set aside 50 koku for every 10,000 koku of rice they collected. After reducing the expenditures of the city of Edo, he had 70 percent of the savings set aside as relief for the needy and as low interest loans for the poor. He also established a vocational training program for the unemployed and the vagrants in Edo. In 1789, in order to relieve the Bakufu's liege vassals who had fallen in debt to the rice brokers, he canceled all the debts that they had incurred before 1784 and reduced the interest rates on those incurred after 1784.

In the hope of increasing agricultural production, Sadanobu encouraged the peasants in the cities to return to the countryside. He issued sumptuary laws prohibiting them from indulging in any wasteful or extravagant activities. This was intended to foster frugality among the peasantry. He also attempted to impose standards of austerity on the townspeople; he even went so far as to attempt to tighten their moral values by curbing unlicensed prostitution, censoring books that he deemed prurient, and banning mixed bathing of persons over the age of six.

In order to cope with the rising tide of unorthodox philosophies, Sadanobu issued the Kansei ban on heterodoxy and prohibited the teaching of any philosophy other than the Chu Hsi version of Confucianism in the Bakufu's schools. He also adopted a policy of denying employment in the Bakufu to anyone who had been trained in unorthodox philosophies.

It was during this period that Russia began probing Japan's northern islands. Sadanobu was not at first concerned about this, and in fact he arrested an advocate of national defense, Hayashi Shihei, for criticizing the Bakufu for neglecting its defenses against external threats. Later he did come to recognize the need to fortify the northern coastal regions.

In spite of his strenuous efforts, Sadanobu failed to solve the basic problems of the Bakufu. He remained in office for only six years, but his puritanical asceticism did manage to cramp the life-style of influential people in the shōgun's entourage, including the ladies in the inner palace.

Sadanobu's departure was followed by an era of laxity under the leadership of the hedonistic Ienari, who was shōgun for the more than fifty years from 1786 to 1837. Even after his resignation, Ienari dominated the Bakufu until his death in 1841. Moral standards declined and graft and bribery became rampant once again. Government expenditures rose along with the considerable personal expenses of the self-indulgent shōgun (he had forty wives and concubines to support). The price of rice remained low, but the cost of other commodities rose sharply. The only steps taken by the Bakufu to deal with its financial difficulties were to repeatedly debase the coinage and make requests of wealthy merchants for financial contributions. Between 1806 and 1813 the Bakufu called upon the merchants and villagers to contribute money three times, and over 1.4 million ryō was collected. The Bakufu's difficulties, however, continued to multiply as famines broke out frequently and, as we will see later, peasant uprisings increased in size and number. In addition to the internal difficulties, pressures from the outside world were becoming more serious.

After Ienari's death another attempt at reforms was made, this time by the chief councilor, Mizuno Tadakuni (1793–1851), in what is called the Tempō Reforms. Like Sadanobu, Tadakuni also endeavored to tighten moral standards, reduce expenses, encourage frugality by issuing many sumptuary laws, and curtail extravagance in food and clothing. In addition, he restricted what he considered to be frivolous and wasteful activities, such as festivals, Kabuki, Nō, and other forms of entertainment. He even sought to curtail the operation of pawnshops, public bathhouses, hairdressers, and the like.

Like Sadanobu, Tadakuni encouraged the initiation of reclamation projects and hoped to increase agricultural production by compelling the peasants who had migrated to the cities to return to the villages. In addition, he sought to curtail secondary work such as weaving because he believed that it reduced the time the peasants could spend tilling the soil.

Tadakuni also sought to curb inflation by the fixing of wages and prices. Convinced that a free flow of goods would reduce high prices, he ended the monopolistic privileges that had been granted to the wholesalers and merchant guilds by the Tanuma administration. This of course resulted in the loss of the fees they had been paying the Bakufu, and to offset this reduction in revenues Tadakuni found it necessary to compel the wealthy Osaka merchants to donate money to the Bakufu. As another means of increasing the Bakufu's income, he sought to bring under its direct control the land held by the bannermen and daimyō in the vicinity of Edo and Osaka. This measure, however, was so vigorously opposed by the parties concerned that he was forced to abandon it. This episode served to unite the opposition against him while providing the catalyst that eventually brought about his dismissal. As was the case with Sadanobu, Tadakuni's austerity program displeased a great many people, including the shōgun's consort. As a result, he was removed from office in 1843, only two years after he had initiated the Tempō Reforms. He made a brief comeback in

1844 but was dismissed again after a short term in office. Many of his reforms were rapidly undone soon after he fell from power.

All the while he was in office Tadakuni encouraged the daimyō to follow his example by urging them to institute similar reforms in their han. Many failed to respond, but some han, such as Chōshū, did in fact initiate their own reform programs. None of these attempts were very effective, but some han did manage to reduce their expenses and tighten official control over the marketing of cash crops. During his tenure in office Tadakuni was also very much aware of the trouble China was having with the British, and he sought to strengthen his nation's military defenses by training the warriors in Western gunnery.

All the reforms initiated by the various Bakufu officials were basically ineffective because, though they were honestly intended to solve the Bakufu's economic difficulties, they were aimed at achieving this by actually preventing changes, that is, by curbing the rising merchant class and money economy. Essentially, the reform programs pointed to a return to the predominantly agrarian, natural economy of early Tokugawa. It was with the best of intentions that the reformers persisted in adopting reactionary measures. But sumptuary laws to enforce simple living and uplift the people's moral standards could not solve the Bakufu's financial problems, nor could these legal maneuvers prevent the disintegration of the closed society. The Bakufu thus approached the middle of the nineteenth century having failed to solve its basic economic difficulties. At this juncture it was confronted with a major external crisis that ultimately brought about its downfall—the arrival of Commodore Perry. Before we turn to this event, however, let us examine more closely the economic difficulties of Tokugawa society.

ECONOMIC PROBLEMS

The basic cause of Tokugawa society's problems lay in the fact that the economy was supported by an agrarian base that, though expanded, was not sufficiently broad to meet either the increasing needs of the ruling class, whose size and standard of living did not remain static, or the rising expectations of the common classes. From the end of the seventeenth century, in particular, commerce began to grow, thus creating an economy evermore incompatible with agrarianism.

Large urban centers emerged and the demand not only for basic necessities but also for what the ruling authorities regarded as luxury goods steadily increased. In order to meet these needs of the cities, the production of nonessential agricultural and industrial goods had to increase and consequently, the number and size of local business entrepreneurs, wholesale dealers, and shippers grew. The sankinkōtai system also served to stimulate economic growth by increasing commercial and industrial activities along the routes that the daimyō crossed in their travels to and from Edo. There were, necessarily, growing expenditures, which the daimyō sought to meet by fostering the production of cash crops and industrial goods that could be marketed to other han. Now that a greater variety and better quality of fabrics, utensils, household goods, and art objects were available, the taste and standard of living of the samurai as well as the wealthier elements in the towns and villages rose substantially. Such improvements, however, also tended to raise the level of expectation of the other segments of the society. An increased imbalance between income and expenditures resulted. Despite the fact that over the years rice production grew at a rate greater than the increase in population, the people, instead of enjoying an augmented sense of ease and satisfaction, became increasingly restless about an economic and financial situation they found uncomfortable and dissatisfying.

We have already discussed some of the economic problems plaguing the Bakufu, and we shall now turn to an examination of those confronting the daimyō and the samurai. Ogyū Sorai observed in the 1720s that whereas thirty or forty years earlier lower-class samurai never wore formal ceremonial suits and were unable to furnish their houses with *tatami* (reed mats), they now not only had better household furnishings and fancy formal suits, but their hair smelled of perfume, and their sword guards were decorated with gold and silver inlays.

To be sure, the daimyō were certainly enjoying much greater luxury if the samurai were living in better houses and wearing finer clothing. According to Sorai,

> In the way in which they comport themselves throughout the day, in their garments, food and drink, household furnishings, dwellings, employment of servants, the conduct of their wives, the retinues that accompany them, the manner in which they travel, the ceremonies of coming of age, marriage and burial—in all these matters they naturally tend to be extravagant in accordance with the trend of the times.[2]

The samurai and the daimyō needed more money to maintain their more elaborate style of living, and their financial needs were made ever the more acute by the recurrent periods of inflation that beset the land. The monetary problems of the daimyō were further intensified by the need to defray the cost of traveling back and forth to Edo and maintaining two residences, one in the home province and one in Edo. The extent to which this cut into the daimyō's budget is illustrated by the example of Saga Han. In the mid-seventeenth century 20 percent of its expenditures were applied to travel costs for the sankin kōtai, and 28 percent was used for its residence in Edo.

The Bakufu added to the financial burdens of the daimyō by requiring them, whenever it felt the need to do so, to participate in public works and other expensive tasks. Saga Han, for example, devoted 4 percent of its expenditures to guarding Nagasaki. In 1754 Satsuma, already in debt for 800,000 ryō, was asked to assist in the construction of a water-control project along the Kiso River in central Honshu. Participation in this project made it necessary for Satsuma to raise more than 200,000 ryō. To obtain the money, the already over-taxed peasants had to be taxed even further. After the completion of the project, the Satsuma official in charge committed hara-kiri to atone for the hardships inflicted upon the people.

In addition to these expenses, the daimyō's financial difficulties were aggravated by such calamitous events as floods, droughts, famines, and fires. Consequently, many han were continuously plagued with budgetary deficits.

There were only a limited number of ways in which the daimyō could cope with the rising costs of their personal and public needs. One way was to borrow from the wealthy merchants, and there were, in fact, some merchant houses that specialized in loaning money to the daimyō and samurai. An interesting example of this was Yodoya Tatsugorō, whose wealth was legendary. So many daimyō had fallen deeply in debt to him that the Bakufu finally confiscated his fortune in 1705. The ostensible reason given for this action was that he was living in an outrageously extravagant fashion, far beyond the limits suitable to a person of his social status.

The Kōnoike family records showed that in 1706 its loans to the daimyō totaled over 278,000 ryō, and by 1795 this amount had risen to more than 416,000 ryō. After the Tokugawa era, the descendants of one merchant family found three cases full of certificates of loans to daimyō amounting to ten million ryō.

In order to extricate the daimyō and the samurai from their indebtedness, the Bakufu sought to compel the merchants to settle for less than full payment of outstanding loans. In some instances it called for the total cancellation of long-standing debts, inflicting great losses upon the merchants. For instance, when Senior Councilor Sadanobu canceled debts in 1789, ninety-six financial agents lost a total of about 1.2 million ryō. Some daimyō, in arranging the terms of a loan, demanded that they be given anywhere from one hundred and fifty to two hundred years to repay the debt. These measures naturally caused many merchant houses to become bankrupt, and induced others to become extremely wary about loaning money to military men. This in turn forced the daimyō and the samurai to abandon their traditional attitude of superiority and appeal to the wealthy merchants for money with lowered heads. In order to cultivate the good will of the merchants, they gave them seasonal gifts, extended special commercial privileges, and accorded them the rights of the samurai, such as the rights to bear swords and receive stipends.

The subservience of the warrior class to the wealthy merchants led one contemporary observer to remark, "When the great merchants of Osaka get angry, the feudal barons of the land quake with fear."[3] Another commentator wrote, "Both large and small daimyō . . . are constantly plagued by their creditors to pay their debts and have no peace of mind worrying about how to make excuses. They fear the sight of moneylenders as if they were demons. Forgetting that they are samurai, they bow and scrape to the townspeople."[4]

Another way in which the daimyō sought to increase their revenues was by taxing the peasants more heavily. There was a limit, however, to this approach. Some han made occasional tax reassessments to take into account the increase in rice production, but there is some evidence to indicate that in many han this was not actually done because of the laborious tasks involved in making thoroughgoing surveys. Many daimyō followed the example of the Bakufu reformers and periodically attempted to reduce their expenses by implementing austerity programs, but these measures repeatedly failed to solve their financial problems. Some daimyō sought to cope with their difficulties by reducing the samurai's stipends, but naturally this only worsened the already serious plight of the samurai. Some other measures that were resorted to were the extraction of forced loans from the merchants and the issuance of currencies valid only in the han.

The daimyō did adopt some measures that yielded very positive results. Many han attempted to increase their revenues by expanding agricultural production. They reclaimed wastelands, initiated water-control projects, built irrigation systems, and introduced improved methods of farming and better strains of seed. As noted below, the acreage under cultivation was substantially increased, and greater yield per unit of land was achieved. It appears, however, that even this increased agricultural yield failed to meet the growing expenditures of the Bakufu and the han.

Another positive measure that was adopted by the Bakufu and the han was the fostering of the production of crops and handicraft goods that could be marketed to other han. As a result, many han came to be known for special products. Some han even concentrated on the production of high quality rice with the intention of competing more effectively for the urban rice market. Many han were known for their textiles, pottery, timber, and fish, while other han managed to produce commodities not readily available elsewhere, such as salt, sugar, indigo, wax, tea, and paper. Villages near major cities like Edo concentrated on producing vegetables for the urban consumers. Some han exploited the mineral resources that had not been claimed by the Bakufu. A few han in the south and the west managed to increase their revenues by engaging in trade with Korea and the Ryukyu Islands; for instance, Tsushima Han, which was officially valued at 20,000 koku, managed to raise its revenues to about 200,000 koku by trading with Korea.

In marketing the commercial and industrial crops many han either established han monopolies or granted monopolistic rights to selected entrepreneurs. In order to compete effectively with other han while increasing their own revenues, han authorities paid the producers of the cash crops minimum prices. This frequently became a source of conflict between the peasants and the authorities.

The Bakufu and the daimyō were feeling the pressures of rising expenditures, but the samurai felt the imbalance between income and outlay even more acutely. As we noted earlier, the samurai had also become accustomed to a more elegant way of life. Their expenses were growing, and their economic woes were further intensified by the fact that they had a fixed income in rice even though the price of rice tended to drop in time of abundant harvest. The price of other commodities, however, not only did not drop, but in some instances rose.

Another economic development that hurt the samurai was the policy adopted by the Bakufu and some daimyō to withhold a certain amount of rice stipends from time to time. In Chōshū as early as 1646 the retainers were asked to "loan" one-fifth of their stipends to the han. Later the amount was raised to one-third and then to one-half of their stipends. These were meant to be only temporary measures, but such reductions often lasted for years. During the time between 1742 and 1762, for example, the Chōshū retainers were asked to take reductions annually, and for seven years in a row they were required to accept reductions of 50 percent. This practice, which was also followed by other han, forced the samurai to fall deeper and deeper into debt, and had the effect of weakening the samurai's sense of loyalty to their lords, who, they felt, were failing in their duty to provide them with adequate means of living. A critic at the end of the eighteenth century observed, "Some daimyō have now ceased to pay their retainers their basic stipends. These men have had half their property confiscated by the daimyō as well, and hate them so much that they find it impossible to contain their ever-accumulating resentment."[5]

Occasionally the samurai would be aided when the Bakufu and the daimyō ordered a cancellation of debts, but before long they were heavily in debt again because the basic situation remained unchanged. Consequently, the poorer samurai were reduced to selling their military equipment and there are instances of a few who even sold their daughters. Some turned to banditry, but the most common solution open to the lower-class samurai was to engage in some sort of handicraft work such as repairing umbrellas, lanterns, wooden clogs, or household utensils. This kind of menial work was considered beneath their dignity, but they were compelled to do it in order to survive. It was not uncommon for some samurai to establish family ties with merchant houses as a means of escape from financial problems. A samurai might adopt a young man from a merchant family or permit his son to marry a merchant's daughter.

In addition, peacetime conditions had brought about a deterioration in the warriors' moral standards. Many samurai began to frequent places of entertainment—the brothels and the theaters—which existed primarily for the pleasure of the townspeople. It was estimated that in the middle of the eighteenth century 70 percent of the patrons of Edo's brothels were samurai. One observer, bemoaning the moral decay of the samurai, surmised that seven or eight samurai out of ten were effete weaklings.

To some extent, the economic distresses and consequent changes in moral standards of the ruling class tended to blur the social distinctions between the samurai and the merchant classes. At the same time, the bonds between the lord and his followers were weakened. These changes, together with the penetration of commercial interests into the rural areas and the growing unrest of the peasantry, were beginning to strain the existing social and political order.

THE LOT OF THE PEASANTS

The peasantry was the segment of the society that supported the national economy and endured hardships and miseries in silence. The expanding money economy was affecting them most adversely and, after the Genroku era, as the Bakufu and the daimyō faced growing financial difficulties, the plight of the peasants appeared to worsen as they were taxed even more heavily.

The infiltration of money and commercial economy into the villages also meant the penetration of Genroku culture. This was true despite the attempts of the Bakufu to keep the villages insulated from the more extravagant ways of the cities. As might be expected, the desire for better living conditions grew among the peasants, and they began to purchase items that the authorities regarded as luxury goods. They also needed money to buy fertilizers and agricultural implements. Their expenses were rising at the same time that the authorities in many han were increasing the rate of taxation in order to meet their growing expenses. This situation became even more serious when, in some instances, the peasants were compelled to pay taxes several years in advance. As we noted previously, there were also numerous additional taxes besides those levied on the rice crop. The peasants were also subject to corvée, the most burdensome being the obligation to provide men and horses for the courier or horse station system.

There is some indication that the ruling class was not uniformly ruthless in its financial demands, but this is not to say that the taxation was not burdensome. Some daimyō, in fact, raised the tax rate to exceed 50 percent, and in a few extreme cases, the peasants were forced to pay 70 percent of the harvest. It should be noted that while many daimyō revised the method of assessment in order to increase the tax yields, the han in the poorer sections of the north and in the mountainous areas were especially stringent in exacting taxes. On the other hand, the Bakufu retained its taxation rate of 40 percent. During the latter half of its rule it usually managed to collect about 1.6 million koku from its assessed holdings of something over 4 million koku. In 1744, by revising the method of assessment, it managed to raise its intake to 1.8 million koku. After 1766, however, its tax revenues gradually declined.

Abuses occurred in all the han when some ambitious officials sought to impress their lords by increasing the tax yields. At the same time, however, there were officials who sought to further and protect the interests of the people and gained renown as practitioners of "benevolent rule."

An important point to consider in assessing the tax burden on the peasants is the fact that no nationwide land survey was made after the Kambun and Empō eras (1661–1681). The area under cultivation, however, had been steadily expanded through reclamation, and the productivity per acre of land was increased substantially through the years by better plant varieties, greater use of fertilizers, and improved methods of farming. The area under cultivation in 1598 was 1.5 million chō, whereas by the Kyōhō era (1716–1736) it had risen to 2.97 million chō. Agricultural production in 1598 was estimated at 18.5 million koku, whereas by the Genroku era (1688–1703) it had risen to 25.78 million, and by 1834 it had reached 30.43 million. In light of the fact that no nationwide land survey had been made since the latter half of the seventeenth century, it is possible that the amount of rice and other crops left in the hands of the villagers may not have decreased even though the tax rates rose. Moreover, in order to encourage the reclamation of wastelands the officials were usually willing to overlook the fact that taxes were not paid on reclaimed plots, or else they imposed only a nominal levy. One study of eleven widely scattered villages indicates that from around 1700 to 1850 the official assessment of productivity varied very little, that is, there was no substantial movement upward. The same was true of the tax rate; no significant changes had occurred in these villages. This of course was a period during which productivity was still increasing.

It would appear then that in spite of the financial pressures facing them, the Bakufu and many daimyō did not tax the peasants as severely as they might have. The growing determination of the peasants to resist additional levies and arbitrary measures may have been partially responsible for this. Furthermore, the changing attitude of the villagers perhaps accounts for the increase in uprisings at a time when the standard of living of the peasants may have been higher than that of their ancestors who lived during the early stages of Tokugawa rule.

There are also strong indications that the larger amount of rice and other products that remained in the villages after taxation did not benefit all the villagers equally, but was in fact primarily directed to the advantage of the wealthier members. The villagers who were likely to increase the yield per acre and to enlarge their holdings through land reclamation were the wealthier farmers. This was the case because of the additional expenses and labor needed for such undertakings. These wealthy and thus prominent villagers were the ones to hold the key village posts, and this enabled them to determine each producer's share of taxation. It appears that in many villages the increased yields and greater holdings were not taken into account in allocating each producer's share of the tax burden.

The fact that the wealthier villagers were benefiting from the taxation system is reflected in the many complaints lodged by the poorer peasants that they were being taxed more heavily than the rich. The clash of interests can also be seen in the growing number of peasant disturbances that were directed against the headmen and other prominent villagers. This is in sharp contrast to the many earlier disturbances, which were led by the village leaders to protest the policies of the Bakufu or han officials.

The rising rate of tenancy also indicates that the gap between the rich and poor peasants was widening. It was illegal to buy or sell land, but this law was frequently circumvented, and even some merchants purchased land in the villages. Most of the land belonging to the poorer peasants, however, passed into the hands of the wealthy villagers who held mortgages on the fields of impoverished farmers. The percentage of tenancy varied greatly from place to place, but it is estimated that in areas where the commercial economy had penetrated deeply, that is, near the major cities and the main roads, it had risen to 50 percent by the nineteenth century. Accompanying this increase in tenant farmers was an increase in the number of hired workers on the larger farms and in the village handicraft industries. A further indication of the growing disparity of wealth in the villages can be seen in the changing pattern of landholding: the number of large and very small holdings increased while medium-sized holdings decreased.

The wealthier villagers, in addition to enhancing their wealth through greater productivity per acre and acquisition of more land, began investing their money in the commercial and industrial enterprises that were developing in the rural areas. Many were already involved in traditional commercial activities such as the lending of money and the selling of daily necessities (*e.g.*, sake, salt, soy-sauce, oil) to the villagers. Now some began to participate in such "manufacturing" enterprises as spinning, weaving, pottery making, and other handicraft industries. Others ventured into the business of marketing the cash and industrial crops that were produced in their villages. At the same time, urban merchants came to the villages to market these crops and became members of the rural communities. The consequence of this was the development of a group of rural dwellers, known as *gōnōshō* (rich farmer/businessman), who came into existence in villages that were affected strongly by the commercial economy.

An early nineteenth-century observer made the following remarks concerning the growing disparity between the rich and the poor villagers: "the wealthy farmers have forgotten their rank, have been given the right to have surnames, wear swords or even have yearly allowances. They are addicted to wearing beautiful clothes, practice military arts, study Chinese books and poetry, and even call courtesans from the prosperous centres to their homes."[6] Essentially, then, they were living like members of the samurai class. In sharp contrast to this, the poorer farmers, he noted, were falling deeper into debt and losing their land. In the less productive sections of the country, the poorer peasants found it difficult to raise a family and resorted to infanticide and abortion. A social critic writing in the later stages of the Tokugawa era claimed that in the northern provinces the number of children killed annually exceeded sixty or seventy thousand.

The fact that the population remained stable and even decreased from time to time after the eighteenth century indicates that a large percentage of the peasantry was leading a marginal existence. In 1721 the population of the common classes was officially noted to be twenty-six million. It fluctuated between twenty-five and twenty-seven million from that date until the end of the Tokugawa era.[7] Figures prior to 1721 are not available, but if we accept an estimated figure of eighteen million for the period 1573–1591, it is conceivable that the population increased by ten million from the end of the sixteenth century to the beginning of the eighteenth.

The population during the latter half of the Tokugawa era was held down by periodic famines and epidemics, and by abortion and infanticide. Mass starvation resulted whenever there were serious crop failures, which were caused by droughts, excessive rainfall, floods, typhoons, cold weather, or locusts. There were in all thirty-five famines in the Edo period. In 1732, for example, swarms of locusts descended upon western Japan, practically ruining the entire rice crop of that region. This is known as the Kyōhō famine, and contemporary estimates held that while it lasted, 969,900 people died of starvation. No doubt this figure is highly exaggerated, but it does, nevertheless, indicate the strong impression that large-scale starvation made upon observers. In 1755 cold weather destroyed the crops in the north, and as a result, in one han alone it was reported that one out of five persons died of starvation. In 1773 droughts preceded a plague that claimed the lives of two hundred thousand people. This death toll rose as the plague spread through the northern provinces, with Sendai Han reporting the loss of three hundred thousand people. This was followed by the great Temmei famine that began in 1783 and lasted until 1787. It was caused by continuous bad weather: excessive rainfall, unseasonably cold weather, and drought. The year the famine started, Mt. Asama in central Japan erupted, causing much death and destruction. The bad weather and persistent crop failures continued year after year and the northern provinces, which were again affected most seriously, experienced such mass starvation that the people were finally reduced to practicing cannibalism. No accurate figure is available on the number of people who starved to death in the Temmei famine, but one contemporary observer wrote, "during the three years of bad crops and famine which occurred since 1783, over two million people in Ōu Province alone starved to death."[8] This is an overestimation, but it is believed that several hundred thousand persons did perish, and much of the northern region remained uninhabited and untilled for years.

In the Tempō era another major famine occurred that lasted from 1833 to 1836. Once again the northern provinces were most severely affected. Tsugaru Han, which was said to have lost eighty thousand persons in a single year during the Temmei famine, lost another forty-five thousand.

The effects of these famines and catastrophes are reflected in the decreases in the population that followed each major outbreak. As a result of the Kyōhō famine of 1732–1733, the population of the common people dropped from 26.92 million in 1732 to 26.15 million in 1744, when the next census was taken. Just prior to the Temmei famine, the population was 26.01 million, but it declined to 25.08 million in 1786, and then dropped even further to 24.89 million in 1792.

PEASANT UPRISINGS

The peasants did not remain completely passive when confronted with the rigid control and exploitation by the ruling class, growing economic hardships, and periodic disasters. There was little they could do about natural calamities, but they could and did protest against abuses on the part of the officials and demand relief in times of famine and disaster.

Recent studies show that between 1590 and 1867 there were 2,809 peasant disturbances. During the early years of Tokugawa rule these disturbances tended to occur more frequently in the poorer regions. Later on, however, they began to break out increasingly often in the more advanced areas, thus indicating that the penetration of commercial economy was causing difficulties in the villages. The number of peasant uprisings rose significantly in the latter half of the Edo period. This was also true of the Bakufu's own domain: from 1590 to 1750 the Bakufu was faced with 146 peasant disturbances in its demesne, while between 1751 and 1867 it was confronted with 401 incidents.

The protest movements took various forms. The peasants could, of course, submit petitions through regular channels, but such actions were not effective since they could so readily be blocked at the lower levels. Illegal actions took the form of mass flights into another lord's domain, forceful demonstrations, violent uprisings, and submission of petitions that bypassed the lower authorities and went directly to the daimyō or Bakufu. With the passage of time, the protest movements tended to grow increasingly violent, and from about 1710 forceful demonstrations and violent uprisings constituted between 40 and 50 percent of all protests. The houses and warehouses of the rich farmers, merchants, and moneylenders were frequently the objects of attack.

In a study that was made of 2,755 peasant outbursts, it was determined that taxation, having been named in 628 of the incidents, was the most prevalent cause of violent action. The other incidents involved the following immediate causes: 355 were directed against some aspect of the administrative system; 214 involved demands for relief and assistance; 158 were rice riots; 146 were directed against abusive Bakufu or han officials; and 134 were protests against arbitrary measures taken by the authorities. In the later stages of the Edo period there was an increase in protests against the village leaders and merchants who had monopolistic rights.[9]

During the latter half of the Tokugawa era, the number of participants and the areas covered by the disturbances tended to grow in scope. In 1738, eighty-four thousand peasants in Iwaki Province in the north participated in a demonstration against excessive taxation. In 1754, one hundred and sixty-eight thousand peasants were involved in an outburst against unfair taxation in Kurume Han in Kyushu. In 1764, two hundred thousand peasants in the Kantō region rioted to protest the burdens of corvée in the horse stations. Following the Temmei famine, violent uprisings involving thousands of peasants broke out with increasing frequency. One of the major riots in the nineteenth century was the 1831 uprising in Chōshū where one hundred thousand peasants rioted, demanding a reduction in taxes and protesting the han's monopolistic policy in marketing industrial crops.

It is interesting to speculate as to why peasant unrest grew in the latter half of the Tokugawa period when, compared to the first half, more food and other commodities were available. The population remained more or less stable after the eighteenth century while rice production increased somewhat, so there must have been more food to go around.[10] A partial answer is found in the fact that this was the time when the three major famines of the Edo period occurred: the Kyōhō famine of 1732–1733, the Temmei famine of 1783–1787, and the Tempō famine of 1833–1836. In the decade or so during and following these major famines, the number of peasant disturbances increased significantly.

This period of increasing unrest also coincided with the growing financial difficulties of the Bakufu and the han. The various measures they adopted to cope with the situation, such as the Kyōhō, Kansei, and Tempō reforms, caused the people inconvenience and hardship. The growth of commercial economy and its consequent effects in the villages also gave rise to unrest by causing dislocations in the countryside. The economic difficulties caused by opening the country to the West touched off a large number of peasant disturbances in the 1860s. We have already made note of the growing conflict between the wealthier villagers and poorer peasants, which also contributed to the increase in agrarian troubles.

Another possible contributing factor that should not be overlooked is that the peasants were getting bolder in challenging the ruling class because the latter had lost some of its militaristic qualities. The samurai were no longer hardy warriors; they were more like gentleman-scholars who had been softened by urban living. Very few samurai lived in the villages where the peasants dwelled, and when these outsiders did appear it was only to collect taxes. Finally, the greater productivity and the improved standard of living being enjoyed by the village leaders and the townspeople must have had the double effect of raising the expectations of the peasants while making them more militant.

In some instances the protestors did succeed in gaining concessions and in having their grievances redressed; but, in all cases of violent or illegal action, the leaders were arrested and punished because any sort of conspiracy or group action was strictly prohibited. In order to ferret out the instigators, the suspected leaders were tortured cruelly and forced to confess. They were then beheaded or crucified. Some were buried alive.

The peasant uprisings were not motivated by any desire to change the social or political order. They were simply protest actions calling for redress of specific grievances. The peasants remained politically unsophisticated partly because of the Bakufu's success in keeping them isolated and politically ignorant. The rulers followed the adage that "the peasants should not be informed but should be made to depend upon the ruling class." Peasant riots did break out, particularly in the Kantō and northern regions, when the Bakufu was being overthrown by the imperial forces. These were called *yonaoshi ikki*, uprisings to reform the society, but they were isolated actions directed primarily against the wealthy villagers.

It was not only the peasants who were forced to resort to violence because of economic difficulties; the urban poor also began to stage violent demonstrations. Inflationary prices and food shortages were the primary causes for these urban riots, which were usually directed against the rice and sake merchants and the pawnbrokers.

Prior to the Kyōhō (1716–1736) era, only eight urban disturbances had occurred, and only one of these involved any violence. After 1717, however, 332 instances of urban conflict were recorded, and most of them entailed rioting and violence. One of the most widespread urban rice riots occurred late in the spring of 1787 in the wake of the Temmei crop failures and famine when fifty separate violent incidents broke out in cities throughout the country.

The Tempō famine also touched off rice riots in the cities, where shortages and inflated prices caused rampant hunger and starvation. This series of disturbances culminated in a major uprising in 1837 in Osaka, which was led by a former police officer and a Wang Yang-ming scholar, Ōshio Heihachirō (1792–1837). Ōshio was outraged at the indifference of the Osaka city commissioners and the rich merchants, such as Mitsui and Kōnoike, to whom he had unsuccessfully appealed for help. Instead of taking any positive action to alleviate the unfair conditions, one of the city commissioners accused Ōshio of violating the ban on making direct appeals to higher officials. Ōshio, as a result, decided that the only course left to him was to lead the people in an uprising against the rich and the established authorities. He had only about three hundred followers, largely impoverished townspeople and peasants from nearby villages, but they managed to set fire to one-fifth of the city. The uprising was quickly crushed, and he was forced to take his own life.

Urban disturbances continued to break out. The crisis facing the Bakufu and established authorities became acute after the advent of Perry, and the number of urban riots increased. Seventy such outbursts were recorded between 1854 and the fall of the Bakufu.

AGRICULTURAL IMPROVEMENTS

Agricultural production, as noted above, did not remain static during the Tokugawa period. A variety of factors contributed to the increased yields in rice and other crops. There was a far greater and more extensive use of fertilizers—in addition to night soil, manure, grass, leaves, and ashes, dried fish and lees of vegetable oil came into use. The variety of plants also increased considerably, and it is estimated that the number of rice varieties swelled from about one hundred and seventy-five in the early seventeenth century to over two thousand by the mid-nineteenth century. Irrigation systems were improved with wider use being made of water wheels and treadmills. In the northern and Kantō regions, sericulture became important as a supplementary source of rural income.

The production of commercial and industrial crops began to increase throughout the country. Cotton, indigo, sugar cane, tobacco, silk worms, tea, wax tree, etc. were produced by the peasants to supplement their income or at the behest of their lords. Despite the increasing production of cash crops and growing commercial activities, Tokugawa Japan was still predominantly an agricultural country, not a commercial one. It is estimated that in the 1860s only about 20 percent of the agricultural products reached the commercial market, whereas a century later the figure had grown to 60 percent.

The fishing industry remained an important part of the Tokugawa economy, as did mining, forestry, and the various handicraft industries. Somewhat larger production facilities, especially in textiles, were emerging at the end of the era. Commercial capital began to enter the process of production to some extent, and the more advanced areas of the economy were showing signs of industrial growth. In view of the overall picture, however, all these changes were not really significant enough to affect the fundamentally agrarian character of the economy.

Not many Tokugawa thinkers concerned themselves with the practical aspects of farming, but there were a few who did. Among the more notable of these were Ōhara Yūgaku (1797–1858) and Ninomiya Sontoku (1787–1856). Yūgaku, although born into a samurai family, was disowned for having killed a man in a duel and spent years wandering around the country. He finally settled in a village in the Kantō region, just as the Tempō famine broke out. Deeply distressed at the suffering of the peasantry, he sought to devise ways in which to assist them. In 1838 he organized a cooperative credit union encompassing four villages. Each member was required to transfer to the cooperative a plot of land worth five ryō, and the profits from this land were then put into a fund that was to be used to assist the members in time of need. Yūgaku also introduced better methods of farming and initiated a land improvement program. In addition, he sought to instill a wholesome outlook into the peasantry and taught that the nature of things and the Way were fixed by the unity of Heaven and Earth. The common people too were created by this unity, so they were obliged to follow the Way. This consisted in practicing filial piety, adhering to one's station in life, and respecting the samurai.

In spite of his positive contributions to agrarian life, and his essentially pro-establishment philosophy, Yūgaku was accused by the authorities of disturbing the existing order in the village and of exceeding his proper station in life by daring to propagate his own philosophy. He was forced to dissolve the cooperative before being incarcerated. After his release he committed hara-kiri.

The other agrarian reformer, Ninomiya Sontoku, referred to as the "peasant sage of Japan," was born into a peasant family and remained a tiller of the soil and a spokesman for the peasantry all his life. His family was plunged into the depth of poverty by the Temmei famine and a destructive typhoon. Through hard work, Sontoku more than restored the family fortune and became a minor landlord of 4 chō. Like Yūgaku he also sought to help his fellow peasants improve their lot. He taught them the importance of making long-range plans and advised them to make an annual budget in which they were always to plan on spending less than they expected to make. He also proposed the establishment of voluntary credit unions, a suggestion that was adopted by a fairly large number of villages in Sagami, where Sontoku came from, as well as in the neighboring provinces. He was active in relief work during the Tempō famine, and as he gained renown as an agrarian expert, he was sought out by many han to assist in revitalizing villages that had fallen into decay.

Sontoku believed that the peasants must be instilled with a philosophy of life that would be fitting to them while enhancing their well-being. Each person, he taught, owes his existence and well-being to his ancestors and society and, therefore, has as his duty the following of the doctrine of Repayment of Virtue, which calls for hard work, thrift, and sharing what one can with others. Sontoku's interpretations of the Way of Heaven and the Way of Man were pragmatic and utilitarian: the Way of Heaven is the way of nature as seen in the physical world; the Way of Man is fixed by man's necessity to survive in nature. Thus, the Way of Man tells us "rice is good and weeds are bad; to build a house is good, to destroy it is bad. . . . All that is convenient for man is good and all that is inconvenient is bad."[11]

Unlike other Tokugawa thinkers, Yūgaku and Sontoku concerned themselves with practical problems and not with theoretical or idealistic moral concepts. This propensity to direct one's attention to practical matters came to be manifested increasingly in the intellectual world of the late Edo period.

INTELLECTUAL CURRENTS: REFORMERS AND CRITICS

During the latter half of the Tokugawa regime, heterodox views came to be embraced by a growing number of thinkers, and Chu Hsi philosophy, the official ideology, no longer dominated the intellectual scene. The Kansei edict prohibiting heterodox studies was issued in 1790 by Matsudaira Sadanobu, and it was intended to combat the rising tide of unorthodox points of view. It could, however, neither curb opinions critical of official policies nor restrict the diffusion of non–Chu Hsi, or for that matter, non-Confucian philosophies.

There were several schools of thought among the heterodox thinkers. Of course these cannot all be neatly classified into fixed categories, but for the sake of convenience we can list the following: the school of thought that was influenced by Dutch or Western learning; the pragmatic, rationalistic critics of the existing order; the nationalists of the Mito school; and the nationalists of the school of National Learning.

The school of Dutch learning (*rangaku*) came into existence after 1720, when the Bakufu relaxed its ban against Western books and permitted works not containing Christian ideas to enter the country. This led a small circle of interested scholars to begin studying Dutch in order to become acquainted with Western science. Japanese-Dutch dictionaries were compiled, and these men started to pursue such subjects as astronomy, physics, electricity, plant studies, cartography, geography, and medicine. The pioneer students of this school included Aoki Kon'yō (1698–1769), who compiled a dictionary of the Dutch language, which he completed in 1758, and Hiraga Gennai (1729–1779), a versatile man who was not only interested in Western science but also in play writing and Western painting. In his scientific work he engaged in botanical studies, conducted experiments in electricity, produced asbestos, and made a thermometer. He also taught Western painting, and among his students was Shiba Kōkan (1738–1818), who became the foremost exponent of the Western style of painting.

The Bakufu was interested in encouraging the study of astronomy and built an observatory in Edo in 1744. Surveying and cartography were also studied at this center, and it was through mastery of these fields that Inō Tadataka (1745–1818) managed to survey the entire Japanese coastline and produce an accurate map of the country. Among the early advocates of the Copernican theory were Miura Baien (1723–1789) and Shiba Kōkan. Baien, though a Confucian scholar, developed a naturalistic philosophy that departed from the traditional theoretical explanation of the nature of things. He believed that the principles underlying the natural world could be understood only by studying things in the physical world, and not by projecting assumptions about human nature onto the natural world. He emphasized the importance of developing a thoroughgoing spirit of inquiry and skepticism, but the comprehensive system of logic that he formulated was too complex to be easily understood by his contemporaries. It was not until very recently that his position in the history of Japanese thought as a unique and original thinker came to be appreciated.

The science that had the greatest influence on the fostering of Dutch studies was medicine. Among the pioneers in this field were Maeno Ryōtaku (1723–1803) and Sugita Gempaku (1733–1817). In 1771 they had an opportunity to watch a dissection being performed, and they were thus able, through direct observation, to compare the human anatomy with the illustrations and descriptions in a Dutch book on anatomy. They were profoundly impressed by the accuracy of the Dutch work and so appalled at the erroneous notions they had formerly held that they set about doing a translation of the Dutch text, which they published in 1774. This was the first openly circulated Dutch book that was translated into Japanese, and it did much to arouse the interest of fellow scholars.

Dutch studies were advanced significantly when Philipp Franz von Siebold, a young German doctor, arrived in 1823 to serve as a medical officer at the Dutch factory in Nagasaki. He was allowed to open a clinic and a medical school outside the city, and it was here that he taught fifty-seven Japanese medical students. In 1828 Siebold got in trouble with the authorities when it was discovered that he was planning to take a map of Japan with him on his projected trip back to Europe. He was expelled from the country as a suspected spy, but he was able to return in 1859 after Japan opened her doors to the West.

The Confucians began to attack Dutch studies as interest in them mounted. Ōtsuki Gentaku (1757–1827), an advocate of Dutch learning, responded as follows to the critics: "Dutch learning is not perfect, but if we choose the good points and follow them, what harm could come of that? What is more ridiculous than to refuse to discuss its merits and cling to one's forte without changing."[12] The scholars of Dutch studies grew increasingly critical of the Bakufu's anachronistic policy of seclusion and began as a result to experience growing official hostility. These men were bringing about an expanded awareness of the outside world and had become a force that could not be ignored.

Russian movements in the north along with stories about European activities in the rest of Asia induced some Japanese thinkers to turn their attention to the problems of national defense. They also considered, though usually in private, the policies that they thought Japan should adopt in coping with the foreign powers. Hayashi Shihei (1738–1793) was one of the first of these thinkers to call for the adoption of appropriate defense measures to meet the impending threat from abroad. He urged the use of Western military science and arms, especially cannons, to repel the foreign naval vessels. The Bakufu, then under the direction of Matsudaira Sadanobu, arrested him for publishing a book dealing with the affairs of state, but he had already set a precedent for such discussions, which others were to follow. In the nineteenth century Takano Chōei (1804–1850), who had studied under Siebold, and Watanabe Kazan (1793–1841), who was a student of the Dutch language, an accomplished painter, and an experienced administrator, expressed their disagreement with the Bakufu's policy of driving away all foreign ships approaching Japanese shores. For this they were both persecuted and driven to suicide.

The practical and rational critics and analysts of Tokugawa society had acquired, in addition to what was noted above about Dutch learning, some knowledge about the West. One of these men, Honda Toshiaki (1744–1821), favored development of foreign trade and colonization in order to strengthen Japan's economy. He believed that the government was responsible for the economic miseries of the people, and he was convinced that the ruling class had to provide vigorous leadership to change Japan into a wealthy, industrial nation like some of the European countries.

Toshiaki believed that in order to strengthen the economy, centralized control had to be established. He felt it was particularly important to bring shipping and trade under state control. "As long as there are no government-owned ships and the merchants have complete control over transport and trade," he wrote, "the economic conditions of the samurai and farmers grow steadily worse."[13] In foreign policy he favored an expansionist course of action and bemoaned the fact that Hokkaido, Sakhalin, and Kamchatka were not being colonized. "Since," he wrote, "it is a national obligation to attempt to increase the size of the country, even if this involves invading other countries, it makes me speechless with despair when I realize that we have permitted all of our possessions to be snatched away by another country."[14] His desire was to make Japan "the greatest nation in the world." Toshiaki was highly critical of the Bakufu and favored drastic changes, but because he did not publicize his ideas, he did not encounter any difficulties from the authorities. Consequently, he also failed to exert much influence on the thinking of his age.

It is interesting to note that men like Toshiaki and Satō Nobuhiro (1769–1850) already recognized key concepts about the necessity of adopting Western science and technology and the importance of developing the nation's economy for military purposes—an idea that was to have full sway in the early Meiji period. Nobuhiro had studied Dutch and was interested in a variety of practical subjects. He was also seriously concerned about the external threat and was deeply disturbed by China's defeat in the Opium War. Like Toshiaki, he believed in strengthening the economy in order to strengthen the nation; that is, he believed in what came to be known as a policy of *fukoku kyōhei* (enrich and strengthen the nation). Nobuhiro served as an adviser to Senior Councilor Mizuno Tadakuni and to several daimyō, so his ideas received the attention of the ruling authorities. His proposal for drastic economic reorganization was not adopted, but when the Bakufu sought to regulate the economy more stringently after 1855, it is believed that Nobuhiro's ideas had something to do with it.

In order to revitalize Japan's economy, he advocated the establishment of a highly centralized totalitarian government that would have the authority to control the entire economic life of the society while fully utilizing and completely regulating all natural and human resources. He suggested that the country's industries be divided into eight divisions with every person being assigned to a given occupation and strictly forbidden from engaging in any other work. The existing political order and the class system were to be abolished, of course, and the ruler given autocratic powers that would allow him to "manage freely the entire nation of Japan as if it were his hands and feet."[15]

Nobuhiro, under the influence of the Shinto nationalism of Hirata Atsutane, whose views are discussed later in this chapter, envisioned Japan extending her divine rule over the rest of the world. "In terms of world geography," he argued, "our Imperial Land would appear to be the axis of the other countries of the world, as indeed it is. Natural circumstances favor the launching of an expedition from our country to conquer others, whereas they are adverse to the conquest of our country by an expedition from abroad."[16] It appears that an awareness of the outside world quickly led to the rise of expansionistic nationalism.

There were a number of other rationalist critics of the existing order who contemplated various ways of strengthening the society. Kaiho Seiryō (1755–1817), for example, advocated that since commerce constituted the basis of the social order industrial activities should be extended to all segments of the society. Shiba Kōkan recognized the superiority of Western science and favored establishing trade with Russia. He also expressed egalitarian ideas: "from the emperor, and shōgun above, to the samurai, peasants, merchants, artisans, pariahs, and beggars below all are human beings."[17] Yamagata Bantō (1748–1821), a scholar who had emerged from the merchant class, also recognized the superiority of Western science and adopted a materialistic, atheistic point of view. He noted the prevalence of conflict between the ruler and the people in Japanese history and, like Shiba Kōkan, asserted that all men were equal.

The nationalists, both the Mito school and the school of National Learning, though not yet in favor of overthrowing the Bakufu, were beginning to put increasing emphasis on the importance of the imperial family. They believed in "revering the emperor and respecting the Bakufu," and they tended to be outspokenly anti-Western. The Bakufu officials were willing to tolerate expressions of respect for the imperial family as long as these were accompanied by similar declamations about the Bakufu, but they were not willing to condone pro-imperial expressions that at the same time implied a criticism of the Bakufu. Followers of Yamazaki Ansai (1618–1682), syncretist of Confucianism and Shinto, were punished by the Bakufu as exponents of pro-imperial, anti-Bakufu sentiments. They were Takenouchi Shikibu (1712–1767), who was exiled, and Yamagata Daini (1725–1767), who was executed. Pro-royalists in the early nineteenth century were careful not to step into the danger zone.

This was true of Aizawa Seishisai (1782–1863) of Mito, one of the earliest advocates of the policy of *sonnō jōi* (revere the emperor and repel the barbarians). He argued in traditional fashion that obedience to one's lord and adherence to the Bakufu's laws signified loyalty to the emperor. In 1825 he wrote a book called *New Proposals* in which he set forth his nationalistic, pro-royalist opinions. This book appeared at a time when Japan's peace was being threatened by the attempts of foreign vessels to enter her ports. In fact, it was in 1825 that the Bakufu issued an order to fire upon all foreign ships approaching Japanese shores. Seishisai's *New Proposals* had a significant impact on the thinking of his contemporaries, and the volume came to be regarded as something of a Bible for the nationalistic patriots of the period.

Seishisai embraced the Shinto concepts of the divine origin of Japan and the uniqueness of the imperial family, who were descendants of the Sun Goddess. He held Japan to be "at the vertex of the earth" and the nation that sets the standard for others to follow. He elaborated upon the concept of Japan's *kokutai* (national polity), a theory that combined elements from Shinto mythology, Confucian ethics, and Bushidō. It was this theory that emerged in the twentieth century as a key element in the ideology of the ultranationalists. Japan's kokutai was unique, Seishisai asserted, because the nation was founded by the Sun Goddess and because the imperial line, which stems directly from her, has survived inviolate through the ages. Concepts of loyalty to the sovereign and filial piety were thus handed down to the Japanese people by the Sun Goddess herself.

Seishisai possessed a narrow, xenophobic point of view, as the following statement of his vividly illustrates.

Today the alien barbarians of the West, lowly organs of the legs and feet of the world, are dashing about across the sea, trampling other countries underfoot, and daring, with their squinting eyes and limping feet, to override the noble nations. What manner of arrogance is this! . . . everything exists in its natural bodily form, and our Divine Land is situated at the top of the earth. . . . It [America] occupies the hindmost region of the earth; thus, its people are stupid and simple, and are incapable of doing things.[18]

As might be expected, he was highly critical of the scholars of Dutch learning. He accused them of being taken in by Western theories and of seeking to transform the civilized Japanese way of life into that of the barbarians. He was also rabidly anti-Christian, contending that Christianity's aim was to devour the countries that it entered.

The nationalists of the Mito school, although they were sympathetic to certain Shinto concepts, were basically Confucians, and as such they sought to reconcile the concept of taigi meibun with loyalty both to the shōgun and to the emperor. Consequently, they did not agree fully with the scholars of National Learning who were critical of Confucianism.

The central figure among the scholars of National Learning during this period was Hirata Atsutane (1776–1843), a zealous Shinto nationalist. In seeking to place National Learning above all other schools of thought, he contended that all learnings, including Confucianism and Buddhism, were encompassed in Japanese learning, "just as the many rivers flow into the sea, where their waters are joined."[19] Atsutane hoped to establish Shinto's supremacy over all other doctrines, and he was almost irrational in his criticisms of Confucianism and Buddhism. He had been exposed to Western knowledge and was influenced to some extent by Christian concepts, which were entering the country through Chinese publications. For example, he equated the early Shinto gods Izanagi and Izanami with Adam and Eve, and in one of his works he quoted the New Testament as if it were a Shinto text.

Atsutane sought to provide Shinto with a clearly defined theology by presenting a monotheistic interpretation of the religion, and by emphasizing life after death. He may have borrowed these two concepts from Christianity. In contrast to Motoori Norinaga, who envisioned two creator gods—Takami-musubi and Kami-musubi—Atsutane contended that Takami-musubi was the sole Creator God who made heaven and earth. He was, Atsutane said, omnipotent, the holiest among the many gods, and ruler over the world from his abode in heaven. In his concept about life after death, Atsutane again departs from the earlier Shintoists, who held that after death, the soul went to the polluted land of *Yomi*. According to Atsutane, the soul enters the land of spirits, where it joins the gods. This earthly life, then, is only a temporary abode for man. It is "the place where we are tested for good and evil. It is a temporary world where we are allowed to live for a short while. The invisible land is our real world."[20]

Atsutane's ethnocentric nationalism was manifested in his belief that Japan, because she was begotten by the gods and thus especially favored by them, ranks far above other countries. People all over the world, he claimed, refer to Japan as the land of the gods, and call the Japanese people descendants of the gods. Even the humblest of the Japanese, being descendants of the gods, are superior to others. He held the Chinese in contempt as being unclean, and although he compared the Dutch to dogs, he did recognize their devotion to intellectual pursuits and their superiority in the sciences. Atsutane was not one of the furious anti-foreigners who insisted on "repelling the barbarians." He sympathized with the seclusionist policy of the Bakufu but favored adopting those elements of Western science and technology that would benefit the country. He did not advocate overthrowing the Bakufu even though he was a Shintoist, and he believed that there was no conflict between revering the emperor and upholding the Bakufu.

Atsutane, however, was fanatical in his opposition to Buddhism. He criticized its ascetic rejection of the mundane world, and he attacked the major Buddhist sects as "enemies of the gods." He renounced the Buddhist concept of satori (enlightenment) and contended that true enlightenment was to be attained by following one's natural inclinations. True enlightenment, he said, "is understood as soon as it is explained to a person. It can be performed at once; it is not a difficult matter at all. It is what a person is born with; it is his nature." According to Atsutane, an enlightened person feels affection for his parents, loves his wife and children, and allows his innate sentiments to have free and natural expression. "Shakyamuni Buddha and Bodhidharma," he argued, "behaved contrary to this way so they were neither enlightened nor followers of the true Way." Consequently, he advocated the abandonment of "all things that smell of Buddhism" and the cultivation of "the Yamato spirit."

Atsutane's influence was widespread. His anti-Buddhist sentiments found considerable support and took concrete form in the anti-Buddhist outbursts that followed the Meiji Restoration. His Shinto nationalist concepts have had a great impact upon the nationalistic thinking of modern Japan.

NOTES

1. E. H. Norman, "Andō Shōeki and the Anatomy of Japanese Feudalism," in *Transactions of the Asiatic Society of Japan*, series 3, vol. 2, pp. 57–58.

2. Maruyama Masao, *Nihon Seijishisōshi Kenkyū (Studies in the History of Japanese Political Thought)* (Tokyo: Tōkyō Daigaku Shuppankai, 1954), p. 120.

3. Sakata Yoshio, *Meiji Ishinshi (A History of the Meiji Restoration)* (Tokyo: Miraisha, 1960), p. 19.

4. Maruyama Masao, *op. cit.*, p. 125.

5. Donald Keene, *The Japanese Discovery of Europe, 1720–1830* (Stanford, Calif.: Stanford University Press, 1969), pp. 168–69.

6. Hugh Borton, "Peasant Uprisings in Japan of the Tokugawa Period," in *Transactions of the Asiatic Society of Japan*, series 2, vol. 16, p. 10.

7. For the total population, two to three million must be added to account for the daimyō and samurai, and their servants, as well as the outcastes, who were excluded from the census. It should be noted that in some instances children were not included in the count either.

8. Keene, *op. cit.*, p. 182.

9. The source for the figures on peasant disturbances is Aoki Kōji, *Hyakushō Ikki no Nenjiteki Kenkyū (A Chronological Study of Peasant Uprisings)* (Tokyo: Shinseisha, 1966), p. 13.

10. During the seventeenth century the rice production increased by about 40 percent while the population may have grown by about 50 percent. From the early eighteenth century, however, the population remained fairly stable until the end of the Tokugawa era while the rice production grew about 18 percent by 1834.

11. Nagata Hiroshi, *Nihon Tetsugakushisōshi (A History of Japanese Philosophical Thought)* (Tokyo: Mikasa Shobō, 1938), p. 237.

12. Keene, *op. cit.*, p. 25.

13. *Ibid.*, p. 176.

14. *Ibid.*, p. 221.

15. Maruyama Masao, *op. cit.*, p. 346.

16. Ryusaku Tsunoda, W. T. de Bary, and Donald Keene, eds., *Sources of Japanese Tradition* (New York: Columbia University Press, 1958), p. 577.

17. Nagata, *op. cit.*, pp. 250–51.

18. Tsunoda *et al.*, *Sources of Japanese Tradition*, p. 596. Reprinted by permission of Columbia University Press.

19. *Ibid.*, p. 543.

20. The source for this and the quotations that follow is Nagata Hiroshi, *op. cit.*, pp. 254 ff.

CHAPTER 10

THE FALL OF THE TOKUGAWA BAKUFU

ARRIVAL OF COMMODORE PERRY

The coming of Perry in 1853 turned out to be an epoch-making event in Japanese history, but even before his arrival the Bakufu's seclusionist policy was already being challenged by the arrival of other foreign vessels. Russia was the first nation to start probing the shores of Japan. In 1771 a Russian adventurer, Baron von Benyowsky, who had been exiled to Kamchatka, seized control of a small vessel with the aid of some other convicts and sailed to Awa in Shikoku. Benyowsky pretended to be a Dutchman and told the Japanese that Russia was planning to attack Hokkaido the following year. This caused consternation among the Japanese officials and stirred the advocates of national defense, such as Hayashi Shihei, into action. In 1878 a Russian merchant ship came to Kunajiri Island off western Hokkaido and asked the local daimyō to enter into commercial relations. This offer to engage in trade was repeated in the fall of 1792 when a Russian ship, the *Ekaterina*, arrived at Nemuro in Hokkaido to return some castaway Japanese seamen. The authorities rejected the offer but told the Russians to sail to Nagasaki and present their request there. Adam Laxman, the commander of the ship, decided, however, to return to Russia without bothering to go on to Nagasaki. In 1804 the head of the Russian-American Company, Rezanov, arrived in Nagasaki and requested the establishment of commercial relations. He too failed to persuade the Bakufu to abandon its seclusionist position.

In the face of increasing Russian activities in the north, especially in Sakhalin and the Kuriles, the Bakufu began to concern itself with the defense of the northern regions, and in 1808 sent a survey team out there and across into eastern Siberia. Under the leadership of Mamiya Rinzō, the group verified the fact that Sakhalin was in fact an island and not a peninsula attached to Siberia. Russian interest in the Far East abated during the Napoleonic Wars, and it was not until 1847, when Nicholas Muraviev was appointed governor-general of eastern Siberia, that she began to press upon Japanese shores again.

England and America were also beginning to display some interest in opening Japan's ports. In 1818 the British sent a vessel to Uraga, near Edo, and asked for the commencement of commercial relations, but they too were summarily turned away. Also arriving on Japanese shores were whaling ships looking for food and water. As a result, in 1825 the Bakufu issued an edict ordering forcible ejection of all foreign ships from Japanese coastal regions. Upon receiving word of the Chinese defeat in the Opium War, the Bakufu began to strengthen its military forces by manufacturing cannons and training men in gunnery. In 1842 the edict of 1825 was relaxed by Senior Councilor Mizuno Tadakuni, and it was ordered that ships drifting accidentally to Japanese shores were to be provided with food, water, and fuel. Fundamentally, however, the basic seclusionist policy remained unchanged. For example, in 1844 when William II of Holland sent a message to the Bakufu courteously explaining the world situation and urging that Japan open her doors, his advice went completely unheeded.

The nation that finally succeeded in persuading Japan to open her ports was the United States. She was becoming a significant Pacific power and consequently sought to develop commercial relations with Asian nations. In addition, the United States had whaling ships roaming the north Pacific that needed supply bases and shelter. Moreover it was felt that arrangements had to be negotiated for the protection and care of American seamen shipwrecked on Japanese shores, who were heretofore treated as unlawful intruders by the authorities.

In 1837 an American merchant ship, the *Morrison*, arrived with the aim of establishing contact with Japan, but she was promptly driven off. The leader of this mission then recommended to the United States government that a naval expedition be sent to open Japanese ports. In 1846 Commodore James Biddle was dispatched with two American warships, but he too failed to achieve his objective. Finally, Commodore Matthew Calbraith Perry was given the assignment and on July 8, 1853, he arrived off the coast of Uraga with four warships. Edo was plunged into a state of crisis when the "black ships" sailed into Edo Bay, ignoring the protesting Japanese on little boats. Perry was determined to accomplish his mission, so he refused to be shunted aside and gave the Bakufu three days to accept President Fillmore's letter to the shōgun asking for humane treatment of shipwrecked seamen, permission for American ships to enter Japanese ports for coal and supplies, and, if possible, trade between the two nations. The Bakufu had no choice but to accede to Perry's demands and allowed him to land in Uraga. He delivered the letter and then departed stating that he would return early the following year for an official reply.

Perry's arrival placed the Bakufu in its most difficult predicament since its founding. It had virtually ignored the outside world for more than two hundred years and now found that it could no longer continue to do so. The Bakufu officials knew that Japan was incapable of withstanding any military assault by the Western powers, but the ruling class was severely divided on how to deal with the difficulties posed by Perry. The blind fanatics favored "repelling the barbarians," but men who were better informed realized that such action was pure folly. The gravity of the situation and the Bakufu's inability to deal with it resolutely made it necessary to include radically new elements in the deliberative and policy-making processes. The Bakufu's officials turned for advice to the imperial court and all the daimyō, including the tozama (outside) lords, as well as to the shōgun's liege vassals. This, of course, gave potential opponents of the Bakufu and the politically ambitious elements an opportunity to move into the center of the political arena. The Bakufu was forced, reluctantly, to abandon its seclusionist policy, and the opposition then used the issue of jōi (repelling the barbarians) as a means to badger and embarrass it. At the same time, the inclusion of the imperial court in the decision-making process made it a rallying point for critics of the Bakufu. Thus sonnō (revering or honoring the emperor) was tied in with jōi as a political weapon with which to assail the Bakufu.

In response to the Bakufu's call for advice concerning the American request, seven hundred memorials were submitted. No one, however, managed to formulate a brilliant solution. Some men suggested that the Bakufu accede to Perry's demands, but a majority of the replies advanced the desirable though unrealistic position that the policy of seclusion be retained while war be avoided at all costs. A few of the respondents, on the other hand, did advocate going to war against the intruders. The most eminent proponent of this policy was the lord of Mito, Tokugawa Nariaki (1800–1860), who contended that "if we put our trust in war the whole country's morale will be increased and even if we sustain an initial defeat we will in the end expel the foreigner." He bemoaned the fact that "In these feeble days men tend to cling to peace; they are not fond of defending their country by war."[1]

There were many men who agreed that the only practical solution would be to stall the Americans as long as possible. This, however, was not a feasible plan simply because Perry did return early in 1854, just as he had promised, and this time he had eight "black ships" with him. The Bakufu's officials were overwhelmed by this show of force and, fearing an attack if Perry's requests were not met, agreed to open two ports—Hakodate in Hokkaido and Shimoda on the tip of Izu Peninsula—to American ships, to treat shipwrecked sailors properly, and to permit a consul to reside in Shimoda. The most-favored-nation clause was also included in the treaty even though the Bakufu did not actually agree to establish commercial relations. This agreement, the Treaty of Kanagawa, was signed on March 31, 1854. England, France, Russia, and the Netherlands soon concluded similar agreements and thus brought to a close Japan's long period of seclusion. In effect this signaled the beginning of the end for the Tokugawa Bakufu, for its opponents and critics could now begin to intensify their attacks against it, criticizing its inability to stand up against the Western powers.

In August, 1856, the American government sent Townsend Harris to Shimoda to press for a commercial treaty. Some Bakufu officials, realizing that the Western powers were far in advance of Japan in military, economic, and technological affairs, concluded that Japan could no longer refuse to establish full diplomatic and commercial relations with foreign powers. Iwase Tadanari, the official who was given the task of negotiating with Harris, was convinced that Japan had to open her doors and persuaded the Bakufu's high officials to accept this fact. Several leading daimyō also became convinced of the wisdom of opening the country, but one of the most influential of them, Tokugawa Nariaki, remained adamant in his opposition and sought to win the support of the imperial court. Emperor Kōmei (1831–1866) was surrounded by advisers who were grossly ignorant of the world situation, and so it was not exceedingly difficult to persuade him that opening the country would be disastrous. He decided, therefore, to support the anti-foreign faction.

In the meanwhile, Harris and the Bakufu's officials concluded their negotiations on a commercial treaty and the senior councilor, Hotta Masayoshi (1810–1864), seeking to allay the very strong opposition led by Nariaki, asked for imperial approval of the treaty. Masayoshi expected immediate imperial consent, but the emperor remained firmly committed to the policy of jōi. It was at this point that Ii Naosuke (1815–1860), who had just been appointed tairō (great councilor), decided that the treaty would have to be signed without imperial sanction. The Bakufu's officials, intimidated by Harris'. information that the British and French fleets, fresh from their triumph over the Chinese, were on their way to extract greater concessions from Japan, finally signed the commercial treaty on July 29, 1858. It provided for the immediate opening of three ports to trade and the addition of two more a few years later. Duties of a varied scale on imports and 5 percent on exports were agreed upon. Edo and Osaka were to be opened for foreign residents by 1862 and 1863. American citizens were granted extraterritorial rights and freedom of worship in Japan. Similar treaties were concluded with England, France, Russia, and the Netherlands.

THE IMMEDIATE CONSEQUENCES

The impact of these contacts with the West was felt immediately in the political realm, even though involvement with foreign nations remained essentially limited until the Meiji government came into existence. The effects of the new relationships also became discernible in the cultural and economic areas, and the treaty ports such as Yokohama with their Western residents began to grow into important centers of Western culture.

In 1860 a Japanese embassy was sent to the United States to exchange ratifications of the treaty, and in 1861 another mission was dispatched to Europe. These trips exposed a considerable number of influential Japanese to the Western world, and some of them, like Fukuzawa Yukichi, a leading Meiji educator, returned convinced of the need to adopt Western practices and institutions. The general mood of the country nevertheless remained strongly anti-Western, so these men were compelled to remain silent until the advent of the Meiji era. The Bakufu, however, did recognize the need to train some officials in Western languages, and in 1857 it opened the

"Institute for the Investigation of Barbarian Books." Initially only Dutch was taught, but by 1860 other Western languages were added to the curriculum, and in 1863 the institute was officially turned into a government college for Western studies.

Various educational programs served to increase the exposure of many Japanese to Western culture. In 1862 the Bakufu sent a group of eight students to study in the Netherlands, and this example was soon followed by several han. In 1863 Chōshū dispatched five students to England and in 1864 Satsuma sent sixteen more there. A number of students also went abroad on their own initiative, and many young men in Japan began to study Western languages with Western missionaries and Japanese instructors who were qualified in this field.

Commerce with the West, although still limited, began to increase in the sixties. Exports exceeded imports until 1866 when the trend was reversed, and the total combined figure, not including arms and ships, exceeded thirty-two million dollars. The chief trading partner was England, with whom 80 percent of Japanese trade from 1859 to the downfall of the Bakufu was conducted. Raw silk was the main item of export; tea, copperware, marine products, and lacquerware were among the other major export commodities. Imported goods included cotton yarn, cotton cloth, woollen fabrics, ironware, and sugar.

The tremendous demand for such items as silk and tea resulted in increased production, but it was quite insufficient to meet the enormous requests for these commodities. The demand for raw silk in particular created serious domestic shortages and inflationary prices. On the other hand, the importation of cotton yarn and cotton cloth had the most adverse effects on the domestic producers. Foreign trade did, nevertheless, have the vitally important consequence of stimulating the growth of some factories in which many workers were brought together under one roof to work using reeling machines or processing tea. These factories were, of course, still limited in number and size, and the dominant mode remained domestic handicraft production.

A feature of foreign trade that particularly disturbed the Bakufu was the inordinate outflow of gold. Gold coins were exchanged with silver at a ratio of about one to five in Japan while the world rate was about one to fifteen. This meant that foreigners could make an enormous profit by first exchanging silver for gold in Japan and then taking the gold to China, where it commanded its full value in the world market. Before the Bakufu corrected the situation by debasing its gold coins in 1860, about 500,000 ryō in gold coins had flowed out of the country.

From a political point of view, the agreement to enter into commercial and diplomatic relations with the Western nations proved to be disastrous for the Bakufu. The anti-foreign faction began to grow increasingly disenchanted with the Bakufu, and it commenced openly to espouse the cause of the imperial court. Thus, the movement "to revere the emperor and repel the barbarians" began to congeal into a formidable force as it gained the support of a growing number of activist warriors known as *shishi* (men of high purpose). Ii Naosuke came under severe criticism for having signed the treaty with the United States without imperial approval, and the opposition to him soon became intermeshed with the struggle over succession to the shogunate.

The struggle to pick his successor unfolded even before the weak and feeble-minded Shōgun Iesada (1824–1858) passed away. One faction, which included the daimyō of Echizen and Satsuma as well as some reform-minded Bakufu officials, favored Nariaki's son, Yoshinobu (1837–1913), also known as Keiki, who had a reputation as an individual of considerable ability and intelligence. The support of the anti-foreign faction was guaranteed him simply by virtue of the fact that he was the son of an avowed anti-Westerner. Keiki was also favored by some proponents of the open-door policy who believed that the old guard among the top Bakufu officials had to be removed.

Ii Naosuke, representing the fudai daimyō who traditionally controlled the top Bakufu posts, led the faction opposed to Keiki. They feared that this succession to the shogunate would mean the control of the Bakufu by Nariaki, who was not only anti-Western but sympathetic to the imperial court as well. In order to block Keiki, Ii supported the candidacy of Iemochi, the shōgun's cousin and eight-year-old head of Kii Han. Ii succeeded in making Iemochi shōgun and then began persecuting those who had opposed his policies or had supported Keiki. He placed Nariaki under house arrest, forced Keiki to retire, contrived the dismissal of anti-Bakufu court advisers, and executed the active samurai opponents and critics of the Bakufu.

Among Ii's victims was Yoshida Shōin (1830–1859), a zealous patriot and the leader of the young extremist warriors of Chōshū (see page 215). Another victim was Hashimoto Sanai, a warrior of Echizen, who was condemned for having worked for the candidacy of Keiki. Unlike the other critics of Ii, Sanai had favored opening the country. Ten warriors, including two who died in prison, were condemned to death, and many others were exiled to offshore islands. From Ii's point of view, he was merely upholding the authority of the Bakufu, for lower level warriors were forbidden from interfering in state affairs. The zealots, however, were no longer bound by such considerations as "knowing their place." In order to avenge the death of their fellow warriors, a group of activists from Mito waylaid Ii in March, 1860, as he was entering Edo castle and assassinated him. This deprived the Bakufu of its strongman, and forced its officials to try to cope with the opposition by winning over the cooperation of the imperial court. Consequently, the center of political action began shifting to Kyoto.

THE MENTALITY OF SONNŌ JŌI

Many proponents of sonnō jōi, the movement "to revere the emperor and repel the barbarians," were young warriors who came primarily from the lower rungs of the samurai hierarchy, although there were a few from the middle segment of that class. Some well-to-do farmers' sons as well as priests and scholars could also be found among their ranks. Mito, Chōshū, Satsuma, and Tosa produced the largest number of these men, but they were to be found in other han also.

These samurai, usually referred to as shishi, were inclined to be fiery extremists as well as fanatical political activists. They were usually expert swordsmen who rigorously upheld such traditional samurai values as duty, courage, and honor. Some of the shishi outgrew their earlier limitations and managed to emerge as perspicacious statesmen; by and large, however, they were men who lacked the vision to discern a meaningful role and place for Japan in the context of the changing world scene. They were not inclined to be reasonable and tended instead to be ruled by their passions. Self-righteous, intolerant, and dogmatic to the extreme, they envisioned themselves as the saviors of Japan, men with a sacred mission. They were convinced that they were on the side of truth, justice, and right, and that they were the only true patriots while those who failed to agree with them were self-serving traitors. The shishi were, in effect, the forerunners of the ultranationalist extremists of prewar Japan.

The shishi constituted only a minority in their han, but the influence they wielded was very strongly felt because of the readiness with which they would use force against those who disagreed with them. There were frequent outbursts of violence as the shishi repeatedly tried to seize power. In Chōshū and Satsuma they eventually did capture the han leadership. Their uprising against the established leadership in Mito, however, was crushed. In Tosa, even though they assassinated a moderate han official they failed to intimidate the han leaders and were finally driven out. Later, however, as the daimyō moved closer to the sonnō position, some of the shishi were restored to their good graces. Their terrorist tactics made the extremists a force to contend with not only in their own han but in Kyoto and Edo as well.

The shishi were as a rule rabidly anti-Western, but they disagreed about the tactics to be used in achieving their ends. Some men favored driving the Westerners out and closing the country; others favored opening the country in order to enable Japan to adopt Western military methods and thus become powerful enough to cope with the Western threat.[2] Some of the Bakufu officials who went along with the open-door policy did so because they felt it was an ineluctable necessity, but at heart they favored the seclusionist policy and the preservation of the old feudal order.

Sonnō jōi sentiments are generally believed to have originated in Mito, with men such as Aizawa Seishisai and the Fujitas (father Yūkoku and son Tōko) among the early advocates. Initially, the proponents of sonnō jōi did not advocate an anti-Bakufu policy, believing that loyalty to both the imperial court and the Bakufu was possible. After the arrival of Perry, however, and the conclusion of the commercial treaties, the sonnō jōi movement took a sharp anti-Bakufu turn.

The man who emerged as the leading spokesman of this movement was Yoshida Shōin, a brilliant shishi from Chōshū, who was the son of a low-ranking samurai. He studied Chu Hsi Confucianism and Yamaga Sokō's military science, read treatises on Wang Yang-ming philosophy, and was exposed to Western technology in Nagasaki. In 1851 he went to Edo and became a disciple of Sakuma Zōzan, a leading student of the Dutch language and Western science. He also traveled to Mito to see Aizawa Seishisai, whose works he had studied earlier. The arrival of Perry had a decisive effect on him and, believing that he should get to know his enemy, he sought to board an American ship to go abroad to study. He was arrested for violating the law of the land, and was turned over to his han to be placed under house arrest. After his release, Shōin started a private school to indoctrinate the young men of his han with his loyalist, nationalistic point of view. Among his students were the future leaders of Meiji Japan, Itō Hirobumi and Yamagata Aritomo, as well as one of the three architects of the Meiji Restoration, Kido Kōin, and the would-be leaders of the extremists in Chōshū, Takasugi Shinsaku and Kusaka Genzui—a truly impressive galaxy of disciples. Shōin believed that the old leaders were completely incapable of solving the national crisis, and so he envisioned the establishment of a new order under the leadership of people like himself and his followers, the "grass-roots heroes." His followers in Chōshū did indeed play a major role in overthrowing the old order.

Shōin was intensely anti-foreign and a loyal adherent to the Shintoistic notion of the divine nature of Japan. "One must," he wrote, "worship and revere the gods. The country of Yamato is . . . the honorable country which was founded by the lordly Gods."[3] His anti-Western sentiments burst forth with the coming of Perry, and he exhorted the Japanese people to unite and drive away the "wily barbarians." He was convinced that new leadership and new ideas had to be injected into the government in order to cope with the national emergency. He did not advocate the Bakufu's overthrow until it signed the commercial treaty with Harris without first receiving imperial sanction. When it finally did so, he turned against it in wrathful indignation that epitomized the feelings of the advocates of sonnō jōi:

> It is clear that the Americans' intentions are harmful to the Land of the Gods. It has been proven that the words of the American envoy have caused the land of the Gods to be dishonored. In view of this, the Emperor, in extreme anger, decreed that relations be severed with the American envoy. This command the Bakufu was obliged to obey without delay but it failed to do so. It behaved with arrogance and independence, and made flattery of the Americans the highest policy of the land. It gave no thought to the national danger, did not reflect upon the national disgrace, and disobeyed the imperial decree. This is the Shōgun's crime. Heaven and earth will not tolerate it. The anger of the Gods and men have been aroused. Now it would be proper to destroy and kill in accordance with the fundamental principle of righteousness. No mercy should be shown.[4]

Shōin used all his resources in opposing the Bakufu and frequently plotted to take direct action against its officials. Six months before his death, he wrote, "As long as the Tokugawa government exists, American, Russian, English, and French control over Japan will continue. The situation is indeed critical. How can any red-blooded person bear to see our great nation which has remained independent and unconquered for three thousand years become enslaved by other nations?"[5] When the commercial treaty was signed with the United States, Shōin was so outraged that he conspired with his followers to assassinate one of the Bakufu councilors. He was arrested, turned over to the Bakufu, and later executed.

Sakuma Zōzan (1811–1864), Shōin's master, was also highly nationalistic, but he responded differently to the advent of the West. Zōzan was a Chu Hsi Confucian, but he was also interested in Western learning and had studied the Dutch language. He was particularly fascinated by Western science and technology, and in recognition of Japan's need to adopt Western military and naval techniques, he became an expert on Western gunnery. He had a wide following as a teacher and influenced many young men. Zōzan, unlike Shōin, favored opening Japan's doors in order to adopt Western science and technology. His attitude toward Western knowledge is reflected in the following statement:

> In teachings concerning morality, benevolence, and righteousness, filial piety and brotherly love, loyalty and faithfulness, we must follow the examples and precepts of the Chinese sages. In astronomy, geography, navigation, surveying, the investigation of the principle of all things, the art of gunnery, commerce, medicine, machinery and construction, we must rely mainly on the West. We must gather the strong points of the five worlds and construct the great learning of our imperial nation.[6]

Essentially, then, he favored the morality of the East and the scientific expertise of the West. He became identified with the policy of opening the country and was assassinated by fanatical sonnō jōi advocates. His faith in Eastern morals and Western science was the very attitude that was to be embraced by many of the leaders of Meiji Japan. Basically, the Japanese were interested in the external aspects of Western civilization while they sought to retain in their inner life those elements that they regarded as being intrinsically Japanese.

THE RISE OF THE ANTI-BAKUFU FORCES

The assassination of Ii Naosuke brought about some readily observable changes in the political picture. As we have already noted, the imperial court loomed larger in the national political scene. At the same time the tozama han, particularly Satsuma, Chōshū, and Tosa, as well as the han related to the Bakufu, Aizu, and Echizen, began to exert their influence on the national political arena. Furthermore, with Ii gone the Bakufu's leadership fell to more moderate officials who sought to neutralize their zealous opponents while effecting an alliance between the imperial court and the Bakufu. Emperor Kōmei agreed to this strategy of cooperation in the belief that the Bakufu would in return adopt the policy of driving out the Westerners. The alliance, known as kōbu-gattai (union of the court and military), was cemented by the marriage of Shōgun Iemochi to the emperor's younger sister Princess Kazunomiya, in early 1862. This policy was supported by the daimyō of Satsuma, Echizen, and Aizu.

The shishi angrily opposed this policy and launched a campaign of terror, assassinating those who had cooperated with Ii in suppressing the shishi as well as those who had supported the marriage of Iemochi and Princess Kazunomiya. Another target of the anti-Western fanatics was naturally enough the foreign officials. Starting with the killing of two Russian sailors in the summer of 1859, a number of Westerners were murdered, among whom was Henry Heuskin, Harris' Dutch language interpreter, who was killed in January, 1861.

The most active elements among the shishi emerged from Chōshū. The lord of Satsuma was able to keep the extremists in his han under control, but the shishi in Chōshū were able to operate in a rather freewheeling manner. The lord of Chōshū was willing to leave the management of political affairs to his chief officials. Around 1860, when the Chōshū leaders adopted a policy of playing an active role in the national scene, the han leadership was in the hands of Nagai Uta, an official who favored a policy of moderation. He sought to play the role of a mediator between the court and the Bakufu when Ii's departure offered Chōshū an opportunity to move into the national political arena. Nagai also favored the policy of opening the country to the West. His ideas were vehemently opposed by the shishi, and his failure to effect a reconciliation between the court and Bakufu offered his opponents, led by Kusaka, a perfect opportunity to discredit him. He was ultimately ordered to commit hara-kiri, and the Chōshū leadership passed into the hands of the proponents of sonnō jōi.

Contrary to the expectations of the advocates of kōbu-gattai, the terrorists managed to swing the court back to a rigidly anti-Western position. Emperor Kōmei dispatched a messenger to Edo calling for the immediate expulsion of the foreigners. In early 1863 the shōgun and Keiki, who had been appointed his guardian, traveled to Kyoto to confer with the imperial court regarding the command. Seeing that the imperial court was dominated by the jōi faction, the daimyō who were opposed to such a policy, including the lord of Satsuma, departed for their home provinces. As a result, the Bakufu officials were forced to agree to implement the policy of jōi and May 10, 1863, was set as the date the policy was to go into effect.

The deadline arrived with the extremists of Chōshū firing upon Western ships passing through Shimonoseki straits. As might be expected, the Western powers were swift to retaliate and three American and French men-of-war attacked the Shimonoseki shore batteries, before landing and completely destroying the gun emplacements. The attacks, however, against the Western vessels passing through Shimonoseki straits nevertheless continued. During the following summer, England, France, the United States, and Holland sent seventeen warships against Chōshū, destroyed its forts, and routed its forces on land. This caused Chōshū to abandon its blind anti-Western stance and begin Westernizing its military forces. In a similar way, Satsuma also underwent a kind of baptism by fire in the summer of 1863, when British warships attacked Kagoshima in retaliation for the killing of an Englishman the previous fall. This encounter resulted in bringing the British and Satsuma officials closer together.

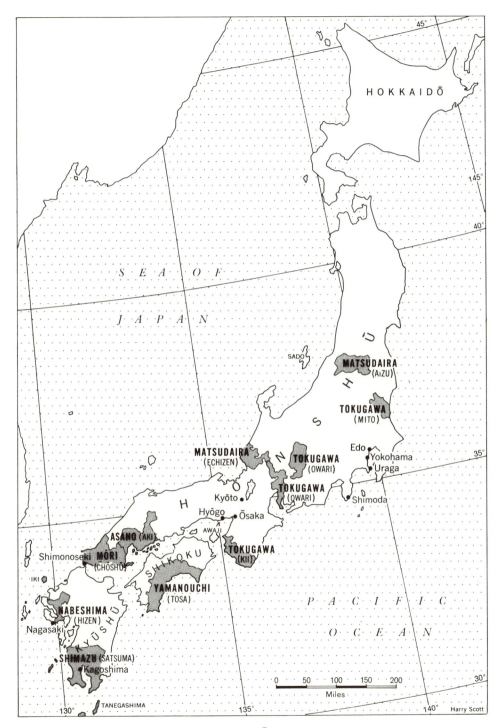

HOKKAIDŌ

SEA OF

JAPAN

SADO

MATSUDAIRA
(AIZU)

TOKUGAWA
(MITO)

Edo
Yokohama
Uraga

MATSUDAIRA
(ECHIZEN)

TOKUGAWA
(OWARI)

TOKUGAWA
(OWARI)

Kyōto

Shimoda

Hyōgo
Ōsaka

ASANO (AKI)

AWAJI

TOKUGAWA
(KII)

Shimonoseki MŌRI
(CHŌSHŪ)

IKI

SHIKOKU

YAMANOUCHI
(TOSA)

PACIFIC

NABESHIMA
(HIZEN)

KYUSHU

OCEAN

Nagasaki

SHIMAZU (SATSUMA)
Kagoshima

0   50   100 150 200
Miles

TANEGASHIMA

Harry Scott

PROMINENT DAIMYŌ DOMAINS, 1867.

In the fall of 1863, the political faction favoring a union between the imperial court and Bakufu finally succeeded, with the support of Satsuma and Aizu, in driving the Chōshū warriors out of the imperial court. The anti-Bakufu court advisers were also expelled from Kyoto. Swordsmen organized to support the Bakufu retaliated against the violence-prone anti-Bakufu shishi, and the lord of Aizu, the constable of Kyoto, kept the city under tight control.

Once the Chōshū radicals and the anti-Bakufu court officials were out of the way, the relationship between the Bakufu and the court improved. In order to fulfill its promise to expel the foreigners, the Bakufu agreed to close the port of Yokohama. The court accepted this pledge as adequate proof of the Bakufu's willingness to reimpose the policy of seclusion.

Chōshū now became the base for all the anti-Western, anti-Bakufu extremists. They succeeded in persuading the han leaders to re-enter Kyoto by force, and in the summer of 1864, the men of Chōshū marched against the imperial seat. They were driven back by the Satsuma-Aizu forces, and in the course of the conflict some of the extremist leaders, including Kusaka Genzui, lost their lives. In the fall, the Bakufu sent a punitive expedition against Chōshū. Having just been rather severely chastised by the Western powers, Chōshū was in no condition to engage the expeditionary army in combat. Consequently, it acceded to the Bakufu's demands that those responsible for the attack against Kyoto be executed. Leadership in Chōshū was then taken over by the conservatives.

The extremists who called themselves the "righteous faction," under the leadership of Takasugi Shinsaku (1839–1867), rebelled against the conservative officials in 1865 and succeeded in re-establishing their political influence. Takasugi had the support of those auxiliary militia units who were trained in Western military techniques and equipped with Western arms. These units had been organized in 1863 by Takasugi, who was authorized to do so in order to defend the han against the Western powers. A fairly large percentage of each unit consisted of peasants because of the fact that non-samurai men were now allowed to join. The samurai, who composed 25 to 30 percent of the personnel, provided the leadership. Masterless samurai and townsmen were also among the militiamen. The establishment of militia units that were open to non-samurai became necessary because upper-class samurai disdained the use of rifles, convinced that it was a dishonor to abandon their swords. Membership in the auxiliary militia opened the way to political success for many lower-class samurai. Future leaders such as Kido Kōin (1833–1877), Itō Hirobumi (1841–1909), Yamagata Aritomo (1838–1922), and Inoue Kaoru (1835–1915) were active in these units.

Even before the crushing defeat by the Western powers, some sonnō jōi leaders in Chōshū were beginning to realize the necessity of adopting Western military techniques and arms. The naval assaults by the Western powers naturally enhanced this already growing awareness. In addition, Itō Hirobumi and Inoue Kaoru had traveled abroad and returned thoroughly convinced that Japan could not return to her former seclusionist position. They began to urge their fellow shishi to accept the policy of broadening contacts with the outside world for the purpose of strengthening the nation. Kido Kōin and Takasugi shared their views. These men ceased concerning themselves solely with the interests of their own han and began thinking of the well-being of the entire nation. They concluded that the establishment of a strong centralized authority was essential if Japan were to withstand the foreign menace.

In order to strengthen Japan, they believed that it was necessary to attend to Chōshū first. Consequently, after Takasugi's rebellion, the han leadership adopted the policy of fortifying Chōshū's military power. Ōmura Masujirō (1824–1869) was given the assignment of building the Chōshū army into a modern military force. Western vessels as well as thousands of Western rifles were purchased through an English arms merchant, Thomas Glover. The money to purchase these ships and weapons was taken out of a special reserve fund that Chōshū had established in 1762 and preserved even when the han budget was running a yearly deficit.

Chōshū was busy strengthening its military forces as a momentous turn of events was occurring on the national scene. The policy of uniting the court and Bakufu was beginning to disintegrate; at the same time, behind-the-scene machinations aimed at bringing together the two rival han, Satsuma and Chōshū, were beginning to meet with some success. A group of daimyō, including those of Satsuma, Tosa, and Aizu, and Bakufu officials headed by Keiki, worked together to maintain harmony between the court and Bakufu after the departure of Chōshū from Kyoto. Soon, however, dissension began to break out because, while the leaders of Satsuma wanted a government controlled by the major han, a faction in the Bakufu was seeking to revive their autocratic powers. The leader of this group was Finance Commissioner Oguri Tadamasa (1827–1868), who was a member of the embassy that had visited the United States in 1860. Oguri hoped to modernize the Bakufu's military forces, reduce the influence of Chōshū and Satsuma, and establish a strong national government under the Bakufu. In order to accomplish this, Oguri favored obtaining the support of a Western power and turned to Leon Roches, the French minister, for advice and assistance.

Shimazu Hisamitsu (1817–1887), who was regent to the daimyō of Satsuma, disapproved of the new trend in the Bakufu and began to entertain the thought of joining hands with his former foe, Chōshū. Prior to this, the radicals in Satsuma, headed by Saigō Takamori (1827–1877) and Ōkubo Toshimichi (1830–1878), had begun agitating for the adoption of an anti-Bakufu position but Hisamitsu had restrained them. Now that he was changing his attitude toward the Bakufu, they came to the fore as key leaders of the anti-Bakufu faction.

The man who served as a mediator between Satsuma and Chōshū was Sakamoto Ryōma (1835–1867), a shishi from Tosa who had outgrown the narrowly anti-Western position he had originally embraced. He now favored opening the country and introducing reforms at the national level. He brought Saigō of Satsuma and Kido of Chōshū together, and in early 1866 the two men agreed upon an alliance.

In June of that year the Bakufu, now led by the centralists, decided to eliminate Chōshū as an obstructive element once and for all and sent a second expeditionary force against it. This time, however, many major daimyō refused to support the move. Satsuma, naturally, declined to go against its recently acquired ally. Chōshū instituted a policy of total mobilization to stop the Bakufu's forces. Its troops were better trained, better armed, and their morale was higher, so it is no surprise that they managed to rout the expeditionary army. This failure revealed the Bakufu's weakness and served to strengthen the determination of the opposition to overthrow it.

Satsuma was also taking steps to modernize its armed forces by purchasing Western arms. Like the Bakufu and other han, Satsuma also had financial difficulties, but the measures it had put into effect during the Tempō era placed it in a far stronger financial position. It repudiated its debts to the merchants, reduced the samurai's stipends, encouraged the production of cash crops, and fostered trade with the Ryukus. In particular, it successfully exploited the sugar cane production on its offshore islands by allowing no other crops to be produced and by keeping stringent controls over the peasants. Those, for example, who produced poor quality sugar were severely punished. The han authorities established a rigid monopoly on sugar, using Draconian methods to ensure its control; for instance, anyone who engaged in the private sale of sugar was put to death. The use of such ruthless measures enabled Satsuma to increase its sugar production to the point where it came to supply more than one half of all the sugar sold in Osaka. Principally because of its sugar monopoly, it managed to accumulate reserve funds, which it was able to draw upon when it began to modernize its armed forces.

Satsuma was a particularly dangerous foe of the Bakufu for numerous reasons. First, it was the second largest han, with an official yield of 770,000 koku. Second, it was located in the most distant part of the country, and this made it difficult for the Bakufu to exert its authority. Third, Satsuma had a far larger percentage of samurai in its population than any of the other han. Here the ratio of samurai to commoners was one to three, whereas the national average was one to seventeen. Fourth, the civilizing influence of the urban centers was much diminished in Satsuma, and the warriors tended as a result to retain a hardier and more militaristic outlook than the samurai of other han.

In evaluating the potential threat against the Bakufu, it should be noted that Chōshū also had a larger ratio of samurai to commoners—one to ten—than the national average. The Bakufu, in sharp contrast to Chōshū and Satsuma, retained fewer samurai than even its own scale called for, based on the official assessment of agricultural productivity. This was also true of Owari and Aizu, both collateral houses of the shogunate. Traditional feudal values along with a deep sense of loyalty and dedication to the han were strongly embedded in the Chōshū samurai. In its productive capacity, moreover, Chōshū was among the top ten han with more than 700,000 koku, well over the official estimate. In view of all these factors, the combination of Satsuma and Chōshū can be seen as posing a very serious threat to the Bakufu.

The opposition han were aided by the fact that the Bakufu lacked strong and resolute leadership. The shōgun died during the course of the second expedition against Chōshū, and although everyone's choice for successor was Keiki, he lacked confidence in his own ability to cope with the situation and hesitated for several months before accepting the offer. He then moved to strengthen the Bakufu by following Oguri's line of thinking. He also turned to the French minister Roches for advice and initiated steps to modernize the army and navy as well as the administrative system.

These moves disturbed the opposition leaders because they feared that if the Bakufu succeeded in introducing reforms and in strengthening its military forces, it could possibly regain its former status as the paramount authority. Consequently, the opponents, led by Saigō Takamori, Ōkubo Toshimichi, and Kido Kōin, moved swiftly to effect the overthrow of the Bakufu. They joined hands with the anti-Bakufu court nobles led by Iwakura Tomomi (1825–1883), the most able of the court aristocrats, and began to make plans for the restoration of power to the imperial court.

THE MEIJI RESTORATION

Sakamoto Ryōma managed to persuade his fellow clansman Gotō Shōjirō (1838–1897) to work for a peaceful solution to the power struggle at the same time that the Satsuma-Chōshū faction was plotting to overthrow the Bakufu. Under the prompting direction of Sakamoto and Gotō, Yamanouchi Yōdō (1827–1872) urged Shōgun Keiki to restore the powers of government voluntarily to the young Emperor Meiji, who had just ascended the throne. Keiki agreed to the proposal and in November of 1867 he formally petitioned the emperor to accept the restoration of power.

In describing his reasons for making this momentous decision, Keiki later explained that he had concluded that the restoration of power to the court was absolutely essential to the resolution of the crisis facing the country. Several loci of power had developed and he was searching for a political system that would incorporate the various factions in such a way as to allow the new government to function effectively. At this point, he wrote,

> Matsudaira Yōdō (Lord of Tosa) submitted his memorial calling for the establishment of upper and lower houses. I decided that this was indeed a good proposal. The upper house would consist of court aristocrats and the daimyō and the lower house would consist of selected han warriors. In this way all matters would be decided by public opinion, and the actual task of restoring imperial rule would be accomplished. As a result I acquired the courage and the confidence to bring about the restoration of imperial rule.[7]

The daimyō of Tosa as well as Gotō Shōjirō wanted to avoid a civil war that might offer the Western powers a chance to intervene and thus compromise Japan's independence. They also envisioned the establishment of a government that would be run along parliamentary lines, with the shōgun serving as the prime minister. Evidently Keiki also expected to become the chief executive of this new government. He may have relinquished his authority as shōgun, but as the head of the Tokugawa domains he was still a major feudal lord. The Tokugawa clan was bound to be a significant force in the new order as long as this situation remained unchanged. The anti-Tokugawa faction, however, had no intention of permitting the Tokugawa family to dominate the new government. They were prepared to destroy the Tokugawa clan by force if necessary, and they had even obtained a secret imperial mandate to do so. In a conference of court aristocrats, and leading daimyō and their retainers, Iwakura, with Ōkubo and Saigō's support, demanded that the Tokugawa family relinquish its entire holdings and that Keiki renounce all his authority.

Yamanouchi Yōdō fought strenuously to preserve a place in the new order for Keiki and the Tokugawa clan, but his efforts were completely undermined by Saigō's machinations. Convinced that an armed conflict was necessary if the Tokugawa clan was to be completely liquidated, Saigō decided to incite the Tokugawa forces into attacking by hiring a large number of ruffians and hoodlums in Edo to provoke their retainers. The latter fell into the trap set by Saigō and raided the Satsuma residence in Edo. News of the conflict soon reached Keiki and he and his advisers felt that they could no longer endure the humiliations being inflicted upon them by the Satsuma-Chōshū faction. They decided to take up arms against them even though this meant defying the imperial court, which was now in the grip of the Satsuma-Chōshū clique. Consequently, the Tokugawa forces were branded as rebels. Even Yōdō of Tosa was forced to join the Satsuma-Chōshū faction against Keiki.

In the ensuing battle, the Tokugawa forces were easily routed at Toba-Fushimi outside of Kyoto. Keiki fled to Edo and permitted his commander, Katsu Kaishū—who was convinced of the necessity of establishing a new order—to surrender Edo without a fight in April, 1868. Keiki was placed under house arrest, and he subsequently retired to Shizuoka. Some loyal Bakufu warriors continued to resist the imperial forces in the vicinity of Edo, but they were soon subjugated. The overthrow of the Tokugawa Bakufu was thus achieved without the country undergoing a major civil war.

The end of more than two hundred and sixty years of Tokugawa rule and the subsequent restoration of imperial rule was primarily a political event, although it has been interpreted by many Japanese historians as the product of the new social and economic forces that developed during the latter part of the Tokugawa era. It is unquestionably true that social and economic problems had begun to trouble the Bakufu, but these had not become serious enough to undermine its political authority. Elements of the ascending social and economic forces—the townsmen and the peasantry—were not the ones that challenged the existing order of things. The opposition faction emerged from the same political, social, and economic background as the Bakufu. Basically the struggle that resulted in the downfall of the Bakufu was an old-fashioned power struggle between traditional feudal power blocs. Specifically, it was a struggle between the Bakufu and, primarily, Chōshū and Satsuma. The failure of the former and the success of the latter was not directly related to the rise of the peasantry, the emergence of the merchant class, and the growth of commercial capitalism. The Meiji Restoration was certainly not a bourgeois revolution. Furthermore, peasant uprisings were not politically motivated or even directly involved in the actual overthrow of the Tokugawa government.

The outcome of the power struggle was the result of a variety of factors. For one thing, the Satsuma-Chōshū forces were militarily better prepared and possessed more able leaders. They did not gain their advantage over the Bakufu through a more significant growth in commercial capitalism or by virtue of a stronger consciousness among the merchants and the peasantry in their domains. Neither did these forces in the Bakufu's domains align themselves with the Satsuma-Chōshū faction to assist them against the Tokugawa clan. The two han were better prepared militarily because they were financially capable of purchasing modern weapons from the West. This was not the result of their having moved from an agrarian to a commercial economy. As we noted, Chōshū had a special reserve fund that was utilized to purchase weapons, and Satsuma maintained strict control over its economy and had a profitable sugar monopoly.

The crucial factor that made the difference in the rivalry between the Bakufu and the opposition han was leadership. A large number of zealous, highly capable shishi who were willing to take drastic actions to achieve their objectives were present in Satsuma and Chōshū. Many new leaders had also emerged from the lower rungs of the samurai class in these han. The Bakufu, on the other hand, lacked strong leadership, and control remained largely in the hands of the more conservative, high-ranking members of the feudal hierarchy.

In the smaller political communities of the han it was easier for able men from the lower ranks of the samurai to gain recognition and be utilized in time of crisis. In the larger political world of the Bakufu, on the other hand, the upper levels of the hierarchy were crowded with unimaginative, conservative men, and the chances of a low-ranking samurai attracting the attention of the higher officials were extremely limited. After he became shōgun, Keiki claimed that he sought to utilize "men of talent," but by that time it was too late. Furthermore, it is entirely possible that if Keiki himself had been rigorously determined to retain political power at all costs, the outcome may have turned out differently. He was severely lacking in determination and willpower, so he hesitated and procrastinated. The inevitable consequence of this was that power slipped away from the Bakufu almost by default.

Probably the single most important factor, however, that contributed to the downfall of the Bakufu was the arrival of the Western powers. The Bakufu, as the authority directly responsible for foreign relations, was confronted with an impossible dilemma. Perry's arrival forced the Bakufu into opening a Pandora's box that brought the imperial court as well as the daimyō and its retainers into the decision-making process. This was followed by a series of crises that were set off by the signing of the commercial treaty with the United States without first securing imperial sanction. The Western powers were demanding still broader contacts and the Bakufu's opponents were thus given additional opportunities to play upon anti-foreign sentiments and to forge an emotionally charged move-ment—the sonnō jōi movement—that cut across han barriers.

The Bakufu was unable to adopt a definitive policy that they could pursue with firmness. It wavered between opening the country and suc-cumbing to the pressures exerted by the exclusionists. The Bakufu staggered along without resolute leadership after Ii Naosuke, who was willing to use strong measures to curb the advocates of sonnō jōi, was eliminated. The lower-ranking samurai, who would not have been permitted to meddle in the affairs of state under normal circumstances, were able to use terrorist means to intimidate and sometimes eliminate their political foes.

The opposition leaders used every opportunity to harass the Bakufu in its management of foreign affairs. The Chōshū proponents of sonnō jōi fired upon Western vessels, and when they were directly confronted by the foreign powers they sought to shift the blame to the Bakufu by claiming that they were following its orders to expel the intruders. In 1867, as the deadline for the opening of the port of Hyōgo approached, the leaders of Satsuma insisted that the Bakufu renege on its agreement to open the port because, as they claimed, it was too close to Kyoto and would be offensive to the imperial court. At the same time, the leaders of Satsuma were in fact themselves dealing with the Western powers by purchasing ships and arms from them. In order to embarrass the Bakufu, the British, in collusion with the Satsuma-Chōshū faction, were pressing for the opening of the port, fully expecting the Bakufu's opponents to block it. In the ensuing crisis the opposition forces were expected to overthrow the Bakufu. Ernest Satow, the British minister's interpreter, recalled "I hinted to Saigō that the chance of a revolution was not to be lost. If Hiogo was once opened, then good-bye to chances of the daimios."[8]

Clearly, the situation that most seriously contributed to the undermining of the Bakufu's authority and self-confidence was the arrival of the Western powers. Without the crisis engendered by this situation, the Bakufu would not have collapsed as soon as it did. The end of Tokugawa rule, needless to say, did not bring about a completely new age and a new society overnight. In the course of the Meiji era significant transformations took place, but the new was built upon the foundations of the old. The attitudes, values, practices, and institutions that molded the Japanese mode of thinking and behavior prior to and during the Tokugawa era continued to govern the thought and actions of the people during the Meiji era and for a long time afterwards. Added to the old, however, were many new elements. These involved not only science and technology, but new political, social, and cultural ideas were also imported. All of these were to contribute to the very difficult period of transition that ensued.

NOTES

1. W. G. Beasley, trans. and ed., *Select Documents on Japanese Foreign Policy, 1853–1868* (London: Oxford University Press, 1955), pp. 103, 107.

2. This latter group would correspond to what Arnold Toynbee calls the "Herodians": "The 'Herodian' is the man who acts on the principle that the most effective way to guard against the danger of the unknown is to master its secret; and, when he finds himself in the predicament of being confronted by a more highly skilled and better armed opponent, he responds by discarding his traditional art of war and learning to fight his enemy with the enemy's own tactics and own weapons." In contrast, the "Zealot" reverts to "archaism evoked by foreign pressure." Arnold Toynbee, *Civilization on Trial and the World and the West* (New York: World Publishing, 1958), pp. 167–73. Perry's arrival brought forth these two types in Japan, and it was the Herodians who ultimately won out.

3. David M. Earl, *Emperor and Nation in Japan* (Seattle, Wash.: University of Washington Press, 1964), p. 183.

4. Maruyama Masao, *Nihon Seijishisōshi Kenkyū* (*Studies in the History of Japanese Political Thought*) (Tokyo: Tōkyō Daigaku Shuppankai, 1954), pp. 355–56.

5. *Ibid.*, pp. 356–57.

6. Naramoto Tatsuya, ed., *Nihon no Shisōka* (*The Thinkers of Japan*) (Tokyo: Mainichi Shimbunsha, 1954), p. 237.

7. Sakata Yoshio, *Meiji Ishinshi* (*A History of the Meiji Restoration*) (Tokyo: Miraisha, 1960), p. 202.

8. Ernest M. Satow, *A Diplomat in Japan* (London: Seeley, 1921), p. 200.

CHRONOLOGICAL CHART

PRE- AND PROTO-HISTORICAL ERAS

?-ca. 250 B.C.	Jōmon culture
ca. 250 B.C.– A.D. 250	Yayoi culture
660 B.C.	Mythical date of the accession of the first Emperor, Jimmu
ca. 100 B.C.	Rice cultivation in wet fields commences.
A.D. 57	The Japanese Kingdom of Nu sends an envoy to the Chinese court of the Later Han Dynasty.
139	The ruler of Yamatai, Himiko, sends an envoy to the Chinese Kingdom of Wei.

YAMATO PERIOD (CA. A.D. 300–710)

ca. 300	The imperial family establishes its hegemony over Japan.
ca. 400	Writing is introduced from Korea.
538 (or 562)	Buddhism is introduced from Paikche in Korea.
562	The Japanese colony of Mimana in Korea is conquered by Silla.
593–622	Prince Shōtoku is regent.
604	The "Constitution of Seventeen Articles" is issued.
607	The Hōryūji is constructed.
645	The Taika Reforms are initiated.
701	The Taihō Code is completed.

NARA PERIOD (710–784)

710	The capital is established in Nara (Heijōkyō).
712	The compilation of the *Kojiki* is completed.
720	The compilation of the *Nihongi* is completed.
743	Private ownership of reclaimed land is permitted.
752	The Great Buddha of Tōdaiji is dedicated.
ca. 780	The compilation of the *Manyōshū* is completed.

HEIAN PERIOD (794–1185)

794	The capital is moved to Kyoto (Heiankyō).
794	Seiitaishōgun is appointed to subdue the Ezo.
858	Fujiwara Yoshifusa is appointed regent.
939–940	Taira-no-Masakado leads a rebellion.
ca. 1002–1019	*The Tale of Genji* is written.
1016	Fujiwara Michinaga is appointed regent.
1086	The cloister government is established.
1167	Taira-no-Kiyomori is appointed chancellor (dajō daijin).
1175	The Pure Land Sect is founded by Hōnen.
1180	Minamoto-no-Yoritomo challenges the Taira family.
1185	The Taira family falls.

KAMAKURA PERIOD (1185–1333)

1192	Yoritomo is appointed shōgun.
1205	Hōjō Yoshitoki becomes regent to the shōgun.
1224	The True Pure Land Sect is founded by Shinran.
1253	The Nichiren Sect is founded by Nichiren.
1274	The first Mongol invasion occurs.
1281	The second Mongol invasion occurs.
1333	The Kamakura Bakufu collapses.
1334	The Kemmu Restoration is established under Emperor Godaigo.
1335	Ashikaga Takauji rebels against the imperial government.
1336	Emperor Godaigo flees to Yoshino and establishes the Southern Court.

ASHIKAGA PERIOD (1338–1573)

1338	Takauji becomes shōgun.
1392	The Southern and Northern courts are united.
1401	The third shōgun, Yoshimitsu, establishes relations with Ming China.
1467–1477	The Ōnin War
1495	Hōjō Sōun captures Odawara.
1506	The painter Sesshū dies.
1543	A Portuguese ship arrives at Tanegashima.
1549	St. Francis Xavier arrives to propagate Christianity.
1568	Oda Nobunaga occupies Kyoto.
1573	The last Ashikaga shōgun is deposed by Nobunaga.
1582	Nobunaga is assassinated.
1586	Toyotomi Hideyoshi is appointed chancellor (dajō daijin).
1587	Christianity is banned by Hideyoshi.
1588–1598	A land survey is conducted under Hideyoshi.
1588	Hideyoshi confiscates arms from the peasants.
1592	Japan invades Korea.
1598	Hideyoshi dies.
1600	Tokugawa Ieyasu triumphs in the Battle of Sekigahara.

TOKUGAWA PERIOD (1600–1867)

1603	Ieyasu is appointed shōgun.
1635	The system of alternate attendance of daimyō in Edo is introduced.

1637–1638	The Shimabara Rebellion
1639	The nation is closed to the outside world.
1643	Buying and selling land is prohibited.
1716	Tokugawa Yoshimune becomes the eighth shōgun and initiates the Kyōho Reforms.
1720	The ban on Western books is relaxed.
1724	The playwright Chikamatsu dies.
1782–1787	The Temmei Famine
1787	Matsudaira Sadanobu becomes rōjū (senior councilor) and initiates the Kansei Reforms.
1792	A Russian vessel commanded by Laxman arrives in Hokkaido, asking for commercial relations.
1793	The novelist Ihara Saikaku dies.
1801	Motoori Norinaga dies.
1825	An edict to drive off foreign vessels is issued.
1833–1837	The Tempyō Famine
1837	Ōshio Heihachirō leads an insurrection.
1841	Rōjū Mizuno Tadakuni initiates the Tempō Reforms.
1849	The woodblock artist Hokusai dies.
1853	Commodore Perry arrives.
1854	The Treaty of Kanagawa is signed with the United States.
1858	Ii Naosuke is appointed great councilor (tairō); a commercial treaty with the United States is concluded; the woodblock artist Hiroshige dies.
1867	Shōgun Keiki restores political power to the imperial court.

MEIJI PERIOD (1868–1912)

1868	A new government is established; Tokyo (formerly Edo) becomes the capital.
1869	Four major daimyō relinquish control over their han to the imperial government.
1871	The han are replaced by prefectures; the postal system is introduced; Tokugawa class distinctions are eliminated; the Iwakura mission is dispatched to the West.
1872	The Tokyo-Yokohama railroad is opened; the freedom to buy and sell land is granted; compulsory elementary education is instituted.
1873	The Gregorian Calendar is adopted (Dec. 3, 1872, of the old lunar calendar is converted to Jan. 1, 1873); universal military conscription and a new land tax are instituted.
1874	A request for the establishment of a national assembly is submitted by Itagaki and others.
1876	The wearing of swords by former samurai is banned.
1877	Saigō Takamori rebels.
1879	The Ryukyu islands become Okinawa Prefecture.
1881	A national assembly is promised by the government.
1884	The peerage is created; The Chichibu uprising occurs.
1885	The cabinet system is adopted; Itō Hirobumi becomes the first Prime Minister.
1887	Electric lighting is introduced.

1888	The Privy Council is established.
1889	The Constitution is promulgated.
1890	The First Diet convenes; the Imperial Rescript on Education is issued; telephone service is introduced.
1894	A treaty revision is agreed upon between Japan and England.
1894–1895	The Sino-Japanese War
1898	The Ōkuma-Itagaki cabinet is formed.
1902	The Anglo-Japanese Alliance is concluded.
1904–1905	The Russo-Japanese War
1910	Korea is annexed; Kōtoku Shūsui and others are executed.
1912	Emperor Meiji dies.

TAISHŌ PERIOD (1912–1926)

1914	Japan enters the First World War.
1915	The Twenty-One Demands are presented to China.
1918	The Hara Cabinet is formed.
1921	The Washington Conference on naval arms limitations convenes.
1923	The Great Earthquake
1925	Universal manhood suffrage is enacted; radio broadcasting commences.
1926	Emperor Taishō dies.

SHŌWA PERIOD (1926–)

1931	The Manchurian Incident
1932	Prime Minister Inukai is assassinated; party government ends.
1933	Japan withdraws from the League of Nations.
1935	Minobe Tatsukichi's Organ Theory is condemned.
1936	Prominent leaders are assassinated by radical militarists; the Anti-Cominteran Pact with Germany is concluded.
1937	War with China breaks out.
1940	Japanese troops move into French Indochina; a tripartite alliance with Germany and Italy is concluded.
1941	Japan attacks Pearl Harbor and the Pacific War begins.
1942	The Battle of Midway (June);
1944	the tide of war shifts. Saipan falls; Prime Minister Tōjō resigns; U.S. bombers carry out massive air raids on Japanese cities.
1945	U.S. troops land in the Philippines and Okinawa; atomic bombs are dropped on Hiroshima and Nagasaki; Russia enters the war; Japan surrenders; Allied occupation under General MacArthur begins.
1946	A new constitution is promulgated.
1948	General Tōjō and others are executed.
1951	The peace treaty is signed in San Francisco.
1952	The Allied occupation ends.
1953	A United States-Japanese Mutual Security Agreement is signed; television broadcasting begins.
1956	Japan is admitted to the United Nations.

1960	A new United States-Japan Mutual Security Agreement is concluded.
1971	The United States agrees to relinquish control of Okinawa by 1972.
1972	Prime Minister Tanaka visits China and normalizes relations.
1973	Arab oil embargo and energy crisis
1975	Emperor Hirohito visits the United States.
1980	Japan produces more automobiles than the United States.
1983	President Reagan visits Japan.

SELECTED BIBLIOGRAPHY

HISTORICAL AND BIOGRAPHICAL DICTIONARIES

Goedertier, Joseph M. A. *Dictionary of Japanese History.* New York: Weatherhill, 1968.

Hisamatsu, Senichi. *Biographical Dictionary of Japanese Literature.* Tokyo: Kodansha, 1976.

Hunter, Janet. *Concise Dictionary of Modern Japanese History.* Berkeley: University of California Press, 1984.

Itasaka, Gen, general editor. *Japan Encyclopedia,* 9 vols. Tokyo: Kodansha, 1983.

Iwao, Seiichi. *Biographical Dictionary of Japanese History.* Tokyo: Kodansha, 1978.

O'Neill, P. G. *Japanese Names.* Tokyo: Weatherhill, 1972.

Papinot, Edmund. *Historical and Geographical Dictionary of Japan,* 2 vols. New York: Ungar, 1964 (reprint of 1910 edition).

Roberts, Laurance P. A. *Dictionary of Japanese Artists.* Tokyo: Weatherhill, 1976.

GEOGRAPHICAL WORKS

Cressey, George B. *Asia's Lands and Peoples.* New York: McGraw-Hill, 1963.

Dempster, Prue. *Japan Advances: A Geographical Study.* New York: Barnes & Noble, 1968.

Isida, Ryujiro. *Geography of Japan.* Tokyo: Kokusai Bunka Shinkokai, 1969.

Trewartha, Glenn T. *Japan: A Physical, Cultural and Regional Geography.* Madison: University of Wisconsin Press, 1965.

GENERAL HISTORIES

Hall, John W. *Japan: From Prehistory to Modern Times.* New York: Delacorte, 1970.

Ienaga, Saburō. *History of Japan.* Tokyo: Japan Travel Bureau, 1956.

Inoue, Mitsusada. *Introduction to Japanese History, Before the Meiji Restoration.* Tokyo: Kokusai Bunka Shinkokai, 1968.

Murdoch, James. *A History of Japan,* 3 vols., each with 2 parts. New York: Ungar, 1964 (reprint of a 1930–1926 edition).

Reischauer, Edwin O. *Japan: The Story of a Nation.* New York: McGraw-Hill, 1990.

Reischauer, Edwin O., and John K. Fairbank. *A History of East Asian Civilization: East Asia the Great Tradition.* Boston: Houghton Mifflin, 1960.

Sansom, Sir George B. *A History of Japan,* 3 vols. Stanford, Calif.: Stanford University Press, 1963.

———. *Japan, A Short Cultural History.* New York: Appleton, 1943.

Totman, Conrad. *Japan Before Perry.* Berkeley: University of California Press, 1981.

SPECIAL ASPECTS OF JAPANESE HISTORY AND CULTURE

Akiyama, Terukazu. *Treasures of Asia: Japanese Painting.* Cleveland: World, 1961.

Anesaki, Masaharu. *History of Japanese Religion.* Tokyo and Rutland, Vt.: Tuttle, 1963.

_____ . *Religious Life of the Japanese People.* Tokyo: Kokusai Bunka Shinkokai, 1961.

Aston, W. G. *A History of Japanese Literature.* New York: Appleton, 1899.

Barrett, William, ed. *Zen Buddhism: Selected Writings of D. T. Suzuki.* Garden City, N.Y.: Doubleday, 1956.

Beasley, W. G., and E. G. Pulleyblank, eds. *Historians of China and Japan.* London: Oxford University Press, 1961.

Benedict, Ruth. *The Chrysanthemum and the Sword: Patterns of Japanese Culture.* Boston: Houghton Mifflin, 1946.

Binyon, Lawrence. *Painting in the Far East.* New York: Dover, 1959.

Boger, H. Batterson. *The Traditional Arts of Japan.* Garden City, N.Y.: Doubleday, 1964.

Borton, Hugh, ed. *Japan.* Ithaca, N.Y.: Cornell University Press, 1951.

Bunce, William K. *Religions in Japan: Buddhism, Shinto, Christianity.* Rutland, Vt.: Tuttle, 1955.

Chamberlain, Bail H. *Things Japanese.* London: Routledge & Kegan Paul, 1939.

Craig, Albert M., and Donald H. Shively. *Personality in Japanese History.* Berkeley, Calif.: University of California Press, 1971.

Dumoulin, Heinrich. *History of Zen Buddhism.* New York: Random House, 1963.

Earhart, H. Bryan. *Japanese Religion: Unity and Diversity.* Rutherford, N.J.: Farleigh Dickinson University Press, 1974.

_____ . *Religion in the Japanese Experience.* Rutherford, N.J.: Fairleigh Dickinson University Press, 1974.

Hall, John Whitney. *Government and Local Power in Japan, 500 to 1700: A Study Based on Bizen Province.* Princeton, N.J.: Princeton University Press, 1966.

Hall, John W., and Richard K. Beardsley. *Twelve Doors to Japan.* New York: McGraw-Hill, 1965.

Hasegawa, Nyozekan. *The Japanese Character: A Cultural Profile.* Translated by John Bester. Tokyo and Palo Alto, Calif.: Kodansha International, 1965.

Hearn, Lafcadio. *Glimpses of Unfamiliar Japan,* 2 vols. Boston: Houghton Mifflin, 1894.

_____ . *Japan: An Attempt at Interpretation.* New York: Macmillan, 1913.

Herrigal, Eugen. *Zen.* New York: McGraw-Hill, 1964.

Hisamatsu, Shinichi. *Zen and the Fine Arts.* Tokyo: Kodansha, 1971.

Holtom, Daniel C. *The National Faith of Japan: A Study in Modern Shinto.* New York: Dutton, 1938.

Honjo, Eijiro. *The Social and Economic History of Japan.* New York: Russell, 1965. (Reprint of a 1935 edition.)

Keene, Donald, ed. *Anthology of Japanese Literature from the Earliest Era to the Mid-nineteenth Century.* New York: Grove, 1955.

_____ , ed. *Japanese Literature: An Introduction for Western Readers.* New York: Grove, 1955.

_____ . *Living Japan.* Garden City, N.Y.: Doubleday, 1949

_____ . *World Within Walls.* New York: Holt, Rinehart and Winston, 1976.

_____ . *The Pleasures of Japanese Literature.* New York: Columbia University Press, 1988.

Kelly, William W. *Deference and Defiance in Nineteenth-Century Japan.* Princeton: Princeton University Press, 1985.

Kitagawa, Joseph M. *Religion in Japanese History*. New York: Columbia University Press, 1966.

Koschmann, Victor J., ed. *Authority and Individual in Japan: Citizen Protest in Historical Perspective*. Tokyo: University of Tokyo Press, 1978.

Lee, Sherman E. *A History of Far Eastern Art*. Englewood Cliffs, N.J.: Prentice-Hall; New York, N.Y.: Abrams, 1964.

McClellan, Edwin. *Woman in the Crested Kimono: The Life of Shizue Io and Her Family*. New Haven: Yale University Press, 1985.

Morris, Ivan. *The Nobility of Failure*. New York: Holt, 1975.

Munsterberg, Hugo. *The Arts of Japan: An Illustrated History*. Tokyo and Rutland, Vt.: Tuttle, 1957.

———. *The Folk Arts of Japan*. Tokyo and Rutland, Vt.: Tuttle, 1958.

———. *Zen and Oriental Art*. Tokyo and Rutland, Vt.: Tuttle, 1965.

Nakamura, Hajime. *Ways of Thinking and Eastern Peoples: India, China, Tibet, Japan*. Honolulu: East-West Center Press, 1964.

Nitobe, Inazo. *Bushidō, the Soul of Japan*. New York: Putnam, 1905.

Okakura, Kakuzo. *The Book of Tea*. Tokyo and Rutland, Vt.: Tuttle, 1956.

Paine, Robert T., and Alexander C. Soper. *The Art and Architecture of Japan*. Baltimore, Md.: Penguin, 1955.

Pickens, Stuart. *Shinto: Japan's Spiritual Roots*.Tokyo: Kodansha, 1980.

Reischauer, Edwin O. *The United States and Japan*. New York: Viking, 1965.

Saunders, Ernest Dale. *Buddhism in Japan; With an Outline of its Origins in India*. Philadelphia: University of Pennsylvania Press, 1964.

Seidensticker, Edward. *Japan*. New York: Time-Life, 1968.

Silberman, Bernard S., ed. *Japanese Character and Culture: A Book of Selected Readings*. Tucson, Ariz.: University of Arizona Press, 1962.

Smith, Robert J., and Richard K. Beardsley. *Japanese Culture: Its Development and Characteristics*. Chicago: Aldine, 1962.

Sugimoto, Masayoshi, and David L. Swain, *Science and Culture in Traditional Japan*. Cambridge, Mass.: MIT Press, 1978.

Suzuki, Daisetsu T. *An Introduction to Zen Buddhism*. New York: Grove, 1964.

———. *Essays in Zen Buddhism*. New York: Harper & Row, 1949.

———. *Zen and Japanese Culture*. New York: Pantheon, 1959.

Swann, Peter C. *The Art of Japan, From the Jomon to the Tokugawa Period*. New York: Crown, 1966.

Takekoshi, Yosaburo. *Economic Aspects of the History of the Civilization of Japan*. 3 vols. New York: Paragon, 1967 (reprint of a 1930 edition).

Tokyo National Museum. *Pageant of Japanese Art*, 6 vols. Tokyo: Tōto Bunka, 1952–1954.

Transactions of the Asiatic Society of Japan. Tokyo: Asiatic Society of Japan, series 1, nos. 1–50, 1872–1922; series 2, nos. 1–19, 1924–1940; series 3, nos. 1–1948– . This collection has a wealth of material on all aspects of Japanese history and culture.

Tsunoda, Ryusaku, W. T. de Bary, and Donald Keene, eds. *Sources of Japanese Tradition*. New York: Columbia University Press, 1958.

Ueda, Makoto. *Literary and Art Theories in Japan*. Cleveland: Case Western Reserve, 1967.

Warner, Langdon. *The Enduring Art of Japan*. New York: Grove, 1952.

Watanabe, Shoko. *Japanese Buddhism, a Critical Appraisal*. Tokyo: Kokusai Bunka Shinkokai, 1968.

Yashiro, Yukio. *Art Treasures of Japan*, 2 vols. Tokyo: Kokusai Bunka Shinkokai, 1960.

EARLY HISTORY TO 1185

Aston, W. G., trans. *Nihongi (Chronicles of Japan from the Earliest Times to A.D. 697)*. New York: Paragon, 1956 (reprint of a 1924 edition).

Borgen, Robert. *Sugawara no Michizane and the Early Heian Court*. Cambridge, Mass.: Harvard University Press, 1986.

Brazell, Karen, trans. *The Confessions of Lady Nijo*. Stanford, Calif.: Stanford University Press, 1973.

Brower, Robert Hopkins, and Earl R. Miner. *Japanese Court Poetry*. Stanford, Calif.: Stanford University Press, 1961.

Campbell, Joseph. *The Masks of God: Oriental Mythology*. New York: Viking, 1962.

Chamberlain, Basil H., trans. *Kojiki (Records of Ancient matters)*. London: Routledge & Kegan Paul, 1932.

Ebersole, Gary L. *Ritual Poetry and Politics of Death in Early Japan*. Princeton, N.J.: Princeton University Press, 1989.

Farris, William W. *Population, Disease, and Land in Early Japan, 645–900*. Cambridge, Mass.: Harvard University Press, 1985.

Field, Norma. *The Splendor of Longing in the Tale of Genji*. Princeton, N.J., Princeton University Press, 1987.

Hurst, Cameron. *Insei: Abdicated Sovereigns in the Politics of Late Heian Japan, 1086–1185*. New York: Columbia University Press, 1976.

Kidder, Edward J. *Japan Before Buddhism*. New York: Praeger, 1959.

Komatsu, Isao. *The Japanese People: Origins of the People and the Language*. Tokyo: Kokusai Bunka Shinkokai, 1962.

McCullough, Helen C., trans. *Tales of Ise: Lyrical Episodes from Tenth-Century Japan*, Stanford, Calif.: Stanford University Press, 1968.

Miner, Earl. *An Introduction to Japanese Court Poetry*. Stanford, Calif.: Stanford University Press, 1968.

Morris, Ivan I. *The World of the Shining Prince: Court Life in Ancient Japan*. New York: Knopf, 1964.

Murasaki Shikibu. *The Tale of Genji*. Translated by Arthur Waley. New York: Random House, 1960. (Also translated by Edward G. Seidensticker. New York: Knopf, 1978.)

Nippon Gakujutsu Shinkokai (The Japan Society for the Promotion of Scientific Research). *Manyōshū: One Thousand Poems*. New York: Columbia University Press, 1965.

Philippi, Donald L., trans. *Kojiki*. Princeton, N.J.: Princeton University Press, 1968.

Sadler, A., L., trans. "Heiki Monogatari (The Tale of the Heike)," in *Tranactions of the Asiatic Society of Japan*, series 1, vol. 46, part 2 (1918), and vol. 49, part 1 (1921).

Sansom, Sir George G. *A History of Japan to 1334*. Stanford, Calif.: Stanford University Press, 1958.

Seidensticker, Edward G., trans. *The Gossamer Years: A Diary by a Noblewoman of Heian Japan*. Tokyo and Rutland, Vt.: Tuttle, 1964.

Sei Shōnagon. *The Pillow Book of Sei Shōnagon*, 2 vols. Translated and edited by Ivan Morris. New York: Columbia University Press, 1967.

Tsunoda, Ryusaku, trans., and L. Carrington Goodrich, ed. *Japan in the Chinese Dynastic Histories: Later Han Through Ming Dynasties*. South Pasadena, Calif.: Perkins, 1951.

Wheeler, Post, ed. and trans. *The Sacred Scriptures of the Japanese*. New York: Abelard-Schuman, 1952.

Young, John. *The Location of Yamatai*. Baltimore, Md.: Johns Hopkins Press, 1957.

THE ASCENDANCY OF THE MILITARY HOUSES:
FROM 1185 TO 1600

Asakawa, Kanichi, ed. *The Documents of Iriki, Illustrative of the Development of the Feudal Institution in Japan.* Tokyo: Japan Society for the Promotion of Science, 1955.

Berry, Mary Elizabeth. *Hideyoshi.* Cambridge, Mass.: Harvard University Press, 1982.

Boxer, Charles R. *The Christian Century in Japan, 1549–1650.* Berkeley: University of California Press, 1951.

Brown, Delmer M. *The Future and the Past: A Translation and Study of the Gukansho.* Berkeley: University of California Press, 1979.

Collcut, Martin. *Five Mountains: The Rinzai Monastic Institution in Medieval Japan.* Cambridge, Mass.: Harvard University Press, 1981.

Cooper, Michael, S. J., ed. *They Came to Japan: An Anthology of European Reports on Japan, 1543–1640.* Berkeley: University of California Press, 1965.

Dening, Walter. *The Life of Toyotomi Hideyoshi (1536–1598).* Tokyo: Hokuseido Press, 1955.

Duus, Peter. *Feudalism in Japan.* New York: Knopf, 1969.

Elison, George, and Bardwell Smith, eds. *Warlords, Artists and Commoners: Japan in the Sixteenth Century.* Honolulu: University Press of Hawaii, 1981.

Hall, John W., Nagahara Keiji, and Kozo Yamamura, eds. *Japan Before Tokugawa: Political Consolidation and Economic Growth.* Princeton, N.J.: Princeton University Press, 1981.

Hall, John W., and Takeshi Toyoda. *Japan in the Muromachi Age.* Berkeley: University of California Press, 1977.

Keene, Donald, trans. *Essays in Idleness: The Tsurezuregusa of Kenkō.* New York: Columbia University Press, 1967.

_____, ed. *Twenty Plays of the No Theatre.* New York: Columbia University Press, 1970.

Kirby, John B. *From Castle to Teahouse: Japanese Architecture of the Momoyama Period.* Tokyo and Rutland, Vt.: Tuttle, 1962.

Kitabatake, Chikafusa. *A Chronicle of Gods and Sovereigns.* Translated by H. Paul Varley. New York: Columbia University Press, 1980.

Mass, Jeffrey P., ed. *Court and Bakufu in Japan.* New Haven: Yale University Press, 1982.

Mass, Jeffrey P., and William B. Hauser, eds. *The Bakufu in Japanese History.* Stanford, Calif.: Stanford University Press, 1985.

Mass, Jeffrey P., *The Development of Kamakura Rule, 1180–1250: A History with Documents.* Stanford, Calif.: Stanford University Press, 1979.

_____. *The Kamakura Bakufu, A Study in Documents.* Stanford, Calif.: Stanford University Press, 1976.

_____. *Warrior Government in Early Medieval Japan.* New Haven: Yale University Press, 1974.

McCullough, Helen, trans. *Okagami: The Great Mirror.* Princeton, N.J.: Princeton University Press, 1980.

_____, trans. *The Taiheiki: A Chronicle of Medieval Japan.* New York: Columbia University Press, 1959.

_____, trans. *The Tale of the Heike.* Stanford, Calif.: Stanford University Press, 1988.

_____, trans. *Yoshitsune: A Fifteenth-Century Japanese Chronicle.* Stanford, Calif.: Stanford University Press, 1966.

Nakamura, Yasuo. *Noh, the Classical Theater*. Trans. Don Kenny. New York and Tokyo: Walker/Weatherhill, 1971.

Reischauer, Edwin O. "Japanese Feudalism," in Rushton Coulborn, ed., *Feudalism in History*. Princeton, N.J.: Princetonn University Press, 1956.

Rodrigues, Joao S. J. *This Island of Japan: Joao Rodigues' Account of 16th Century Japan*. Translated by Michael Cooper. Tokyo: Kodansha, 1973.

Sansom, Sir George B. *A History of Japan, 1334–1615*. Stanford, Calif.: Stanford University Press, 1960.

Shinoda, Minoru. *The Founding of the Kamakura Shogunate, 1180–1185*. New York: Columbia University Press, 1960.

Varley, H. Paul. *Imperial Restoration in Medieval Japan*. New York: Columbia University Press, 1971.

––––––. *The Ōnin War: History of Its Origins and Background, with a Selective Translation of the Chronicles of Ōnin*. New York: Columbia University Press, 1967.

Waley, Arthur. *The Nō Plays of Japan*. London: Allen & Unwin, 1911.

THE TOKUGAWA PERIOD: POLITICAL, SOCIAL, AND ECONOMIC AFFAIRS

Arnesen, Peter J. *The Medieval Japanese Daimyo*. New Haven: Yale University Press, 1979.

Bix, Herbert P. *Peasant Protest in Japan, 1590–1884*. New Haven, Conn.: Yale University Press, 1986.

Bolitho, Harold. *Treasures Among Men: The Fudai Daimyo in Tokugawa Japan*. New Haven: Yale University Press, 1974.

Borton, Hugh. "Peasant Uprisings in Japan of the Tokugawa Period," in *Transactions of the Asiatic Society of Japan*, series 2, vol. 16 (1938).

Hall, John W. *Tanuma Okitsugu, 1719–1788, Forerunner of Modern Japan*. Cambridge, Mass.: Harvard University Press, 1955.

Hall, John W., and Marius Jansen, eds. *Studies in the Institutional History of Early Modern Japan*. Princeton, N.J.: Princeton University Press, 1968.

Jannetta, Ann B. *Epidemics and Mortality in Early Modern Japan*. Princeton, N.J.: Princeton University Press, 1987.

Kaempfer, Engelbert. *History of Japan*, 3 vols. Translated by J.G.S. Schenchzer. Glasgow: MacLehose, 1906.

Katsu, Kōkichi. *Musui's Story: The Autobiography of a Tokugawa Samurai*, Teruko Craig, trans. Tucson, Ariz.: University of Arizona Press, 1988.

Ooms, Herman. *Charismatic Bureaucrat: A Political Biography of Matsudaira Sadanobu*. Chicago: University of Chicago, 1975.

Perrin, Noel. *Giving Up the Gun, Japan's Reversion to the Sword, 1543–1879*. Boulder, Colorado: Shambhala, 1980.

Roberts, John C. *Mitsui Empire: Three Centuries of Japanese Business*. New York: Weatherhill, 1973.

Sadler, A. L. *The Maker of Modern Japan: The Life of Tokugawa Ieyasu*. London: Allen and Unwin, 1937.

Sansom, Sir George B. *A History of Japan, 1615–1867*. Stanford, Calif.: Stanford University Press, 1963.

Sheldon, C. D. *The Rise of the Merchant Class in Tokugawa Japan*. Locust Valley, N.Y.: Augustin, 1958.

Smith, Neil Skene, ed. "Materials On Japanese Social and Economic History: Tokugawa Japan," in *Transactions of the Asiatic Society of Japan*, series 2, vol. 14 (1937).

Smith, Thomas C. *The Agrarian Origins of Modern Japan*. Stanford, Calif.: Stanford University Press, 1959.

———. *Nakahara, Family Farming and Population in a Japan Village, 1717–1830*. Stanford, Calif.: Stanford University Press, 1977.

———. *Native Sources of Japanese Industrialization*. Berkeley and Los Angeles, Calif.: University of California Press, 1988.

Toby, Ronald P. *State and Diplomacy in Early Modern Japan*. Princeton, N.J.: Princeton University Press, 1984.

Totman, Conrad D. *Politics in the Tokugawa Bakufu, 1600–1843*. Cambridge, Mass.: Harvard University Press, 1967.

———. *Tokugawa Ieyasu*. South San Francisco: Heian, 1982.

Vlastos, Stephen. *Peasant Protests and Uprisings in Tokugawa Japan*. Berkeley and Los Angeles, Calif.: University of California Press, 1986.

Walthall, Anne. *Social Protest and Popular Culture in Eighteenth Century Japan*. Tucson, Ariz.: University of Arizona Press, 1985.

Webb, Herschel. *The Japanese Imperial Institution in the Tokugawa Period*. New York: Columbia University Press, 1968.

Wigmore, John H. *Law and Justice in Tokugawa Japan*, 2 vols. Tokyo: University of Tokyo Press, 1969.

THE TOKUGAWA PERIOD: INTELLECTUAL DEVELOPMENTS

Ackroyd, Joyce, trans. *Told Round a Brushwood Fire: The Autobiography of Arai Hakuseki*. Tucson, Ariz.: University of Arizona Press, 1980.

Arai, Hakuseki. *Lessons for History*. Translated by Joyce Ackroyd. St. Lucia, Queensland: University of Queensland, 1982.

Bellah, Robert N. *Tokugawa Religion: The Values of Pre-Industrial Japan*. Glencoe, Ill.: Free Press, 1957.

Dardess, John W., *Confucianism and Autocracy*. Berkeley: University of California Press, 1983.

Dore, Ronald P. *Education in Tokugawa Japan*. Berkeley, Calif.: University of California Press, 1965.

Earl, David M. *Emperor and Nation in Japan: Political Thinkers of the Tokugawa Period*. Seattle: University of Washington Press, 1964.

Elison, George. *Deus Destroyed: The Image of Christianity in Early Modern Japan*. Cambridge, Mass.: Harvard University Press, 1973.

Harootunian, H.D. *Things Seen and Unseen: Discourse and Ideology in Tokugawa Nativism*. Chicago: University of Chicago Press, 1988.

Keene, Donald. *The Japanese Discovery of Europe, 1720–1830*. Stanford, Calif.: Stanford University Press, 1969.

Koschmann, J. Victor. *The Mito Ideology: Discourse, Reform, and Insurrection in Late Tokugawa Japan*. Berkeley and Los Angeles, Calif.: University of California Press, 1987.

Maruyama, Masao. *Studies in the Intellectual History of Tokugawa Japan*. Translated by Mikiso Hane. Tokyo: University of Tokyo Press, 1974.

Matsumoto, Shigeru. *Motoori Norinaga, 1730–1801*. Cambridge, Mass.: Harvard University Press, 1970.

Najita, Tetsuo. *Vision of Virtue in Tokugawa Japan*. Chicago: University of Chicago Press, 1987.

Najita, Tetsuo and Erwin Scheiner, eds. *Japanese Thought in the Tokugawa Period, 1600–1868: Methods and Metaphors*. Chicago: University of Chicago Press, 1978.

Nakai, Kate Wildman. *Shogunal Politics: Arai Hakuseki and the Premises of Tokugawa Rule*. Cambridge, Mass.: Harvard University Press, 1988.

Norman, E. H. "Andō Shōeki and the Anatomy of Japanese Feudalism," in *Transactions of the Asiatic Society of Japan*, series 3, vol. 2 (1949).
Nosco, Peter, ed. *Confucianism and Tokugawa Culture*. Princeton, N.J.: Princeton University Press, 1984.
Ogyū, Sorai. *The Political Writings of Ogyū Sorai*. Trans. J. R. McEwan. London: Cambridge University Press, 1962.
Ooms, Herman. *Tokugawa Ideology, Early Constructs, 1570–1680*. Princeton, N.J.: Princeton University Press, 1985.
Passin, Herbert. *Society and Education in Japan*. New York: Bureau of Publications, Teachers' College and East Asian Institute, Columbia University, 1965.
Sansom, Sir George B. *The Western World and Japan*. New York: Knopf, 1950.
Yamamoto, Tsunetomo. *Hagakure: The Book of the Samurai*. Translated by William S. Wilson. Tokyo: Kodansha, 1978.

THE TOKUGAWA PERIOD: CULTURAL DEVELOPMENTS

Ando, Tsuruo. *Performing Arts of Japan: Bunraku, the Puppet Theater*. New York and Tokyo: Walker/Weatherhill, 1970.
Blyth, Reginald H. *Haiku*, 4 vols. Tokyo: Hokuseido Press, 1950–1952.
Bowers, Faubion. *Japanese Theatre*. New York: Hill & Wang, 1959.
Chikamatsu, Monzaemon. *The Major Plays of Chikamatsu*. Trans. Donald Keene. New York: Columbia University Press, 1961.
Ernst, Earle. *The Kabuki Theatre*. New York: Oxford University Press, 1956.
Henderson, Harold G. *An Introduction to Haiku*. Garden City, N.Y.: Doubleday, 1958.
Hibbett, Howard. *The Floating World in Japanese Fiction*. New York: Grove, 1960.
Hillier, J. *Japanese Masters of the Colour Print*. London: Phaidon, 1954.
Ihara, Saikaku. *Five Women Who Loved Love*. Translated by William T. de Bary. Tokyo and Rutland, Vt.: Tuttle, 1956.
———. *The Life an Amorous Woman and Other Writings*. Trans. Ivan Morris. Norfolk, Conn.: Laughlin, 1963.
Michener, James. *The Floating World*. New York: Random House, 1954.
Tanizaki, Junichiro. *Secret History of the Lord of Musashi and Arrowroot*. New York: Knopf, 1982.
Toita, Yasuji. *Performing Arts of Japan: Kabuki the Popular Theater*. Trans. Don Kenny. New York and Tokyo: Walker/Weatherhill, 1970.

THE LAST YEARS OF TOKUGAWA RULE

Alcock, Sir Rutherford. *The Capital of the Tycoon: A Narrative of Three Years' Residence in Japan*, 2 vols. New York: Harper, 1863.
Beasley, W. G., ed. and trans. *Select Documents on Japanese Foreign Policy, 1853–1868*. London: Oxford University Press, 1955.
Black, John R. *Young Japan: Yokohama and Yedo 1858–79*, 2 vols. London: Oxford University Press, 1969.
Craig, Albert M. *Chōshū in the Meiji Restoration*. Cambridge, Mass.: Harvard University Press, 1961.
Harootunian, H. D. *Toward Restoration: The Growth of Political Consciousness in Tokugawa Japan*. Berkeley: University of California Press, 1970.
Jansen, Marius B., *Sakamoto Ryōma and the Meiji Restoration*. Princeton, N.J.: Princeton University Press, 1961.
Satow, Sir Ernest M. *A Diplomat in Japan*. London: Seeley Service, 1921.

Totman, Conrad. *The Collapse of the Tokugawa Bakufu, 1862–1868.* Honolulu: University Press of Hawaii, 1980.

Walworth, Arthur. *Black Ships Off Japan: The Story of Commodore Perry's Expedition.* New York: Knopf, 1948.

Yamamuro, Kozo. *A Study of Samurai Income and Entrepreneurship.* Cambridge, Mass.: Harvard University Press, 1974.

ABOUT THE BOOK
AND AUTHOR

This newly revised edition drawn from Professor Hane's classic text, *Japan: A Historical Survey*, presents a rich account of early Japanese history for students. Important elements of this past persist in present-day Japan more tenaciously than is sometimes realized. Hane traces the key developments of premodern Japanese history, including the establishment of the imperial dynasty, early influences from China and Korea, the rise of the samurai class and the establishment of feudalism, the culture and society of the long Tokugawa period, the rise of Confucianism and Shinto nationalism, and, finally, the end of Tokugawa rule.

Although the book is structured around major political developments, Hane also carefully integrates the social, economic, cultural, and intellectual aspects of Japanese history. His revisions incorporate important recent scholarship on this formative period of Japan's history.

Mikiso Hane is professor of history at Knox College and has written extensively on Japan for over twenty years.

INDEX

245